# Whitemarsh
## Information Systems Corporation

# Enterprise Architectures

### Michael M. Gorman

Whitemarsh Information Systems Corporation
2008 Althea Lane
Bowie, Maryland 20716
Tele: 301-249-1142
Email: Whitemarsh@wiscorp.com
Web: www.wiscorp.com

Designations used by companies to distinguish their products are often claimed as trademarks. In all instances where Whitemarsh Press is aware of a claim, the product names appear in initial capital or all capital letters. Readers, however, should contact the appropriate companies for more complete information regarding trademarks and registration.

This publication is designed to provide accurate and authoritative information in regard to the subject matter covered. It is sold with the understanding that the publisher is not engaged in rendering legal, accounting, or other professional services. If legal advice or other expert assistance is required, the services of a competent professional person should be sought. FROM A DECLARATION OF PRINCIPLES JOINTLY ADOPTED BY A COMMITTEE OF THE AMERICAN BAR ASSOCIATION AND A COMMITTEE OF PUBLISHERS.

ISBN 978-0-9789968-2-6

Printed in the United States of America

# Table of Contents

# Figures

# Tables

# Preface

A lack of demonstrable integration across various architecture classes is what prompted this book. It is common for different teams to be assembled across the enterprise to "do their thing." One group does the enterprise's[1] architecture while another group does data models, and some third group does Business Information Systems [2] plans.

The result is often three large piles of paper, and in the case of data models, really neat looking diagrams. Sometimes, Picasso comes to mind as the artist. Then, everybody sits back and waits for the magic caterpillars to butterfly transformations to occur. Nothing seems to happen. A "Winter of discontent" sets in. Everybody searches for the Spring, but it is nowhere to be found.

This book shows that not only can Spring happen, but also that three architecture-based product sets, that is, the enterprise's architecture, the data models, and the Business Information System plans are actually part of a larger collection of architectures that are tightly coupled, interdependent, integrated, and non-redundant. In the process of creating the architecture product sets over the past 40+ years, its become painfully obvious that two architectures are missing, and that one architecture, data models, is badly engineered.

The two architectures that are missing are Database Object Classes and Resource Life Cycle Analysis. Database Object Classes are needed to

---

[1]. As defined within this book, an enterprise is merely a term to relate to a collection of organization units that have common collections of data, processes, activities within a business or a company and sometimes beyond corporate affiliations as in the case of data interchanges. An enterprise is therefore not just a synonym for business or a company. Rather, it is intended to convey a common data, process, and activity view across the organizational units sharing that view.

[2]. In this book, a business information system is a set of application-specific software that created, manipulates, evolves or deletes data–most commonly–from a database through a database management system in support of some mission area of the enterprise. A business information system is class of information system, and it is distinguished from other classes such as a computer's operating system, or "systems software" information system such as telecommunications management, database management systems, and end-user security management.

---

overcome the real business perception problems that were caused by the popularity of the relational data model.

The Resource Life Cycle Analysis is needed because of two reasons. First, Resource Life Cycle Analysis enables the creation of an integration lattice work between the enterprise's architecture products and the enterprise's databases and business information systems. The second reason is that not only does Resource Life Cycle Analysis makes Business Information Systems Planning possible in realistic time frames and with reasonable resources, it enables these plans to be repeatable, reliable, and malleable.

The architecture that is badly engineered is data models. After extensive research into what data architects and data modelers actually do, a layered data architecture approach is clearly more appropriate. This approach is not fundamentally new. Rather it sets down into actual practice what is actually done. This approach is more practical, is accomplished all the time by data architects and data modelers but without persistence and repeatability. The result is a collection of data architecture products that support maximal reuse, complete integration, and very controlled redundancy.

In addition, the data architecture approach completely integrates the only two ISO/ANSI standards in this area: ISO 11179 for data element metadata, and ISO/ANSI SQL for comprehensive, portable, and interoperable data model development.

This book sets out five distinct architectures. While that's good, what integrates the work and the work products from all these architectures? It is the Knowledge Worker Framework. This framework, first explicitly posited in 1992, was squarely founded on a database project methodology that has been successfully evolving over the past 30 years. Further, the organization, sequencing, and work products in the Knowledge Worker Framework are those that satisfy 100% of the U.S. General Accountability Office's reasons for information technology system failure. These reasons were discovered from analysis of eight multi-hundred million dollar information technology failures.

It is not enough however, to just assert integration. It must be proven. Thus, there is an underlying metadata repository system that supports the creation, manipulation, evolution, and integration of all the work products. It is upon this highly engineered, experience-fired foundation that this book is based.

# 1

# Enterprise Architectures

The objective of this book is to present an approach to the creation of architectures that should exist across the enterprise to ensure integration of data, semantics, and policy. To that end, this book addresses material about five architectures:

- The Enterprise's architecture.
- The Database Object Class architecture.
- The Data architectures.
- The Resource Life Cycle Analysis architecture.
- The Business Information Systems Plans architecture.

The book starts with explaining just what enterprise architectures are, and the components that should exist in a quality architecture. The book then sets all five architectures within the Knowledge Worker Framework. The Knowledge Worker Framework both has unique products and also products from the five architectures. The Knowledge Worker Framework serves as an overarching framework. Finally, the book describes the all-important role of the metadata repository as the mechanism for integration and non-redundant representation of all the work products.

This book shows that the five architectures are important to comprehensively manage the work products of knowledge workers. This book further shows that all these materials reinforce each other, are integrated, and enable enterprises to understand their past, operate the present, and plan for the future.

This chapter is all about enterprise architectures, that is, what are they, and why the architectures are necessary.

## 1.1   What are Enterprise Architectures?

The term, Enterprise Architecture contains both Enterprise and Architecture. In Wikipedia, enterprise contains no special definition. Rather, the Wikipedia states that "almost any business or organization can be called an enterprise." From the Whitemarsh book, Data Interoperability Community of Interest Handbook, an enterprise is:

> ... a term to relate to a collection of organization units that have common collections of data, processes, activities within a business or a company and sometimes beyond corporate affiliations as in the case of data interchanges. Ideally, there is also a common governance of these items. An enterprise is therefore not just a synonym for business or a company. Rather, it is intended to convey a common data, process, and activity view across the organizational units sharing that view.

As to architecture, the Wikipedia states that an architecture is:

> ... the design of the total built environment, from the macrolevel of town planning, urban design, and landscape architecture to the microlevel of creating furniture. Architectural design usually must address both feasibility and cost for the builder, as well as function and aesthetics for the user.
>
> Planned architecture often manipulates space, volume, texture, light, shadow, or abstract elements in order to achieve pleasing aesthetics. This distinguishes it from applied science or engineering, which usually concentrate more on the functional and feasibility aspects of the design of constructions or structures

The architectures contained in this book are in the class: Science and Engineering. Specifically, the Wikipedia provides a definition for Enterprise Architecture as follows:

> Enterprise architecture is the practice of applying a comprehensive and rigorous method for describing a current and/or future structure and behavior for an organization's processes, business information systems, personnel and organizational sub-units, so that they align

*with the organization's core goals and strategic direction. Although often associated strictly with information technology, it relates more broadly to the practice of business optimization in that it addresses business architecture, performance management, organizational structure and process architecture as well.*

## 1.2    Five Contained Architectures

The definition set out in the previous section sets out the context for the five enterprise-related architectures identified in Table 1.

| Enterprise Architectures | |
| --- | --- |
| **Architecture Class** | **Brief Description** |
| Enterprise | In the architecture for the enterprise itself, the engineering and structure of the enterprise's mission, organizations, functions and database domains are provided such that they can be extended and/or integrated with other more technical architectures such as hardware, business information systems, and business events. |
| Database Object Classes | A Database Object Class architecture is a self-contained set of data structures, processes, states and state-transformation systems that advance a collection of highly engineered data within the domain of a database management system (DBMS). |
| Data | A data architecture is the set of data-specific structures that enable enterprise-wide data and semantics integration critical to data interoperability. |
| Resource Life Cycle Analysis | A Resource Life Cycle Analysis is a set of enterprise resources, each set within a life cycle of major state transformations of those resources. These Resource Life Cycles can be interconnected, and used as a lattice work to attach the enterprise's inventory of database and business information systems, which in turn, greatly assists in the formation of Business Information Systems Plans. |

| Enterprise Architectures | |
| --- | --- |
| **Architecture Class** | **Brief Description** |
| Business Information Systems Plans | A Business Information Systems Plan is a highly engineered sequence of the development of databases and business information systems throughout the enterprise so as to cause maximum reuse and to accomplish the building and evolution of databases and business information systems in a business-rationale-based and highly ordered fashion. |

**Table 1.** Examples of Enterprise Architectures in a Knowledge Worker environment.

The five architectures presented are all contained within the framework for the knowledge worker. The first architecture, the enterprise's architecture provides the overall context within which the knowledge worker operates. The enterprise's architecture identifies and describes the enterprise's mission, organization and functions. It also defines the data which ultimately provides the "proof of execution" of the operating enterprise.

The second architecture, Database Object Classes represent the objects that are valued, updated, employed, and deleted by the knowledge worker as the enterprise's business is conducted. Proof of mission accomplishment exists in the form of data. The data must be consistent, highly engineered, integrated, and non-redundant. Database Object Classes provide such constructions.

The third architecture, data, enables a high degree of engineering across all the enterprise's databases. That's not enough, however, because many enterprises have thousands of databases that are incoherent, in semantic conflict, not integrated, and very redundant. Key to enterprise-wide data engineering are the three levels of generalization above and one level of detailed interfaces below the level of the operating databases.

The highest level of generalization above the operating databases, Data Elements, enables the singular definition of the maximally used business facts and the setting of these business facts within business concepts and controlled value domains. These business facts, once defined are reused many times across the data model generalization levels so as to provide semantic consistency, value domain, and data type management.

The second highest level of generalization above the operating databases, Specified Data Models, enables the specification of standardized functionally-based data models of concepts that ultimately, as whole or partial collections, get used over and over during the construction of implementable database models. These Specified Data Models are used many times to effect standard data structures, semantics, and meaning across enterprise database models.

The first level of generalization above the operating databases, that is, the Implemented Data Models, represents data models of databases that may ultimately become one or more variations of the operating databases. Additionally, whole or partial data structure collections from these Implemented Data Models may be employed in one or more of the operating databases.

The point to these "above" levels of generalizations is that these enable order from data specification chaos, integration and reuse of semantics from the current discord, and control or even elimination of large scale redundancy of data across the enterprise. Ultimately, database should promote harmony, civilized discourse, and not be the cause of the bureaucratic food-fights.

The one level of detailed interfaces below the level of the operating databases is the level of data exchange between database and business information systems. The exchange level has two forms, technology bound, and technology independent. The technology bound level, SQL views, support the direction interaction between the database management system (DBMS) databases and the business information systems. The second form, technology independent, is commonly seen in the form of XML, which has two parts: definition, and data stream. These two parts are either composed by a business information system, or shredded into a database's required structure by the DBMS. This enables data to be put and/or retrieved by DBMS-disconnected business information systems. XML is not however a know-nothing, do-everything data exchange environment. The four layers above the XML layer (that is, Data Elements through Operational Data Models) must already exist for XML to be effective.

The fourth architecture, Resources Life Cycles, are an enterprise resource's organizing architecture. The key premise is that every enterprise consists of a finite set of well-known resources that are created, manipulated, and ultimately dissolved by the enterprise. Examples include locations, facilities, products, monies, staff, real and abstracts, and the like. Enterprise operations are thus seen through the operating life cycles of resources.

Resource Life Cycles are able to be interconnected, one life cycle with another. Collectively, the interconnected Resource Life Cycles form a lattice work through which missions, organizations and functions are operationally viewed, and upon which database objects and business information systems are integrated and coalesced.

The fifth architecture, Business Information Systems Planning, is an architecture that reflects the build and evolution sequence of all information technology projects. This Business Information Systems Planning architecture is built directly from the foundation of the Resource Life Cycle Analysis architecture, which in turn was built from the database objects, data, and enterprise architectures.

All together, these individual architectures enable the enterprise to engineer, evolve, and know answers to the following questions:

- What is the enterprise's mission, organization, functions and domains of data?

- What is the key policy-based engineered data that has to be coherent, integrated, and non-redundant?

- What are the enterprise resources and how do they progress individually and in concert to achieve enterprise missions in the most efficient and effective manner possible?

- What is the overall Business Information Systems Plan, and in what sequence must the database and business information system projects must be accomplished to achieve just-in-time readiness?

Key to all these architectures is the organizing framework for the knowledge worker, that is, the Knowledge Worker Framework. This framework organizes and interrelates these five interconnected and contained architectures and enables all the architecture work products to be integrated, and non-redundantly stored in one metadata repository. This metadata database repository, hereinafter called the Metabase[3], supports the creation,

---

[3]     Metadata is a generic term that identifies all classes of information technology specifications across the enterprise. Hence all data and process
(continued...)

manipulation, and reporting of only what the enterprise needs to exist and thrive.

The material about the Knowledge Worker Framework contains, at varying levels of detail, descriptions about all the products, including the products contained in the architectures encompassed by the Knowledge Worker Framework. The chapters on the individual five architectures, for example, Database Object Classes, provide additional levels of detail about Database Object Class components, reasons for the need for Database Object Classes, the relationship among the components of Database Object Classes, and the relationship between components Database Object Class and components from other architectures.

## 1.3    Remainder of this Book

The chapters in this book set out the engineering and the content of the Knowledge Worker Framework and its five contained architectures. This chapter started with the enumeration of the architectures and stated why each needs to exist and how all the architectures are integrated into an overall whole.

Chapter 2 describes architectures in general and identifies the critical components and measures of successful architectures. Bad architectures are just above not worth having, and may even be counterproductive if they cause the creation of work products that are not able to be integrated, or are supported by methodologies that have not been detailed or proven, end-to-end. Good architectures are fully detailed. Every work product is expertly engineered, is supported by a high-quality methodology, and is able to be integrated with all the other work products within a given architecture and across architectures. Notwithstanding the high degree of engineering, good

---

[3](...continued)

specifications are metadata. All requirements could also be considered metadata. A metadata repository is a database within which all metadata is stored. A metabase database is a metabase. Whitemarsh has employed the term, Metabase, in this context since 1982. A metadata repository system is a software system that captures, stores, reports, and manages all metadata. The system that manages a metabase is the Metabase system. Sophisticated metadata repositories are multi-user and support the capture and reporting of metadata in a non-redundant, integrated manner across the enterprise.

architectures are just highly proceduralized common sense. Common sense is the acid test, and the inverse of common sense is non-sense.

Chapter 3 fully describes the Knowledge Worker Framework, row by row, and column by column. Every cell is detailed including a high level description of every work product that results for the cell contained work processes. All cells are, of course, completely integrated.

Chapter 4, the Enterprise's Architecture, describes the contents of the enterprise's architecture and describes at a high level how the enterprise's architecture is created. This chapter also describes the work products, how they are interrelated, and how these work products fit with the work products of the other architectures.

Chapter 5, Database Object Classes, defines what a Database Object Class is, how it contrasts with other types of objects, and what unique role Database Object Classes play in a database environment. This chapter also presents how Database Object Classes can be implemented in SQL DBMSs that are not object-oriented and how these classes can be implemented in SQL:1999 and above complaint DBMS that are object-oriented. This chapter also describes the work products, how they are interrelated, and how these work products fit with the work products of the other architectures.

Chapter 6, Data Architecture, starts with a presentation of the various classes of the database architectures that most commonly exist within enterprises, be they small or large. The chapter then proceeds to fully define each of the five data model generalization levels, that is, Data Elements, Specified Data Models, Implemented Data Models, Operational Data Models, and View Data Models. The chapter sets out the work products that must be created for each model, and then how all these work products are thoroughly integrated one with the other.

Chapter 7, Resource Life Cycle Analysis, defines just what Resources and Resource Life Cycles are, what business objectives are fulfilled by their employment, where these fit within all the other architectures. While valuable in their own right, Resource Life Cycles also serve as a key linking mechanism between the Enterprise's Architecture, Database Object Classes, and Data Architectures on the one hand and Business Information Systems Plans on the other hand.

Chapter 8, Business Information Systems Plans, explains their necessary characteristics. These characteristics have been glaringly unfilled by other Business Information Systems Plan development methodologies. This explained methodology is the next logical step from the prior architectures and employs all their work products. The Business Information Systems Planning methodology then leverages the large quantity of project methodology and metrics' templates to produce Business Information Systems Plans that are reliable and repeatable, and are malleable as new technologies unfold.

Chapter 9, The Role of the Metabase, shows how the Metabase should be employed to store all the work products from these architectures. Metadata repositories that store just operational or technical metadata miss about 99% of their true value to the enterprise. Clearly, if we focus solely on the optimization of the past we will never be able to plan, see, and accomplish the future. It is through the exposition, optimization, and recasting of our missions, organizations, functions, database objects, databases and business information systems that the future will be unfolding in ever better forms.

Chapter 10, Summary and Conclusions, brings together the goals and summary of every chapter and sets out the way ahead: a work plan for success.

It needs to be said, and remembered that this book is not a theory book. If it had been, it would have been written 25 or more years ago. Rather, this book is the consequence of the evolution and development of enterprise architecture and data management practice that has been conducted in industry and government since the early 1970s.

Every product in every chapter of this book is fully detailed in other Whitemarsh books, and is fully supported by detailed methodology, courses, workshops, and of course, the Metabase, Metabase. In short, this book is a professional practice book and is another integral component of the Whitemarsh Data Management Series.

## 1.4    Questions and Exercises

1.      Are you aware of stand-along architecture projects such as the one-big data model, or a Business Information Systems Plan? What was its value? Did it integrate with existing metadata? Did it become expensive shelf-ware? What was management's attitude towards it over time?

2.      What are the effects of a bad architecture? How do you know if one is bad? Do you follow it nonetheless or try to have it fixed?

3.  How many different kinds of architectures are there in Information Technology? Can there be just "one for all reasons" that is specific, unambiguous, useful, and able to be accomplished?

4.  Do the five architectures in this book address the needs of the Knowledge Worker? What are other architectures? Are there common components across architectures? How are common components defined, valued, and kept in synch?

5.  Does this book provide a practical definition for the enterprise? Architecture? Enterprise Architecture? How would you define these terms? Compare and contrast with the book's definitions.

6.  Why should there be five data model generalization levels? What purpose does each serve? How are the levels interrelated? Does the interrelationship make sense? What would be the benefit to all these levels? Costs?

7.  Should architectures be designed such that they tell stories? How do you update your architectures? How often? Are the updates in one architecture automatically carried over to another when there are common components? If yes, what's the benefit. If not, what's the cost?

# 2

# Components of an Architecture

Chapter 1 set out the overall scope of enterprise architectures, listed those architectures and indicated how those architectures directly affect the knowledge worker.

This chapter describes architectures in general and identifies the critical components and measures of successful architectures. This chapter starts with a description of how an architecture process is engineered and sets out the metrics through which every architecture process should be evaluated.

The chapter shows that it is completely unrealistic to have just one architecture for the whole enterprise. There must be multiple architectures, and while each might be individually designed, built and maintained, there has to be a strategy and mechanism to integrate and maximally reuse the architecture work products into a unified whole. This chapter concludes with a summary.

As stated in the first chapter, bad architectures are just above not worth having, and may even be counterproductive if they cause the creation of work products that are not able to be integrated, or are supported by methodologies that have not been detailed or proven, end-to-end.

Good architectures are fully detailed. Every work product is expertly engineered, is supported by a high-quality methodology, and is able to be integrated with all the other work products within a given architecture and across architectures.

Notwithstanding the high degree of engineering, good architectures are just highly proceduralized common sense. Common sense is the acid test, and the inverse of common sense is non-sense.

## 2.1    Engineering an Architecture Process

Within the scope of the architectures described in this book, the four components of any process within an IDEF-0 diagram come to mind. Figure 1 shows a process cell in an IDEF-0 model.

Some process, that is, the interior of an architectural cell, is taking one or more inputs under one or more constraints and creating one or more outputs through the execution of one or more mechanisms. Essentially that is how all processes operate regardless of diagraming technique or formally declared methodology. Because this transformation operates under a rigorous methodology that would, in all likelihood, be under a well-engineered governance, the results are repeatable and reliable. The process description of this cell fits well with the key elements of the Wikipedia enterprise architecture definition in Chapter 1.

Each cell within in a framework of cells should be assessable as to its completeness and quality. Figure 2 illustrates the ideal contents of cells. Since a cell is essentially an encapsulated process that has inputs, outputs, constraints and mechanism, the process should be best practice in that particular area.

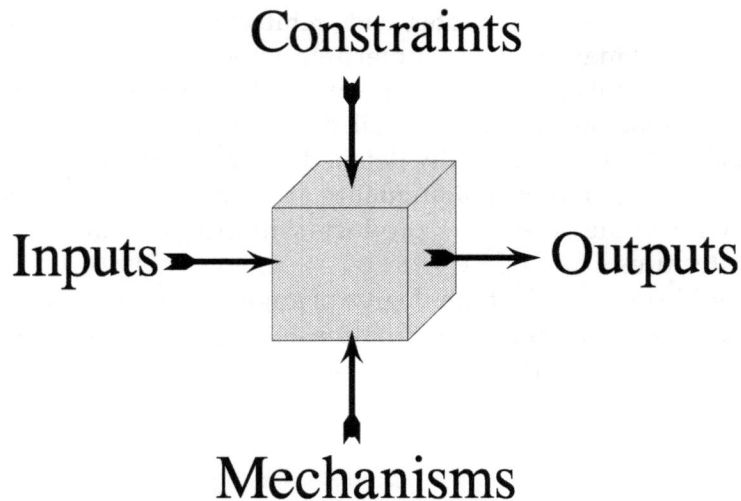

**Figure 1**. IDEF-0 process cell construction.

## Framework

Best Practice
Metrics
Deliverables
Quality Measures
Skills Requirements
Tools & Techniques

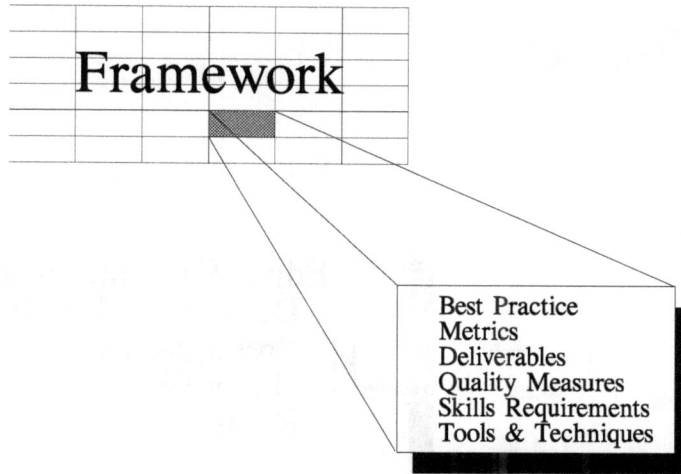

# Framework Cell Contents

**Figure 2.** Measures of a tool's infrastructure contents.

If the individual cell processes have high cohesion and low coupling (explained below), as new best practices arise old ones can be replaced. It is also important to be able to judge the quality of any cell "deliverable." For example, that an enterprise data element must conform to the complete metadata infrastructure for ISO standard 11179 (that is, Part 3) rather than conforming to just a naming convention, that is, Part 5. Key also is the skill and knowledge requirements of staff accomplishing the cell's contents.

Ultimately, the process associated with every cell results in a segment of a work breakdown structure within a methodology that has to be allocated resources, scheduled, and the like. Knowing the required skills of staff enables the proper quantity of time to be allocated because of any given staff assignment.

As to a mechanism, the appropriate set of tools and techniques need to be determined. For example, if the best tool is selected but results in a stove-pipe of metadata that cannot be integrated with other tools' metadata nor be exported to a Metabase, that "best-tool" is of marginal value. In short, every cell is not an isolated island of analysis or design. Rather, each cell is part of an integrated whole.

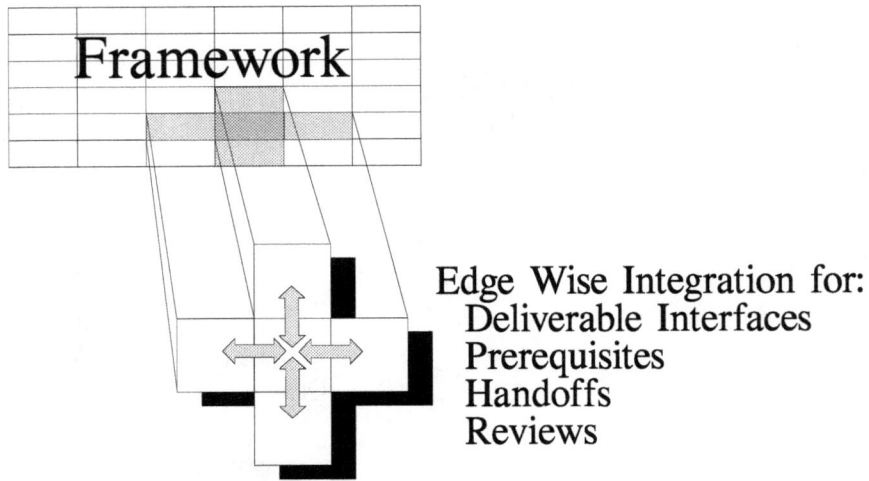

**Figure 3**. Relationships between cells and adjacent or related cells.

## 2.2    Architecture Process Integration

Architecture processes, as represented in framework cells, must relate to each another. Figure 3 shows that every cell is at least related to its adjacent cells. This is not, however, always the only case. In the Knowledge Worker Framework which is described below, the mission cell, which is Row 1, Column 1, is related to the Business Organization's cell which is Row 1, Column 6. But the Organization's cell is related to the R1, Column 5 Business Function cell. In short, while there may be a general "perception" order, that is, left to right and top to bottom, that is not always an interrelationship-order. The relationship order can be quite different. That is because all cell inputs and outputs are stored in a Metabase of metadata-tables and relationships that have a natural order all their own. To exclusively force adjacency relationships can result in a very unnatural looking framework or a very unworkable Metabase. Frameworks and repositories, while related are not just mirrors of each other.

Figure 4 shows that these IDEF-0 cells can be interlinked. In this figure, 10 cells are interlinked through some sort of inputs and outputs. That is, the output of some cell is input to one or more different cells. If the process model

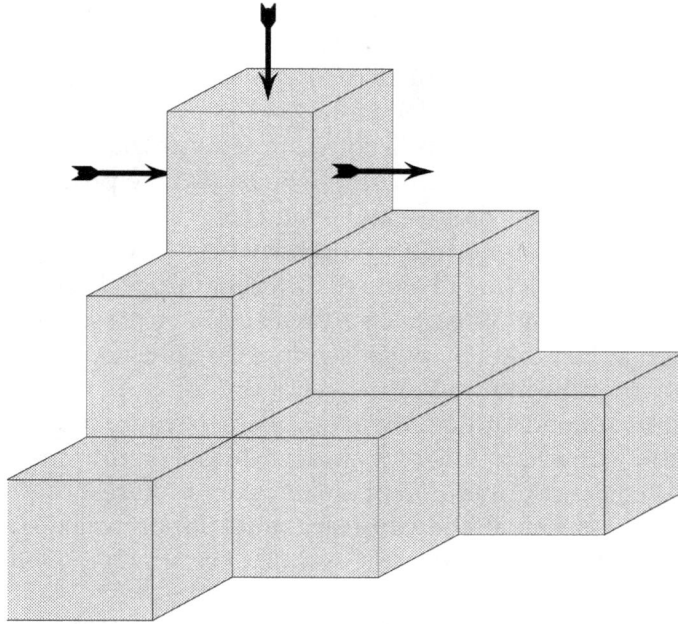

**Figure 4**. Complex networks of process cells.

is well partitioned then each cell is in a "3rd Normal Form." This is a database term that was coined in the 1970s by Edgar Codd. When that term is adapted to process, three things are implied:

- Single agenda.
- The name implies the purpose.
- Single set of inputs and/or single set of outputs.

In the middle 1970s, there arose two terms associated with software engineering, coupling and cohesion. These terms were created and/or popularized by Larry L. Constantine and Edward Yourdon.

Again, from Wikipedia, "coupling is the degree to which a program module relies on another module." The stronger the coupling, the less the separate modules or component parts can stand on their own.

From Wikipedia, "cohesion is a measure of how well the lines of source code within a module work together to provide a specific piece of functionality . . . High cohesion tend to be preferable because high cohesion is associated with several desirable traits . . . Including robustness, reliability, reusability, and understandability, whereas low cohesion is associated with undesirable traits such as being difficult to maintain, difficult to test, difficult to reuse, and even difficult to understand."

As an example, if there was a software module that computed interest as an amount, but within the module there were also the processes to compute delinquency, late charges, and even accept address and telephone number changes, then that module would have very low cohesion. It would be just a jumble of code doing all sorts of different things. If, in contrast, there were multiple software modules, each with a single purpose wherein all the code contributed to just that one purpose, then the cohesion would be high.

For coupling, the internal processes of the software modules are completely self-contained and merely require one or more inputs that are generated by some other module or from an external environment. An example would be the computation of an amount of interest due on a loan. Input would be the principal, the monetary units (if not implied), the interest rate over a period of time, and amount of time over which the interest is to be calculated. Here's an example. From the web link, http://www.moneychimp.com/calculator/mortgage_calculator.htm, there are three inputs, Loan Amount, Interest Rate, Years to Pay, and then one output, the monthly mortgage amount. This is an example of high cohesion because the process is completely encapsulated and there's only one method of entry (i.e., the three values), and one output, the mortgage amount. This is

| Inputs | | |
|---|---|---|
| Loan Amount: | $ | |
| Mortgage Rate: | 7.5 | % |
| Years to Pay: | 30 | |
| | Calculate | |
| Results | | |
| Monthly Payment: | $ | |

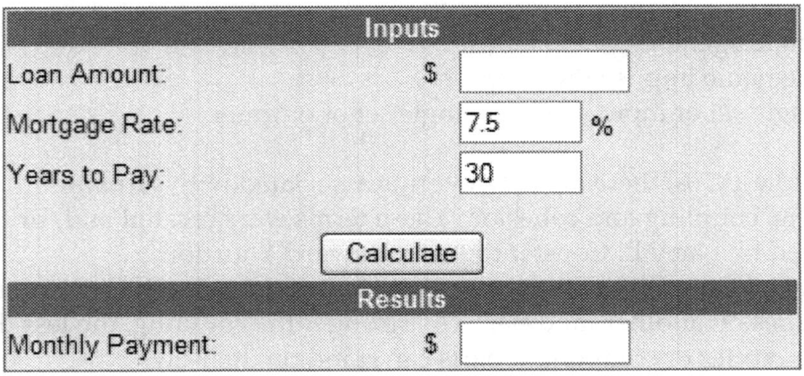

**Figure 5**. Mortgage calculator screen.

also an example of low coupling because there are no apparent dependencies between this module and any other. This calculator is shown in Figure 5.

## 2.3  One Architecture for all Reasons

Figure 4 might imply that there would be one overall architecture. If that were the case, then it would be too big for any lever to raise. Figure 6 shows the plea from Archimedes, "give me a place to stand and I will move the earth."

But since Archimedes is still waiting for his lever, so too would we be waiting for any lever that could raise an enterprise's complete and total architecture. Figure 7 illustrates the intersection of three architectures. Each architecture, for example, software, data, hardware, or telecommunications will almost always have some common elements. People, organization, location, and time are examples. Key to intersecting these architectures is determining the common elements and ensuring that there is low degree of coupling across the architectures, and a high degree of cohesion within the ells of any one architecture.

**Figure 6**. Lifting the one-world architecture.

Figure 7 might conversely imply that architectures are entirely independent one from another. That too is unrealistic. Architectures can also be nested as well. For example, the M1 A2 Abrams Battle Tank is a class of a weapon system's architecture. Within the tank's architecture there would be the fire-power, counter-measures, propulsion, communications architectures.

## 2.4   Integrated Architectures

The materialized instances of the architectures for the M1 Abrams Battle Tank would be machine guns and canons, explosion deflecting shields, propulsion, and radios. Each architecture would form some sort of diagram relevant to Figure 7, and collectively they would all end up looking like Figure 8.

The overall tank is an architecture. Within its architecture are all its contained architectures for fire-power, counter-measures, propulsion, communications, and so on. How these architectures are connected is through two main systems, which too, are architectures: electrical, and data. The key

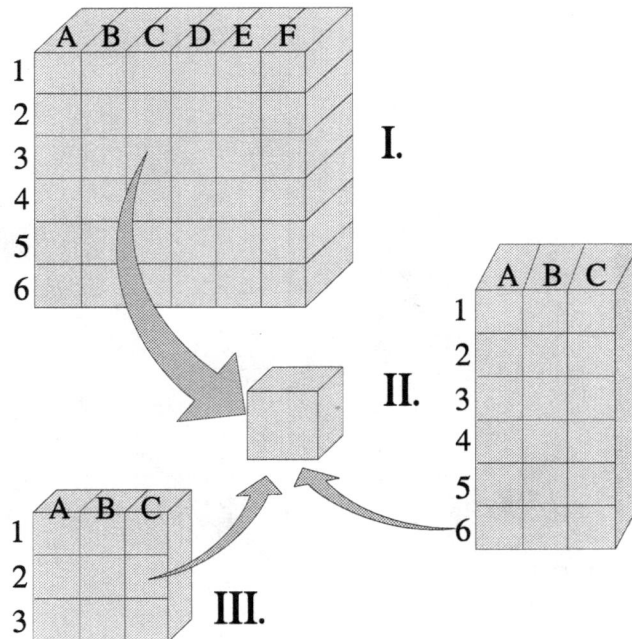

**Figure 7**. Intersecting three architectures.

**Figure 8**. M1 A2 Abrams Battle Tank.

point here is that to have integrated architectures is to have some mechanism of integration across the individual architectures.

Among hardware architectures, the integration mechanisms are commonly electrical and data. Similarly, between computing software architectures the integrating mechanisms are both hardware on which common software runs, and the data "messages" that are exchanged between the software modules. A quality operating system is also an underlying enabling computer software architecture for applications. Similarly, a database management system (DBMS) is a common data definition, access and security architecture of business information systems, interactive users, and for commonly accessible data-based interfaces across a collection of users.

Data messages are either structurally proprietary to the software that is sending or receiving, or they are independent of proprietary structures.

An example of a proprietary structure would be a fixed-format data record design that is defined inside a computer program, and is such that only that specific computer program can read or write those data records.

An example of an independent data structure is XML (extensible markup language). The XML contains two parts: One for types, and the other for instances. The type part contains the definitions and semantics for all the instances. The instances part are the XML-formatted data records themselves.

While the type-language can stand alone, the instances part has little value without the type-language "Rosetta Stone." Two software systems can thus exchange data without knowing each other's internal data format. The sending system composes the exchange data into a type and instances stream, and the receiving system uses its "secret decoder ring" to read the type's file, and through that, understand the instances.

Extending the XML paradigm one exchange-layer further, computing systems can now be independent of even knowing where each other resides, that is, which hardware, or which operating system, or even be independent of a given database management system. It is accomplished by the SOA (Service Oriented Architecture). An SOA environment operates analogously to a cell-phone network. There is a sending phone which creates a series of transactions, for example, a phone call from a car to a home, and includes within each of those messages both the ability to find the receiving phone and also the ability to re-assemble the phone message parts such that they make a coherent phone call.

In all these cases, there are individual architectures and highly engineered and universally accepted interface standards across the architectures. Without interface architecture standards, interoperability is fatally crippled. Since Whitemarsh's focus is data management, the architectures described in this book concentrate on data interoperability among knowledge workers.


## 2.5    Architecture Components Summary

The objective of this chapter was to clearly set out that there's real engineering required for quality architectures. All the work products must be thoroughly identified, engineered, and integrated. Because there's no practical way to have just one architecture, all the different architectures must be such that their work products are able to be stored and integrated within one Metabase.

If the Metabase exists, is on the critical path of all knowledge worker efforts, and is of high quality, overlapped work will not be done multiple times. That will also prevent the need for re-casting existing work because of work product conflicts.

Without quality engineering, bad architectures will likely result and be counterproductive. That will require significant rework because their underlying methodologies that have not been detailed or proven, end-to-end.

In the end, the shortest route to success in terms of both times and money will be through good architectures that are fully detailed, have had their work products expertly engineered, are supported by high-quality methodologies, and are integrated with all the other work products within a Metabase.

Remember always that good architectures are just highly proceduralized common sense; else it is just very expensive non-sense.

The next chapter, Knowledge Worker Framework, describes the framework, row by row, and column by column. Every cell is detailed including a high level description of every work product that results for the cell contained work processes. All cells are, of course, completely integrated.

## 2.6    Questions and Exercises

1.    How have you engineered your architectures? Are the cells like an IDEF-0 model with constraints, inputs, outputs, and mechanisms? Do you have quality control and integrity constraints on the contents of every cell to ensure completeness?

2.    How do you plan for an architecture? Are architectures part of normal activities? Or, is an architecture a response to a crisis?

3.    Can you make use of work products from other architectures easily through data access and loading tools? Are updates to one architecture automatically propagated to all other architectures? Are your architecture meta-models all part of the overall metadata architecture of you enterprise?

4.    How would you rate the coupling and cohesion across your set of architectures? Give both good and bad examples.

5.    How should architectures be integrated and made non-redundant? Can you query, report, and update your architecture work products with normal report writers and programming languages? If so, what's the benefit. If not, what's the cost in flexibility?

6.  Can or should there be on architecture for all reasons. If not then what are examples of different architectures? What would be your strategy for integrating them?

7.  Are the architectures in this book adequate for the Knowledge Worker? What are other architectures? What purpose would they serve? What strategy would you undertake to justify the creation of new class of architecture?

8.  Do you believe that stove-pipes of metadata leads to stove-piped databases and business information systems? If yes, what is the cost of such stove-pipes? If not, how have you avoided the lack of integration? What was the cost of avoidance?

9.  Should existing stove-pipes of metadata be integrated? How would you justify recasting these stove-pipes into one or more of this book's architectures?

# 3

# Knowledge Worker Framework

Chapter 2 focused on the engineering of architectures including whether there are multiple architectures, and given that there are, their independence, or interdependence. The later is clearly the case. Architectures also reside within the framework of the knowledge worker.

This chapter fully describes the Knowledge Worker Framework, row by row, and column by column. Every cell is detailed including a high level description of the key work products that result from the cell contained work processes. All cells are, of course, completely integrated. The Knowledge Worker Framework is needed because it encapsulates the other architectures. The Knowledge Worker Framework enables the definition of integratable work products that are stored in the Metabase. As the work products from one architecture are stored in the Metabase, these work products jump-start the efforts of other work products in another architecture effort.

The Knowledge Worker Framework is explained in detail in other material from the Whitemarsh website. Additionally, it is supported by a very detailed methodology, papers, and the Metabase system which holds, interrelates, and makes non-redundant all the Knowledge Worker Framework's work products.

## 3.1    What is a Knowledge Worker?

A knowledge worker is someone who primarily works with information and abstract concepts. Another type of worker is the real product worker. White collar workers such as clinicians and clinical support personnel are knowledge workers because they develop care plans, provide treatments, and record results. Alternatively, workers on a manufacturing line and for example, food service personnel are not knowledge workers because they are primarily focused on the creation and/or assembly of real products.

Both knowledge workers and real product workers share common characteristics including plans, schedules, estimates and result assessments. Notwithstanding, the fundamental work methods and environment that underlie the knowledge worker and the real product worker are different at the core. Thus, trying to make one a clone of the other is both frustrating and invalid.

Due to the abstract nature of their work, information required by knowledge workers can best be stored, assimilated and used as objects, which are encapsulations of data and processes. To most effectively support knowledge workers, the enterprise should strive to create object-oriented environments.

These two concepts, knowledge worker and object-oriented environments are brought together into technology architectures since both uniquely characterize the ideal working environment.

The knowledge worker's environment involves both automated and non-automated activities. Some non-automated activities involve the use of automation, for example, once a patient receives a treatment from a clinician (non automated activity), the characteristics of the treatment, and the clinicians observations about the patient's reaction to the treatment are typically recorded in some automated system. A knowledge worker's framework must therefore address both manual and automated activities.

Knowledge workers perform groups of functions to accomplish their designated job or to accomplish some aspect of the enterprise's mission. Knowledge workers may perform these function groups in different combinations depending on the enterprise's organization. For example, if an organization is highly distributed into multi-functional units, there may be staffs that perform diverse groups of functions. Conversely, a highly centralized organization may have certain staff devoted to specific and highly specialized functions. The knowledge worker is therefore a complex multi-faceted person who performs diverse functions of varying complexities for one or more organizations.

Knowledge workers need a framework within which all their work products are created, stored, and interrelated. All the architectures are thus set within the Knowledge Worker Framework.

The Knowledge Worker Framework's work products are completely defined, integrated and non-redundant. They are supported by an in depth methodology, books, other papers, workshops, seminars, and of course the Metabase software system that stores, interrelates, updates, and reports all

Knowledge Worker Framework products through a multi-user SQL database and system.

## 3.2    The Killer Nature of Stove-pipes

The business focus of Whitemarsh is data management. Short Paper 2, *Data is Executed Policy*, from the Whitemarsh website states the following:

> Data is the "what" that remains after policy is executed. Thus, Data is Executed Policy. When an organization creates policies, it necessarily creates as its companion, procedures. Together, policy and procedures are set into place to the run the business. As the business runs, data, the consequence of policy execution, is created and stored in databases. These databases become the persistent memory of the organization.
>
> "Data" specifications are thus policy definitions. Similarly, process specifications are procedure definitions. Consequently, all data (i.e., policy) specifications are metadata. All process (i.e., procedure) specifications are also metadata. A metadata database (e.g., Whitemarsh Metabase) is a database for all Policy and Procedure Specifications.
>
> Any policies and procedures not specified or transformed to metadata, and which do not result in database data are not only just anecdotes, they also cannot lead to enterprise persistent memory.

Business information system and database "stove-pipes" are what exists when you do not have an enterprise-wide data architecture. A stove-pipe is the catch phrase for a completely enclosed system from combustion to exhaust. From "WordSpy," (http://www.wordspy.com/), an analogous use of *stove-pipes* exists in organization modeling in which departments, managers, and employees have a narrow and rigid set of responsibilities. Given stovepipe organizations, their contained business information systems and databases are almost always also "stove-pipes." That is, the defined data and processes are peculiar and/or unique to the engineering and culture of the owning organizations, managers, and staff. Stove-pipes are thus directly opposed to enterprise-wide integrated people, organization, database and business information systems models.

It is common to have a 20% to 30% overlap across a large collection of data and business information system processes. If there are 500 databases in an enterprise, and if the business information systems for each database cost $1 million, then across the $500 million, between $100 to $150 million would have been redundantly expended, or worse still, expended on conflicting and redundant databases and business information systems.

In another example of the cost of information technology stove-pipes, the very method of designing database and business information systems themselves can be very expensive unrelated to any functional duplication across enterprise business information systems. A common metric for constructing a business information system and associated database is a function point. From Wikipedia,

> A function point is an ISO recognized software metric to size a business information system based on the functionality that is perceived by the user of the business information system, independent of the technology used to implement the business information system.

Function points commonly cost about $400 each to create. Thus, a 5,000 function point sized system would cost about $2 million. But through advanced techniques that involve software engineering and generation, a function point cost can be reduced to $50. That's an 8:1 reduction.

The point to all of this is that architectures are critical, and architectures, properly engineered and integrated across the enterprise, can both dramatically reduce the development of database and business information systems overlap, and can also reduce the actual cost of creating individual business information systems and databases. The architectures that are relevant to data management are:

- Enterprise Architectures.
- Database Object Classes.
- Data.
- Resource Life Cycle Analysis.
- Business Information Systems Plans.

All five of these architectures exist within the overarching framework for the knowledge worker.

## 3.3    Knowledge Worker Framework

The Knowledge Worker Framework, first posited in 1992, is essentially an architectural framework that, from Wikipedia, is ". . . a skeleton upon which various objects are integrated for a given solution." In this case, the scope of the integrated solution is the "knowledge worker." In the case of the Knowledge Worker Framework, the "object" may be a representation of a real object such as a mission, or may be a wholly contained architecture such as the enterprise's architectures, Database Object Classes, and the data architectures. The architectures contained in the Knowledge Worker Framework are listed in Table 2.

A quick review of all the cells in the Knowledge Worker Framework, presented in Table 3, shows that not all the cells are represented in the five architectures listed in Table 2. That's acceptable because not everything has to be represented in one architecture or another. An architecture is intended to have high cohesion and low coupling. Each of the five architectures listed in Table 2 exhibit those characteristics in that they can stand alone and are not dependent on one another.

| Knowledge Worker Framework Contained Architectures | | |
| --- | --- | --- |
| **Architecture** | **Rows** | **Columns** |
| Enterprise | Scope and Business | Mission through Organizations |
| Database Object Classes | System and Technology | Database Object Class |
| Data | Business, System, Technology, Deployment, and Operations | Database Object Class |
| Resource Life Cycle Analysis | Business | Database Object Class |
| Business Information Systems Plans | Scope through Technology | Mission, Database Object Class, and Business Information Systems |

**Table 2.** Knowledge Worker Framework contained architectures.

These architectures are however interconnected, and the mechanism of connection is the Metadata database. In Whitemarsh, this metadata database is called a Metabase. Whitemarsh has been using the string, Metabase, since the early 1980s, and has been designing and building Metabase systems for more than 30 years. Metabases are neither unique nor new. They are however essential to a well ordered, efficient and effective knowledge worker environment in our enterprises.

Databases are commonly seen as the intersection of collections of tables. If a database had only one function-based and narrowly focused collection of tables, it would be called a stove-pipe database. Collections of stove-pipe databases commonly suffer from differently named and discordant semantics for the same thing, and the same names for different things. For example, Region Id in one database is the country's Tax Id number assigned to the corporation. In another database, Region Id might be an auto-generated integer number. In a third database, Region Id might be a crafted code representing a geographic region of the country.

In other databases there are many different names for a person's gender. Notwithstanding that the meaning is easily discovered, some of these value domains are M and F, Male and Female, 0 and 1, and 1 and 2. If combined all together without "scrubbing" a real mess would result, including the fact that in this example there are seven distinct gender codes.

Analogously to real-data databases, the metadata databases that contain the metadata-based work products of all these architectures must be melded, have consistent semantics, and all overlaps merged. It is just not enough to have collections of architectures. If they are unintegrated, redundant, and semantically discordant, they are just stove-pipes, but this time, of metadata.

Table 3 presents the Knowledge Worker Framework. It consists of rows and columns. There are six rows, Scope through Operations represent perspectives on the work products as they are created in an every increasing level of specificity. The rows are not just transformations, one unto the other, however.

| Knowledge Worker Framework | | | | | | |
|---|---|---|---|---|---|---|
| | | Man-machine Interface | | | | |
| | | Machine | | Interface | Man | |
| Deliverables | Mission | Database Object Class | Business Information System | Business Event | Business Function | Organization |
| Scope | List of Business Missions | List of Major Business Resources | List of Business Information Systems | List of Interface Events | List of Major Business Scenarios | List of Organizations |
| Business | Mission Hierarchies | Resource Life Cycles, Data Elements, Specified Data Model | Information Sequencing and Hierarchies | Event Sequencing and Hierarchies | Business Scenario Sequencing and Hierarchies | Organization Charts, Jobs and Descriptions |
| System | Policy Hierarchies | Database Object Class Models | Business Information System Designs | Invocation Protocols, Input and Output Data, and Messages | Best Practices, Quality Measures and Accomplishment Assessments | Job Roles, Responsibilities, and Activity Schedules |
| Technology | Policy Execution Enforcement | Implemented Data Model | Business Information Systems Application Designs | Presentation Layer Business Information System Instigators | Activity Sequences to Accomplish Business Scenarios | Procedure Manuals, Task Lists, Quality Measures and Assessments |
| Deployment | Installed Business Policy and Proce-dures | Operational Data Model | Implemented Business Information Systems | Client-server Windows, Batch Execution Mechanisms | Office Policies and Procedures to Accomplish Activities | Daily Schedules, Shift and Personnel Assignments |
| Operations | Operating Business | View Data Models | Operating Business Information Systems | Start, Stop, and Messages | Detailed Procedure Based Instructions | Daily Activity Executions, and Assessments |

**Table 3.** Knowledge Worker Framework.

There are six columns, Mission through Organization. The mission column stands alone. The Database Objects and Business Information Systems column are the "machine" columns. The Business Function and the Organization columns are the "man" columns. The "man" and "machine" column sets are intersected by the Business Event interface column. This keeps the columns properly grouped and separated from each other in an industrial engineering fashion.

Enterprises commonly create computing supports for knowledge workers under the assumption that the functions they perform and the organizations through which they act are fixed and seldom change. Not only are these assumptions wrong, but when the functions and organizations do change, computing environment changes seldom keeps pace because they are time consuming to specify, difficult to implement, and slow to accomplish. Slow-to-react computing environment changes, therefore, become the very reason why information technology support to business functions and organizations cannot keep pace with the demands of change. What is needed are computing environments that are object-oriented, sensitive to knowledge worker functions and organizations, and that can react to the demands of change in a timely fashion.

What follows is a brief explanation of the Knowledge Worker Framework through an explanation of the rows and the cells belonging to each of the rows. Following the row explanations are the column explanations. While the content of the individual cells are essentially the same, they are presented somewhat differently because in a row-based perspective, for example, the business row, proceeds from missions through organizations, while the column perspective, for example Database Object Class, proceeds on a row by row basis from the "birth" or discovery of Database Object Classes through to the operating enterprise. Ultimately, though, there are no conflicts.

## 3.4    Knowledge Worker Framework Rows

The rows of the Knowledge Worker Framework are largely borrowed, with slight modification, from the Business Information Systems Architecture Framework of John Zachman. The Zachman framework's columns are the six interrogatives set into a particular order of What, How, Where, Who, When, and Why. The Zachman framework, as illustrated at:

www.frameworksoft.com, contains illustrative cell contents that imply products required for information systems.

The Whitemarsh Knowledge Worker Framework did not adopt the Zachman framework columns. This difference is not to just be different for difference's sake, but a difference that resulted from a through analysis of the reasons for information technology systems' failure. The analysis was made of reports from the United States General Accountability Office (GAO) on large-scale information technology system failures. Eight multi 100 million dollar U.S. Federal agency information technology system efforts were studied. Once the reasons for information technology system failure were uncovered, they were allocated to the Zachman framework. From the allocation, it became quite clear that the Zachman framework addressed less than 10% of the reasons for information technology system failure. The failure was not because of the rows, but because of the columns, and the work products implied by the columns.

The Knowledge Worker Framework, in contrast to the Zachman framework, was created "bottom-up" after 25+ years of research and refinement into the creation of a methodology to serve the needs of knowledge workers in database centric environments. When the reasons for information technology system failure were allocated to the Knowledge Worker Framework, the reasons were all addressed. This should not come as a surprise because the Knowledge Worker Framework was not invented. Rather, it was derived over many years of iteration and refinement, and was specifically targeted to the knowledge worker's scope.

The most important value derived from the Knowledge Worker Framework are the identified cells within which the reasons for information technology failures occurred. The overall allocations of percent are provided in Table 4.

There are a number of key observations from Table 4. These, also set out in a summary fashion in Table 5 are:

- First, 41% of the reasons for failure occur because of problems in the first two rows, that is, scope and business. Said another way, every if everything was done perfectly only 59% of the reasons for failure would have been addressed. There wasn't sufficient identification and/or analysis of the enterprise's missions, organizations, or functions. It was impossible to succeed because the problem space was not sufficiently understood. That often occurs because there is too much emphasis on database and business information systems design.

| Knowledge Worker Framework | | | | | | | |
| --- | --- | --- | --- | --- | --- | --- | --- |
| | | Man-Machine Interface | | | | | |
| | | Machine | | Inter-face | Man | | |
| Deliver-ables | Miss-ion | Data-base object Class | Business Infor-mation System | Busi-ness Event | Busi-ness Fun-ction | Organi zation | Row Totals |
| Scope | 5 | 2 | 3 | 1 | 3 | 4 | 18 |
| Business | 5 | 3 | 2 | 1 | 6 | 6 | 23 |
| System | 3 | 2 | 2 | 1 | 12 | 8 | 28 |
| Tech-nology | 1 | 0 | 0 | 0 | 8 | 6 | 15 |
| Deploy-ment | 0 | 0 | 0 | 0 | 5 | 5 | 10 |
| Opera-tions | 0 | 0 | 0 | 0 | 3 | 3 | 6 |
| Col. Totals | 14 | 7 | 7 | 3 | 37 | 32 | 100 |

*Note:* All numbers are expressed as percent allocations of errors to cells. The 12 gray cells are information technology Cells

**Table 4.** Percent Allocation of the GAO reasons for information technology failure to the cells of the Knowledge Worker Framework.

- Second, 29% of all the reasons for failure occur to improper analysis and configuration of just the mission, organization, and function columns within these same scope and business rows. This is just a subset of the first above. If these three areas are insufficiently identified, analyzed, and reviewed then the analysts do not understand what the enterprise is, how it is organized, or what it does.

- Third, 50% of all the reasons for failure occur in the eight cells that are between the System and Operations rows of the Business Function and Business Organization columns. These errors occur because organizations and functions are not properly reconfigured subsequent to a database and/or business information system implementation. Continuing the old processes, policies, procedures, organizations, and methods of work in the face of new supports from databases and business information systems is a recipe for disaster.

- Fourth, only 5% of all the reasons for failure occur within the information technology cells. That is, within the Database Object Class, Business Information System, and Business Event columns that are between the System, Technology, Deployment, and Operations rows. Or to put it another way, 95% of all the reasons for failure lie outside information technology.

| U.S. General Accountability Office Reasons for Information Technology System Failure | |
|---|---|
| **Percent** | **Reasons for information technology Failures Description** |
| 41% | A lack of proper identification, analysis and configuration of enterprise architecture Scope and Business Rows across all six of the columns. That is, Missions, Database Object Classes, Business Information Systems, Business Events, Business Functions and Business Organizations. |
| 29% | A lack of proper identification, analysis and configuration of enterprise architecture Scope and Business Rows of just the Missions, Business Functions and Business Organizations columns. |
| 50% | A lack of proper re-engineering of the business functions and organizations as a consequence of re-engineered databases and business information systems. |
| 5% | A lack of proper engineering and development of databases and business information systems. |

**Table 5.** Summary of U.S. General Accountability Office Reasons for Information Technology System Failure

All of this leads to one and only one conclusion. Organizations that fail to get missions, organizations, and functions correct within the first two rows are almost certain to fail in the development of databases and business information systems.  These cells are the sole provinces of enterprise or subject matter experts, not information technology experts. Information technology experts should not participate, but if they do, they are likely to jeopardize success. That is because information technology experts are likely to see these cells only from an information technology perspective.

What enterprise and subject matter experts need is not for information technology to accomplish the first two rows, nor accomplish the 50% culture-change cells, but there needs to be a good methodology, CASE/Repository systems, and business information system generators so that the enterprise and subject matter experts can get the requirements as accurate as possible before the information technology staff begins any database design or business information system development.

Another point is that to get information technology systems "right" there must be attention paid to 100% of the metadata implied by the Knowledge Worker Framework. And finally, that all this metadata from all the frameworks should be integrated (or at least federated) and non-redundant.

The sections that follow present the rows of the Knowledge Worker Framework along with a description of each row.

## 3.4.1  Scope Row

The Scope row discovers, enumerates, interrelates, and, at a high level, details the contents of the six columns. Thus, discovered, enumerated, interrelated, and described are the enterprise's missions, Database Object Classes, Business Information Systems, Business Events, Business Functions, and Business Organization.

Missions are the essence of the business. Accomplished well, missions are timeless and are independent of both "who" and "how." It is from a foundation of missions that the remaining 35 cells are developed. While missions are created top-down, their completeness and content are validated through both organization and functional analysis. Organizations are bureaucratic groupings of individuals that generally have a common objective and are evaluated as to cost and effectiveness in the completion of their mission. Functions are the human activities that are accomplished by the organizational staff in support of mission accomplishment.

Database Object Classes are the major business-based groupings of enterprise data that proceeds through a well ordered set of states. Business information systems are identified, briefly described and are related to the Database Object Classes.

Business events represent the intersections between [human] functions performed by enterprise staff from within their organizations and the business information systems. Business events are triggered by functions and are set within both calendar and business cycles.

Missions and organizations are interrelated. Functions are related to the mission-organization pairs. Database domains (not listed) are derived from missions and are analyzed to support the discovery of Database Object Classes.

Through this top row, an analyst is able to say which organizations perform which functions, and which business events need assists from business information systems to employ which business data all in support of enterprise mission. This row, across all the columns tells a complete story.

## 3.4.2  Business Row

The Business row details the objects that have been discovered and presented in a high-level way from the first row. In addition to further detailing, the Missions, Organization, and Functions are all set within hierarchies.

The Organization cell additionally shows organization charts, and job descriptions. The Business Functions and Business Events cells show sequencing as well as hierarchies. The Business information systems cell shows an increased quantity of detail.

The Database Object Class cell contains the discovered enterprise resources and their corresponding Resource Life Cycles. Resources are the fundamental components of the business that proceed through major states. The set of ordered states is called a Resource Life Cycle. Examples of resources are facilities, staff, reputation, intellectual property, real property, and the like.

A Resource Life Cycle includes its instigation, a set of state transforms, and then finally a dissolution. For example, employee requisition, employee candidates, employee new-hire, employee assigned, employee evaluated, and employee separated. These Resources and Resource Life Cycles are important because they provide the lattice work through which the databases and business information systems are developed and evolved, and over which business information systems are created.

While related, Database Object Classes and Resources are different. A Database Object Class is pure data that encapsulates states and processes. Resources, in contrast, are significantly more complex and may be related to many Database Object Classes, Business Information Systems, and even whole databases.

Discovered in the database object cell also are the enterprise-level data elements, and the various data models of concepts that ultimately are employed as data model templates for building database designs. An enterprise-level data element is a business fact that may be employed in many business functions, databases and their tables, and business information systems.

This row also tells whole stories. Not only are there missions, organizations, and functions along with their interrelationships, but there are also noun-intensive descriptions, that is, database domains of the data required by the missions. These noun-intensive descriptions are distilled into both Database Object Classes and also enterprise-wide data elements. The Database Object Classes are configured into a high level enterprise entity relationship diagram.

What is now conveyable are the missions, the data required to fulfill the missions, and the business information systems that cause the data to be entered, retrieved and manipulated.

From the right side of the row, staff through organization-based functions instigate business events that, in turn, employ the business information systems to fulfill their knowledge worker roles. These business events are set within both business cycles and calenders so that from the first through the last column the analyst can really understand the scope and operation of the business.

### 3.4.3  System Row

The Systems row is the first row devoted to a "systems perspective." It presumes that the work products created for this row will be employed during the creation of a system. Not all systems are to be information technology systems, however. Some systems are just a systematic set of policies that guide the accomplishment of a highly engineered set of human activities, that is, functions.

For example, there might be a systematic manner through which attendees at a conference are given materials and/or badges. A line is formed, and an Id is presented. A box of registration materials is located and the registration entry is found. A conference badge is produced, and is given to the attendee along with any appropriate conference materials.

Conversely, an order entry system might be a combination of both human-functions and information technology system support. Finally, there might be an entire information technology "batch" system that obtains data from a database and stores it into a data warehouse database.

The cells in the Database Object Class, Business Information Systems, and Business Event for this system's row are created regardless of whether the system is IT-based or manual. In the conference registration example, if all the data are manual, it still has to be defined and entered on some engineered form so that it can be processed in a regular, repeatable, and a systematic manner.

The Mission cell would contain the policy hierarchies that govern the functions that are executed within the organizations and that might govern the rules executed by any system.

In the Database Object Classes cell, the full definitions of Database Object Classes would be found including the data structures, states, table-transformation processes, and entire database object transformation processes. Or, in the case of the manual system, the data and processes found on the forms.

The Business Information Systems cell would contain the design (versus implementation) specifications of any of the business information systems needed to transform the Database Object Classes. In the case of the manual system, these processes would not be in the Business Information System cell. Rather, they would be represented in more detailed levels of the Business Function specifications.

The Business Event cell would contain the business event models across the invocation protocols, and all the expected inputs and outputs. The Business Events would at this point be integrated with the Business Functions that invoke them and the Business Information Systems that they invoke.

The Business Function and the Business Organization models are clearly outside the scope of IT. The work products from these two columns have both an "as-is" and a "to-be" flavor about them. What is critical to know is how the "as-is" functions and organizations will change into the "to-be" functions and organization as a consequence of implementing a Business Information System. If the culture of the enterprise, as evidenced in organizations and functions does not change as a consequence of a new way of conducting business then why have the new business information systems?

Specifically for the Business Function's cell, there would be the creation of functional best practices, quality measures to ensure that the right processes were carried out, and then follow-through assessments on results over time. There's nothing like a "report-card" to keep one's attention. It would also be valuable to have the new functional descriptions evaluated by peer-level businesses, assuming of course that such peer-reviews would not compromise proprietary business practices.

In the Business Organization's cell, there may well be a need to recast job descriptions, methods of organizations that would remove stove-pipes, the ability to seek support through virtual support groups or communities of interest. These revised job descriptions would contain additional responsibilities, modifications to training, and possibly new organizational reporting requirements. All together, the quantity of time required to perform functions within the new organizations should go down because of increased efficiencies, and should show increased quality and effectiveness because of new assists provided by the new business information systems.

From Table 4, the sum of the percents across the Business Function and Business Organization columns from the System through the Operations rows is about 50%. Simply, that means that if all the other cells are done correctly, 50% of the reasons for failure still exist if there has not been a change in the way the enterprise is organized or the functions that are executed to then take advantage of the new business information system's environment. This could be a very expensive lesson indeed.

## 3.4.4  Technology Row

The Technology row, is similar to the Systems row in that it represents a detailing and a new set of work products needed to support either policy specification, Business Organization and Business Function specification, or a furthering of the efforts in support of IT. Thus, the cells in the Database Object Class, Business Information Systems, and Business Event for this technology row are really information technology cells. If there is not a business information system, these cells would likely not be developed as their data would be represented through manual forms, and the detailed processes within the Business Functions column would completely dictate execution.

Given that there is a business information system involved, the Database Object Class models are configured into actual database designs that are then implemented via database management systems. The Business Information Systems column work products are detailed into actual business information system designs.

The mission's cell focuses on the creation of the various enforcement mechanisms for policy execution. In the conference registration procedure above it might include a set of check boxes that require the production of a picture-id that could be used to match against the registration process. If there is a business information system that would be enforcing the registration, maybe the system would produce a picture of the registrant from an initial registration process that might have been on-line. In the case of a conference that would allow non-employees, then the enforcement might be to have a successfully executed fee payment transaction for the conference.

Analogously in the Business Organization and Business Function cells, there would be a further detailing of the various functions and organizations that would be created or revised. For Business Functions, all the activity sequences would be set out and integrated with the various organizations responsible for their accomplishment. Similarly, the Business Organizations would have the various procedure manuals, task lists, quality measures and assessments engineered that would evaluate the organization as a whole.

In the Business Events cell, the actual presentation layers that represent the interfaces between business functions and the business information systems exist and are designed to ensure that there are good human factors interfaces.

## 3.4.5  Deployment Row

The Deployment row presumes that the new environments, from Mission through Business Organizations are ready to be deployed prior to operations. Essentially, this overall row is a roll-out of all the work products so that they can be employed.

In the Mission cell, the various business policy procedures are installed and the various persons performing their organization-based functions are trained. Business Organizations and Business Function cells are similar in that what is installed, trained, and made operational are the office policy and procedures necessary to accomplish activities on a function by function basis, and with respect to Business Organizations, the daily shift schedules, personnel assignments and the like.

As to the Database Object Class cell, the various database designs are bound over to the specific DBMSs that are to operate the databases. In the Business Information Systems column, the systems are deployed on the various hardware. Included of course would have to be any hardware and computing environment procurement activities.

The Business Events cell is where the deployed functions meet the business information systems. In this column's deployment, tests of ease of use and effectiveness would be accomplished to ensure that the projected functional and organization improvements are realized.

## 3.4.6  Operations Row

The Operations row represents the new operating environment. The mission cell would be the operating business. Feedback mechanisms would occur from every set of organization-based functions. This enables a feed back cycle to at least one row above. There would be a similar set of operations for the Business Functions and the Business Organizations. It is very important to have feedback mechanisms including the gathering of operational and performance statistics.

The Database Object Class cell is finally defined in terms of SQL Views that interact with the various databases regardless of the form of data, that is, either fixed formats or XML. The business information systems are set into operation so as to fulfill the needs of the various Business Functions. Finally, Business Events are the day-to-day activity interrupts that are ad hoc, set within business cycles or calendars.

## 3.5  Knowledge Worker Framework Columns

The Knowledge Framework columns represent an unfolding and/or detailing of a collection of work products required over a common domain. These are described in the sections that follow.

### 3.5.1 Mission Column

The mission column represents the rationale or basis for the knowledge worker environment. The first row, Scope, presents the list of missions. The sets of missions are those that form the basis of the enterprise. If a mission is missing then so too is an important aspect of the business. Missions are either external or internal. External missions are those that support the income of the business. Internal missions are those that employ the business's income to operate the business in support of its external missions. For example, if the external mission of the business is to sell a specific product line, then the internal missions are those that support sales, for example, human resource management, research and development, manufacturing, inventory and distribution, and sales management.

Missions are mechanisms for enterprise database partitioning. Once missions are listed, they become the criteria for including or excluding entries in the remaining 35 cells. Additionally, once missions are delineated, one or more missions can be chosen to pursue through the remainder of the framework. Each mission may also be pursued by different analysis and design teams. The only real down side to this approach is the necessary integration once different subordinate mission Implementations are accomplished. If the top two rows (scope and business) are completed prior to breaking the work into separate projects, the end result is more easily integrated.

The Business cell of a mission contains mission hierarchies. Each mission, for example, product sales, or human resource management is represented as a hierarchy of text paragraphs and is presented in an "accomplished-form." That is, the mission is described as if it were completed in a completely ideal manner. Completely removed are any indications of either Who, Who, or Technology.

The Systems cell contains hierarchies of the policies that must be present to accomplish various missions. Business policies must be present to accomplish an enterprise's mission. Each policy must be set out such that it can be easily understood, commonly rationalized, and its adherence must be easily assessed.

The Technology cell represents fully specified and implemented view of enterprise policies that are executed and/or enforced. When the policies are set within the organizations and the functions to which they apply, they must represent common sense to the maximum extent possible. Confusion and misunderstanding lead to uneven execution and uneven results.

The Deployment cell represents the actual "in the field" sets of policies whose execution result in data that is collected, updated, and reported. Data is executed policy. Deployment of policies must include all the necessary training, and if necessary the "hot-line" support to adjudicate the best and most efficient way of carrying out the policies. Of necessity, policy deployments are set within organizational and functional re-engineering efforts.

The Operations cell represents the ongoing and executing set of policies that carry out various aspects of the enterprise' missions. As operations occur it must be quickly and easily determine whether policies are being accurately carried out. Organizations and functions must exist to promote good policy execution, and the appropriate reporting and correction when established policies are being violated.

## 3.5.2  Database Object Class

A Database Object Class is a collection of traditional (that is, formatted and structured data) and nontraditional (that is, video, sound, and unstructured text) data. Database Object Classes proceed through precisely defined states starting with the null state, and then a series of discrete business defined, interlinked non-null states, and finally a null state. Database Object Classes are squarely based on policy analysis for its data structure formulation, and on procedure specification for the proper valuation, modification, migration, and reporting of Database Object Classes.

The Scope cell contains the list of the major resources of the enterprise. Included for example would be organizations, assets, reputation, intellectual property, income and expenses. These resources are key indicators of the major classes of data that are to be discovered and designed into databases.

The Business cell contains three major items: Resource Life Cycles, Data Elements, and Specified Data Models. Not listed are database domains. The Resource Life Cycles are detailed from the Resources that are identified and described in the scope row. As already stated, a resource is a fundamental of the business about which information is collected, funds are expended, or is sold and expensed. Examples are people, contacts, fixed assets, and the like. All business resources are set squarely within the business' missions.

In the Business cell, the resources are decomposed into their Resource Life Cycles. Resource Life Cycle (RLC) was developed by from Ron Ross.[4] Resource life cycles form the basis of the Business Information Systems Plans. Each Resource Life Cycle contains the major state names from the business resource's life cycle. From Ron Ross' book, the Resource Life Cycle for parts might be:

- Define part types
- Establish suppliers
- Acquire parts
- Accept part requests
- Ship parts
- Maintain parts

From a foundation of missions defined within the mission's column, database domains are identified from the mission leaves. Database domains are noun-intensive descriptions of the data necessary to accomplish the mission. From the database domains, the nouns, which are essentially undifferentiated entities are triaged into three groups: Database Object Classes, enterprise data elements, and classes of properties.

Enterprise data elements are the business facts important to the enterprise that may be represented in one or more data models that are created in the Business, System, Technology and Deployment models.

Database Object Classes are collections of data specifications about a single subject. For example, a Company database object would contain company identification information, company products, company locations, company staff assignments, and the like. Finally, a property class is collection of business facts about one simple topic. An example would be the business facts that are necessary to represent a company address.

---

[4]  *Resource Life Cycle Analysis, A Business Modeling Technique for IS Planning* (Database Research Group, Boston, 1992) is a technique for identifying the components of a business that is subject to information systems. The resource life cycles are the basis from which database objects are identified, designed, implemented and deployed.

The Business row also contains the Specified Data Models, which are data models of concepts. These concept data models[5] are employed in the creation of the data models in the subsequent rows.

Within the Business cell, the identified Database Object Classes and database domains need to be cross referenced. Having a database domain without Database Object Classes or vice versa is an analysis error. Similarly, not having a Resource Life Cycle node without one or more Database Object Classes is also an analysis error.

The Technology cell represents Database Object Classes completely through Implemented Data Models within the persistent data language, SQL. As ANSI SQL evolves, and as DBMS vendors implement greater quantities of the standards's features there should be fewer and fewer proprietary database facilities. Today, the majority of the database object processes and database object information systems are SQL vendor proprietary. Notwithstanding the quantity of vendor proprietary code, it is all commercial off the shelf (COTS) software, and firmly based on the technology independent Database Object Class specifications contained in the systems view.

The Deployment cell for Database Object Class represents the actual instances of distributed database data models. Most commonly, these data models operate through the SQL language under the control of a DBMS. If all the cells above the deployment cell have been accomplished carefully, there will be a great deal of interoperability across all the deployed databases. That is because many operational databases will share the same Implemented Data Model, which, in turn, will have been built using commonly constructed data models of concepts that finally, are based on enterprise-wide data elements.

The Operations cell, represent the running databases that interact with business information systems through views. Well engineered business information systems supported by quality database management systems will be able to share data across the databases. Alternatively, the data may be expressed from the business information systems not in terms of SQL views

---

[5]     Note: A data model of a concept is not a conceptual data model. The former is a fully defined data model, and the later represents a "fuzzy" form of a data model that, through data model "baking" becomes more well-formed, that is, a logical data model, and thereafter through more "baking," a physical data model. This is a critical difference. In Whitemarsh, Specified Data Models are data models of concepts. This is a difference with a real distinction.

but as XML formatted schemas and instance streams. These, in turn, would be available for use by other business information systems.

### 3.5.3   Business Information System Column

A business information system is a computer-based data processing system that accomplishes database object state transformations from within the context of business functions. Different business functions may cause the execution of the same business information system. If, in any of the business functions that employ a business information system, the database object value state transformation is not accomplished, the entire set of database object transformations is rolled back so that the database object returns to its prior state.

The Scope cell identifies the business information systems required to support the resources. The list is simple, one business information system per business resource[6]. If, for example, a business resource is people, the business information system would be the human resource management business information system. Similarly identified and named are finance, customer management, facility's management, project management, and asset management business information systems.

The Business cell for business information systems contains the business information system hierarchies necessary to carry out the business information system requirements of the database object transformations inferred by the business Resource Life Cycles. Named components within each detailed business information system clearly identify the nodes within each Resource Life Cycle. For the Parts business resource, the necessary business information systems might be as depicted in Table 6.

Within the systems view, each identified business information system component, for example, Adjust Parts Inventory, is detailed in terms of its logic, screens, file accesses, and reports. Included at this level are the necessary connections to the specific aspects of each database object data structure. Identified and connected as well are the database object processes,

---

[6]     Within the Technology cell, each business information systems from the system's row may become multiple information systems that are implemented on different hardware, operating systems, and that operate through different DBMSs.

and the necessary database object information systems that begin and structure the processes necessary to modify the database object's structure from null to an allowed non-null state.

The critical difference between the database object information system and the business information system is that the database object information system is completely specified and totally implemented within ANSI standard SQL language while the business information system is completely specified and totally implemented within either an ANSI standard 3GL (e.g., COBOL, C) or a vendor proprietary 4GL (e.g., Clarion, FOCUS, and Power Builder).

| Parts Resource Life Cycle Nodes | Business information system Hierarchies |
|---|---|
| Part type definition | Create part type,<br>Maintain parts (insert, maintain, and delete part) |
| Supplier establishment | Create supplier,<br>Maintain suppliers (insert, maintain, and delete supplier) |
| Parts acquisition | Enter part receipt<br>Adjust inventory |
| Order management | Reserve part for order<br>Adjust order line item<br>Report inventory status |
| Parts shipment | Build bill-of-lading<br>Establish shipment<br>Acknowledge shipment receipt |
| Parts maintenance | Adjust parts inventory<br>Replace existing inventory |

**Table 6.** Cross reference between Resource Life Cycle Nodes and Business Information Systems.

The reason that the database object information system is expressed entirely in ANSI/SQL syntax is so it can be ported from one ANSI standard conforming SQL DBMS to another almost without regard to operating system, hardware platform, and presentation layer. In contrast, business information systems interface directly with end users. In client/server parlance that means that the business information systems include a "presentation layer."

Because of the business information system presentation layer, which is almost always operating system and computer platform dependent, porting business information systems can be problematic. It's even more problematic if the database-centric table processing rules have to be encoded in each business information system because not only are the presentation layer based business information systems bloated, the very same business rules have to be coded through a number of different languages. Database Object Information Systems enable the table process rules to be encapsulated within the DBMS.

Within the technology cell, business information systems consist of traditional components, that is, detailed designs for screens, files, reports, processes, menus, and the like. To accelerate implementation, business information system generators should be used whenever possible. Assuming they are, four benefits immediately accrue:

- Detailed design is quicker because the business information system generator builds so many of the system components.

- Coding errors within generated programs are virtually eliminated thus making unit test time close to zero.

- Generated system design documentation is commonly an automatic byproduct of business information system generators

- Long term maintenance is easier because of the three previous benefits.

Within the Deployment cell, business information system components are deployed. Included are equipment, acquisition of network support, and creation of an information technology support infrastructure for training and hotline. For example, the actual systems, programs, menus, and data files. When these components are generated, these only have to undergo normal configuration management.

Finally, within the Operations cell, the business information system components that take in data, produce reports and perform calculations execute. That is, accomplish the requirements of the business event that were instigated by a business function operating within a business organization.

### 3.5.4  Business Event Column

Business Events are the interfaces between the two "machine" columns of the framework and the two "man" columns. The main reason there is a column formally dedicated to the interfaces between man and machine is to preserve their independence, and to set these events squarely within calendar and business cycles. The "man" columns are able to be crafted to fit different and individual functional styles within different and unique organizations.

The Scope cell contains the list of business events required to accomplish business information systems as they support business functions. For the "Parts" example, above, the business events are: Perform Parts Acquisition and Maintenance. Each listed business event acts as a surrogate for the set of business event sequences and if necessary, hierarchies. Each sequence or hierarchy is represented by one member of the business event list.

The Business cell contains the various business event sequences and hierarchies. For example, using the "parts" example from above, the information in the columns surrounding parts is presented in Table 7

| Resource Life Cycle Node | Business information system | Business Event | Business Function |
|---|---|---|---|
| Part type definition | Create part type | Invoke part creation | Create new part information for business |
| Supplier establishment | Create supplier, | Invoke supplier creation | Establish new supplier of parts |
| Parts acquisition | Enter part receipt | Invoke part receipt | Acquire parts from supplier |

**Table 7.** Resource Life Cycle cross relationship with Business Information Systems and Business Events.

The Systems cell contains the specifications of the invocation protocols, input and output data, and the various messages that must be exchanged between the business information systems and the business functions. In the example of Parts, the input information is the specification of the data that must be submitted to establish a new part or supplier, or the specification of a report that is produced by a business information system in support of a particular business function.

The Technology cell contains the precise specifications of the man-machine interface for the different types of involved technology. For example, one business function may cause the creation of the data necessary to instigate a batch report. Another business function may have to create input data in a specific sequence and format. A final example might be the format and the mode of a generated report.

The Development cell of a business event contains the actual developed forms, computer screens, data entry instructions, and the instructions for acquiring and handling reports that ultimately form the operating environment.

The Operations cell embraces the day-to-day operational aspects of interfacing business functions and business information systems. This involves ensuring that there are enough data entry forms, sufficient paper for reports, computers, and telecommunications networks.

## 3.5.5   Business Function Column

A Business Function is a procedure accomplished by someone within an organization to complete some aspect of a business' mission. Business functions almost always exceed the bounds of business information systems. For example, a business function to acquire a new part of a company's inventory might involve identification, gathering examples, analysis for engineering, durability, cost, and repair. Finally, a part is selected for inclusion. Then and only then is the information about the part encoded onto a data entry form as required by the appropriate business event, and then entered into a database through a business information system.

Business functions are commonly a matter of style. Different business organizations can have the same business function style, and the same business organization can have different business function styles. The greatest disaster that can befall a large scale business information system is that its design is derived from a hierarchical decomposition of the business function's lowest levels. When that happens and there is the slightest change to the business functions, the business information systems must also change. The business information system gets whip-sawed. Or, stated differently, whenever the business functions get a *cold*, the business information system, at best gets a *pneumonia*, and at worst, *dies*.

The Knowledge Worker Framework is engineered to keep business information systems and business functions independent one from the other. Only when the business functions change to the extent that they need additional or different business information systems are business information systems impacted by business function changes. These changes typically occur only after there has been a business mission change.

The Scope cell of business functions is the list of the highest level business functions. These functions should closely parallel missions. Missions however, are different from business functions. Business missions are the ultimate targets of the enterprise. Not all missions are necessarily accomplished in the manner they are described. Business functions, however, are always accomplished else the business does not operate. Careful attention should be paid to any differences in business functions that need to be created once a new business information system's environment is put into place. The key questions are: What are the existing functions, what are the new functions, what functions have to be changed or even retired?

Business functions change over time far more frequently than do business missions. Consider for example any large insurance company. Clearly its missions deal with finding clients, offering insurance, performing underwriting, selling and administering policies, and paying claims. These missions have been the basis of insurance for several hundred years.

Business functions however, may change far more often. Insurance almost certainly was only sold through direct contacts with insurance agents. Today, solicitations come in the mail almost every day, and the agents call only during dinner. Payments formerly made through the agent who came to the door on a "debit" route can now be automatically deducted from checking accounts. Claimants used to await the individual insurance agent to inspect damage can now have their claims filed and adjudicated over the phone. Formerly, payments presented by the insurance agent can now be wire transferred or paid on-line to claimant accounts.

Sometimes however, the same business function is performed differently by different organizations. Another difference between mission and function is that missions are described independently from the *how* and *who, and technology* that accomplish them. Business function is the *how* description. Within any business function, the missions are presumed, but the *who* is not known whenever business functions are performed by all business organizations. Whenever the same business function is performed by multiple organizations, but differently, then the business function description is described and then allocated to the specific organization. Business information systems engineering is part of the *technology*.

Within the Business cell, each business function is described in terms of the scenarios performed to accomplish some aspect of the business' mission. Each business function hierarchy is set down along with the sequencing of the steps within each hierarchy. If different business organizations perform the business function, the scenario descriptions can be different so long as the ultimate objectives of the function are clearly identified and are obvious to those who perform the function. As with the Scope cell, great care needs to be exercised to assess the current versus the new. Are functions going to be sequenced differently? What are the changes, and how will they affect the current staffing, current skill mixes, and the like? All these questions need to be asked and answered because any new information technology without corresponding human functions changes will only cause ultimate failure. The GAO studies from which the reasons for information technology failure were uncovered prove that without question.

Within the System cell, each business function contains the exposition of the best practices, quality measure, and accomplishment assessments. These materials represent the idealized methods an organization can employ to accomplish business functions. Supporting each best practice are the various performance targets and assessments that judge satisfactory accomplishment. Whenever business functions are performed differently, there must be style independent assessments. Again, with the cells above, great care must be taken to discover the right set of new "best practices." Existing staff will not look too kindly on knowing that their current practice is now being replaced with "best-practice." The staff will naturally ask, "haven't we been doing our best-practice?" Time and care must be exercised because any imposed new best practice may be subtly sabotaged by knowledge workers unwilling to change. Conversely, any thoroughly untested practice may sabotage an already existing best-practice.

Within the Technology cell, business functions are detailed into their specific activity sequences that accomplish the business scenarios. Each set of activities is stylized to fit the specific organization carrying them out. The activity sequences are evaluated against the best practices and assessment criteria to ensure that the activities accomplish the desired result. As with the above cells, any new specific activity scenarios will have to be carefully worked out so that there is "buy-in" to the new procedures. All organizations will not work exactly the same way. Activity scenarios will likely be different because of different cultures, age groups, and other dynamics.

The Deployment cell represents the actual office procedures employed by organizations performing business functions. These deployed activities must be supported by necessary operational policies, procedures, and whatever technology supports that many be required. By this time in the process of unfolding a new business information systems environment, all must be ready and be willingly received or else the new business information system's deployment is in grave jeopardy. There must have been thorough testing in realistic laboratories of the new functions, new business events, new business information system presentation layers, and the like. If there is not marked improvement in productivity, data quality, ease of use, reporting, and the like, failure may be right around the corner. It is critical to remember that 50% of the reasons for failure still exist once a business information systems is deployed.

The Operations cell represents the detailed instructions that exist within an office and a schedule to actually perform the business function's work. These office procedures should be taught, monitored, and constantly evaluated for maximum efficiency, effectiveness, and minimum cost and risk. At this point in the unfolding of new functionality, success or failure has been predetermined by the care taken in the above cells. No questions should remain when the business information systems are turned on.

## 3.5.6  Organization Column

An organization is a formally constituted group of persons chartered to perform business functions to achieve some aspect of a business' mission. While small businesses often have the same organization from one location to another, large businesses do not. In fact, as businesses become larger and more diversified, organizations become different, stylized, and whenever management changes, business organizations often change in lock-step. Even when the mission of the enterprise fundamentally stays the same, there are business organization changes. It is also quite common to change business function to match the new styles adopted by the business organization changes.

Business organizations are capable of change at a far greater rate than can the business information systems that support them. Thus, while organization changes might only cause mild disruptions, business information systems changes occur only after great expense and significant disruption. Because of these two dynamics, it's ideal not to have to change a business information system whenever a business organization and/or business function change.

To achieve this ideal, the Knowledge Worker Framework is engineered to keep business functions and business organizations independent one from the other, and both independent from business information systems. Only when the business organizations change to the extent that they need additional or different business functions are business functions impacted. The most common changes are those that cause business functions to be transferred from or into different business organizations. Those changes seldom ever impact business information systems. The only business organization changes that impact business information systems are those that typically occur after there has been a business mission change.

Within the Scope cell, the list of the business organizations performing the business functions is provided. It is critical to have a clear comparison between the "as-is" organizations and the "to-be" organizations. It is likely that the "as-is" organizations will have grown up over time to handle the existing set of business information systems, Database Object Classes, and business functions that may well be replaced. If these organizations are not analyzed to see how they might be reconfigured, the real benefits of the new business information systems may never be realized.

Within the Business cell, the various organization charts, jobs and their descriptions are provided. These provide an understanding of the types of persons who will be performing the business functions. In a manner similar to the Scope cell, the "as-is" organization charts, jobs, and descriptions need to be assessed and possibly reconfigured to be the appropriate set of "to-be" organization charts, jobs, and descriptions. Resistance to change should never be under estimated. Great care and planning, and a large quantity of meetings may have to occur to convince the existing staff to change. This would especially be true if there's any hint of outsourcing and/or even "off-shoring" certain functions.

Similar with the two cells above, the System's cell would contain the detailed job roles, responsibilities and activity schedules are provided to better understand when and how the business functions are accomplished. It is likely that over the years there have been subtle changes to the formally constituted and written "as-is" versions of all the job descriptions. Consequently, the "as-is" job descriptions might have to be created from scratch to accurately reflect the current situation before any "to-be" versions of these materials can be created. Once the "to-be" versions are created, a "differences" assessment can be made that would cause the creation of requirements for the development of new training materials, trainers, additional or different technology infrastructure, and the like that must be created prior to any new functionality deployment.

Within the Technology cell, the various new and/or revised procedure manuals are created along with their task lists, the quality measures that ensure that the activity is successfully accomplished by the specific organizational unit, and the specifications of exactly how the activities are assessed. These materials are created and updated on an as needed basis.

Within the Deployment row, the daily schedules, shift and personnel assignments are created. These are integrated with the various business functions. Since organizations can vary, there may be different configurations that perform business functions. The measures of equivalency are the best practices, measures, and assessment criteria created as part of the business function system viewpoint.

Within the Operations cell, organizations are deployed and accomplish the full set of business functions necessary to carry out the business' missions.

## 3.6    Knowledge Worker Framework Summary

This chapter described the Knowledge Worker Framework, row by row, and column by column. Every cell is detailed including a high level description of key work products that result from the cell-contained work processes. All cells are, of course, completely integrated.

This chapter also provided a high level view of the processes necessary to create each work product. Detailed process steps are provided in other Whitemarsh materials.

The Knowledge Worker Framework is just that: a framework for the knowledge worker. The percent of reasons for information technology system failure from Table 4 clearly indicate the framework's real value. If all the cells are accomplished appropriately there's a high probability of success. But, if only the information technology cells are done perfectly, there's still 95% of the reasons for failure. If the cells from the mission, organization and function cells are not done from the system row down, there's still 50% of the failure reasons. These 50% cells are those that would reflect the changed culture regarding organizations, functions, and policy.

Table 4 also shows that even if the "system" that is being contemplated is not an information technology system then there is still a very good reason to use this framework's cells as 66% of all the cells are outside the domain of IT. A close reading of the text from the non-IT cells describes non-IT activities.

Prior to moving onto the Knowledge Worker Framework contained architectures, Figure 9 shows an overall interaction among the columns from the framework. The single headed arrows means 1:M (one-to-many). The manner of reading this diagram is as follows. One mission requires one or more Database Object Classes to fulfill its objective. Similarly, a Database Object Class may be required in one or more missions.

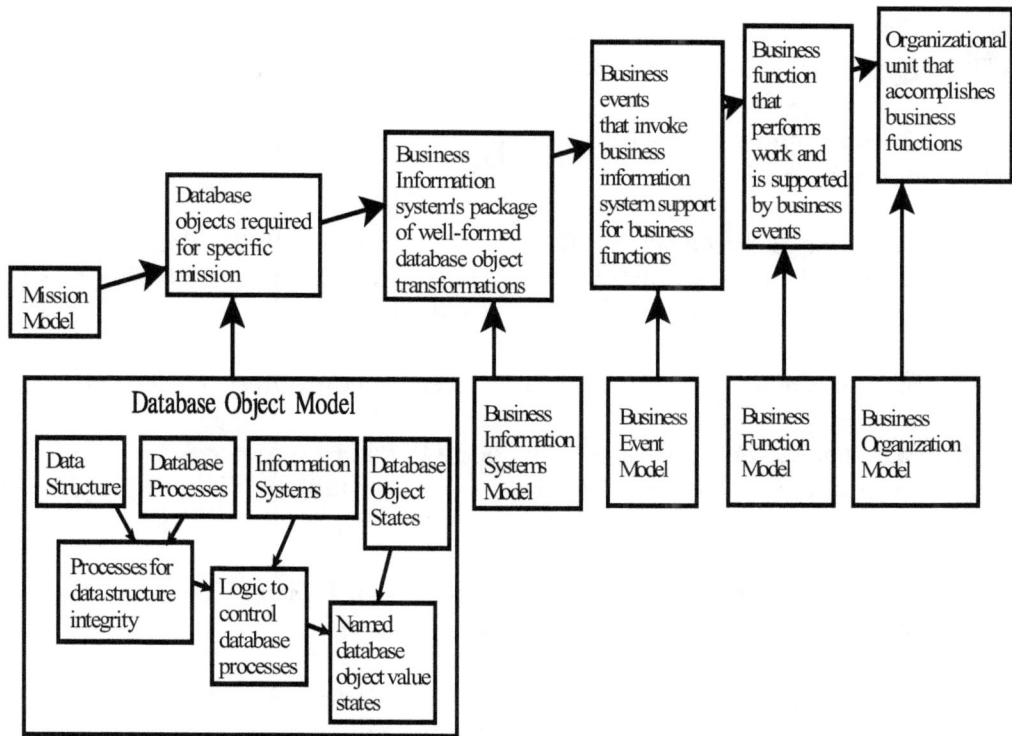

**Figure 9.** Overall relationship across Knowledge Worker Framework columns.

The relationships between the Mission Model and the Database Object Class Model are many-to-many.

Similarly, a Database Object Class may be needed in one or more business information systems, and a business information systems may require data from or put data into one or more Database Object Classes. The remainder of the diagram is read in a similar manner.

The next chapter, Chapter 4, the Enterprise's Architecture, describes the contents of the enterprise's architecture and describes at a high level how the enterprise's architecture is created. This chapter also described the work products, how they are interrelated, and how these work products fit with the work products of the other architectures. What is actually being created within the enterprise's architecture are the set of work products of the Knowledge Worker Framework's first two rows as enumerated in Sections 3.4.1 and 3.4.2 above.

## 3.7    Questions and Exercises

1.    Does the concept of a Knowledge Worker make sense? If yes, why? If not, why not?

2.    Compare and contrast the Knowledge Worker with the Process Worker. What about both is the same? Different? Which is harder to manage? How do you measure success with each?

3.    Should Knowledge Workers be "slaves" to computers or vice versa?

4.    Who should engineer the Knowledge Worker Framework? Information Technology? Or business management? Or both in a cooperative arrangement?

5.    What are your experiences with "reasons for failure?" The same? Different? If different, how and by how much?

6.    Does your organization have a process for addressing failures and amendments to processes or environmental factors that may have contributed reasons for failure? If yes, has it worked, that is, you've

improved? Or yes, but no improvement and why is that so? If no, then why not? How then do you improve?

7.  Do the rows in the Knowledge Worker Framework make sense? Can you see the unfolding, transformation, and operations of your environment through the rows? If yes, then why? If not, what's missing and why?

8.  Is there anything magical about the rows? Should there be more? Fewer? Explain.

9.  Do the columns in the Knowledge Worker Framework make sense? Can you see the unfolding, transformation, and operations of the major work product classifications within your environment through the columns? If yes, then why? If not, what's missing and why?

10. When you examine the columns, work product by work product, does the sequence down through the column make sense? Would you move work products up or down?

11. The columns of the Knowledge Worker Framework are related to each other via many-to-many relationships. What purpose does that serve? How will it benefit your organization?

12. The work products within the Knowledge Worker Framework cells are somewhat related to each other. Should all relationships be restricted to column-adjacency boundaries? Can work products within cells be related to other work products in different cells that are not adjacent? If yes, then wouldn't the methodology through which the Knowledge Worker Framework is accomplished be more than just a top-down and left-right methodology? How about the metadata repository for the work products? Wouldn't it be a traditional database with tables, relationships, and the like? How would you accomplish all this?

13. When a framework is adopted and followed by multiple and separate teams on different projects, should the work products be clear and unambiguously so that they can be commonly understood?

14. What is the benefit of being able to "use" another team's work products in your architecture project? Do you copy it, or do you

"attach" to it? If copy then how do you keep synchronized? If
"attached" then how are you notified of changes and how do you
figure the effects of the changes?

15.    The Knowledge Worker Framework clearly separates mission from the
other five columns. Is that good? What's the effect of getting the
mission wrong? How do you prevent it from being wrong?

16.    The Knowledge Worker Framework separates the two "man" columns
from the two "machine" columns, and intersects "man" and
"machine" with the Business Event column. Is this a good strategy? If
yes, why? If not, why not?

17.    Do you agree that 50% of the reasons for failure occur after systems are
deployed? What's been your experience with "Change Management?"
Is it planned enough? What are the effects of bad "Change
Management?"

# 4

# Enterprise's Architecture

Chapter 3 was entirely focused on the Knowledge Worker Framework. It is within that framework that the architecture in this chapter and in the following chapters reside. The Knowledge Worker Framework is not just another framework. It has been crafted and evolved over many years and was inductively arrived at from very high quality database project methodolgoies.

This chapter, the Enterprise's Architecture, describes the contents of the enterprise's architecture and describes at a high level how the enterprise's architecture is created. This chapter also describes the work products, how they are interrelated, and how these work products fit with the work products of the other architectures.

## 4.1    The Enterprise's Architecture Scope

An enterprise's architecture is the engineering and structure of the enterprise's mission, organizations, functions and database domains so that they can be extended and/or integrated with other more technical architectures such as hardware, business information systems, and business events.

The title of this book is Enterprise Architectures. The title implies that the book is about the various classes of architectures that exist within the enterprise. This chapter describes the enterprise's architecture. Essentially, the first two rows of the Knowledge Worker Framework are the enterprise's architecture.

The enterprise's architecture from the point of view of the knowledge worker comes directly from rows 1 and 2 of the framework shown in Table 3. That is, the Scope and Business rows. There are many other architectures within the enterprise such as finance, products, location, and within information technology, there are architectures of hardware, and networks. All of these architectures would have similar rows, but probably different columns. The column represents the different major product groupings about which the architecture is created.

## 4.2    The Enterprise's Architecture Components

A review of the products shown in Table 3, and then the row sections, 3.5.1 and 3.5.2 and then the Scope and Business rows of the column sections, 3.5.1 through 3.5.6 identify the enterprise's architecture products and explain their contents from both a row and column perspective.

Figure 10[7] depicts the Metabase high-level data model for storing the data contained in the enterprise's architecture. Table 8 enumerates and describes each of the components.

## 4.3    Enterprise's Architecture Process Flow

In the enterprise's architecture, the Missions, Business Organizations and Business Functions are all captured in their hierarchical manner. Missions and Business Organizations are then interrelated to make Mission-Organization pairs. Business Functions are related to the Mission-Organization pairs making valid triples, Mission-Organization-Function.

While not described in Table 3, it is also important to collect the management levels and positions and then related these to the various Mission-Organization-Function triples. Once the Missions are created, they can be cross referenced with the Business Organizations. No relevant organization should be without at least one mission. Else why have the organizations?

---

[7] Throughout this book, the "line with arrow head" conventions are as follows: 1. A line from a component to itself with one arrow-head is a recursive relationship. Ex. Mission contains mission. 2) A line between a component and itself with an arrow head on both ends of the line is a network relationship. Ex. From Figure 17, a concept can contain multiple concepts, and a concept can be contained in multiple concepts. 3) A line between two components with a single arrow head is a one-to-many relationship. Ex. Mission has zero, one, or more Database Domains. 4) A line between two different components that has an arrow head at both ends represents a many-to-many relationship. Ex. Business event can involve many Business Information Systems, and a Business Information System can be involved in many Business Events.

---

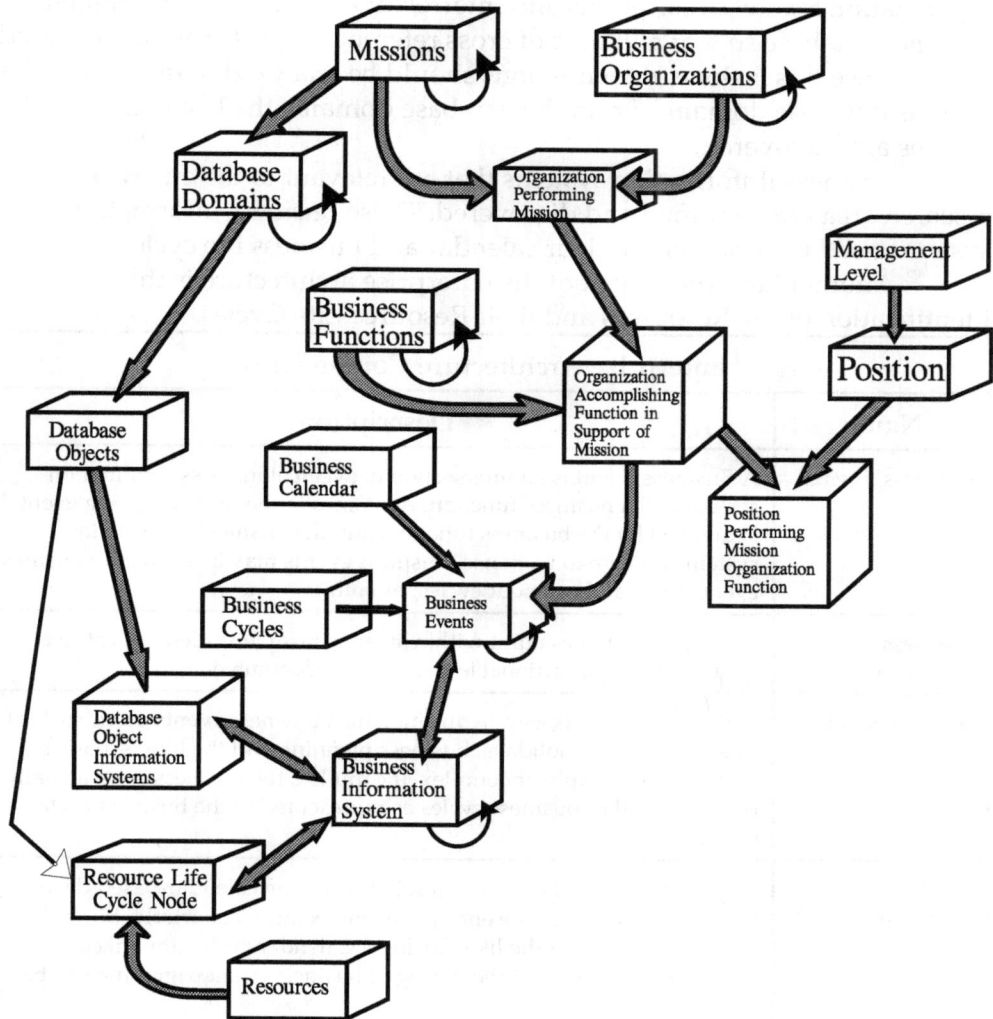

**Figure 10**. Enterprise architecture products and interrelationships.

Business Functions are also a good cross-reference check on the missions. Once the Missions, Organizations, and Business Functions are created and cross-referenced there should be a good view of the enterprise under study. It is common to have the Mission, Organization, and Business Function documents 25 or more pages each. All these hierarchically organization textual descriptions and interrelationships should be entered into the Metabase so that all kinds of cross reference reports can be produced.

Once this is done, then missions should be analyzed to determine the various database domains. From the database domains the Database Object Classes are discovered.

Business iInformation systems that are relevant to the enterprise research area are identified and discovered. These business information systems need to be set within their calendar and business life cycles.

Another key component of the enterprise architecture is the identification of the Resources and their Resource Life Cycles.

| Enterprise Architecture Components | |
|---|---|
| Name | Description |
| Business Events | A Business Event is an intersection between a business information system and a business function. A business event is a triggering event. It is invoked by the business function, and the business information systems execute in response. Business events may be set within business event cycles and calendar cycles, or both. |
| Business Organizations | An Organization is a unit within an enterprise. It is hierarchical so any quantity of organizational levels can be represented. |
| Business Cycle | A Business Cycle is a cycle during which business events occur such as financial reports, holidays, business planning and the like. A business cycle may be simple or complex. If complex, the business cycle actually consists of other business cycles as represented in the business cycle structure. |
| Business Calendar | A Business Calendar Cycle is a set of recurring calendar-based dates that are of interest to the enterprise. For example, quarterly, bi-weekly, monthly, daily, and the like. Business Calender cycles are linked to Business Events so that the timing of business event triggering can be known. |
| Business Functions | A Business Function is a set of hierarchically organization text that describes the activities performed by a position within an organization. Business functions are entirely human-based and if support is needed from a business information system then a business event is triggered. Business functions are independent of organizations and may be allocated to more than one business organization. |

| Enterprise Architecture Components | |
|---|---|
| **Name** | **Description** |
| Business Information Systems | A Business Information System is a computer-based business information system that is being managed through the Metabase. It is known by its characteristics, its operation cycles (business and calendar), subordinate business information systems, employed databases, views, and associated Resource Life Cycle nodes. |
| Database Domains | A Database Domain is a hierarchically organized set of noun-intensive descriptions associated with a mission leaf. Analyzed database domains lead to the identification of Database Object Classes, enterprise data elements, and property classes. Property classes, in turn, often become tables in databases. |
| Database Object Classes | A Database Object Class is a large collection of data and processes that are tied together for business-based reasons, and when instantiated, proceeds through well defined states. A database object can exist in two forms: a collection of interrelated database tables, or the set of a column-based nested structures within a table. The rows that comprise an object are transformed from one valid state to another via database object table processes and database object information systems. Database objects are related to one or more database domains. |
| Database Object Information Systems | A Database Object Information System is a collection of processes defined within the domain of the DBMS usually as a stored procedure that transforms one or more rows of a database object from one valid state to another. A database object information system accomplishes one or more database object table processes. |
| Management Level | Management level is a named and defined level of bureaucratic management within an organizational setting. Examples could be executive, senior, mid-level, and first-level. |
| Missions | Missions are hierarchically organized textual descriptions that define the very existence of the enterprise, and that are the ultimate goals and objectives that measure enterprise accomplishment from within different business functions and organizations. An enterprise is incomplete if one of its missions is not defined. Not all enterprises accomplish their missions simultaneously or in an ideal state. Missions are accomplished over time and are subject to revisions. |

| Enterprise Architecture Components | |
|---|---|
| **Name** | **Description** |
| Organizations Performing Missions | An Organization Performing Missions, that is, a Mission-Organization is the association of an organization with a mission. There can be multiple organizations associated with a mission and an organization can be associated with multiple missions. The description contained within the Mission-Organization may be more refined than the description contained in either the mission or the organization. |
| Organizations Accomplishing Functions ... | An organization accomplishing a function in support of a mission, that is, a Mission-Organization-Function is the association of a mission-organization with a function. A mission-organization can be associated with multiple functions and a function can be associated with multiple mission-organizations. One or more mission-organization-functions may be associated with a business information system. When they are, business events are created. |
| Positions | A Position is a named and defined collection of work tasks that can be performed by or more persons. Positions are often assigned to one or more organizations. |
| Positions performing missions ... | A Mission Organization Function Position Role is the assignment of a position to a particular function within an organization as it accomplishes a mission. Once a position is assigned, its role can be described. |
| Resource Life Cycle Analysis Node | A Resource Life Cycle Node is a life cycle state within the resource. If the resource is employee, the life cycle node may be employee requisition, employee candidate, employee new hire, assigned employee, reviewed employee, and separated employee. |
| Resources | A Resource is an enduring asset of value to the enterprise. Included for example are facilities, assets, staffs, money, even abstract concepts like reputation. If a resource is missing then the enterprise is incomplete. |

**Table 8.** Enterprise's architecture components.

Once these are all identified, described, and entered into the Metabase, the Database Object Classes and Resource Life Cycle nodes are intersected. Database Object Classes and Business Information Systems are interrelated though the creation of a Database Object Information System. Database Object Class details are discussed in the Database Object Classes architecture section.

The objective of the enterprise architecture effort is to clearly know what the enterprise is, what are its critical components, and to set all the descriptions of these components into their proper relationship with other components. Done completely, but at a reasonably high level, the enterprise's purpose and scope should be quite clear. These products become the foundation from which all databases and business information systems are identified and defined. These products also become the context for all policy specification, implementation, and adherence. Finally, these products become the context for all organizational and functional details. All these lower levels are shown in the System through Operations rows of Table 3.

## 4.4    Enterprise's Architecture Summary

The objective of this chapter was to describe the first of the contained architectures, the enterprise's architecture. It is fitting that this architecture is accomplished first as this architecture provides context for all the other architectures. However, if other architectures are done in parallel, that's acceptable just so long as the work products that exist across the architectures are reconciled. While there may be overlapping work products there must only be one definitive set. For example, if there's a Resource and one or more of its Resource Life Cycle nodes cannot be discovered from within the enterprise's missions, then an analysis error has been made. Such errors must be resolved.

This chapter also identified and described all the component parts of the enterprise's architecture, and also set out the high-level process flow that creates the enterprise's architecture.

Chapter 5, Database Object Classes, defines what a Database Object Class is, how it contrasts with other types of objects, and what unique role Database Object Classes play in a database environment. Chapter 5 also presents how Database Object Classes can be implemented in SQL DBMSs that are not object-oriented and how these classes can be implemented in SQL:1999 and above compliant DBMS which are object-oriented. Finally, Chapter 5 describes the work products, how they are interrelated, and how these work products fit with the work products of the other architectures.

## 4.5 Questions and Exercises

1. What has been your experience with developing and using an enterprise's architecture? If good, how and what have been its benefits to strategic, tactical and operational work environments?

2. What's the effect of an enterprise's architecture on your projects? Is the enterprise's architecture followed as a controlling guidance? If yes, why and what have been the benefits and drawbacks? If not, what was used as the context to justify a project?

3. How often do you update your enterprise's architectures? Why is it updated? Is it an all or nothing update process? Can there be incremental updates to part of an architecture?

4. Do "outsiders" accomplish your enterprise's architectures? If yes, why? What are the benefits? If no, what have been the benefits or drawbacks? Is there "ownership" if an "outsider" does your enterprise's architectures?

5. Figure 10 shows the components and relationships in the enterprise's architectures. Do you agree with these? Too many? Too few? Please explain your answer.

6. Should the effort to develop/update and enterprise's architecture be woven information technology the yearly planning cycle? If so, how? Is your organization engineered to participate in these efforts?

7. Are "systems" built that are not justified by the enterprise's architectures? Who makes the case for the exceptions? Or, are exceptions the rule? What happens to the credibility of the enterprise's architectures if they are not followed?

8. Can you see how to tell "stories" with the enterprise's architecture components? Are stories/scenarios an effective tool? If yes, why? If not, why not?

# 5

# Database Object Class Architecture

Chapter 4, Enterprise's Architecture, was the first architecture to be described because it is a broad architecture in that it addresses all the columns of the Knowledge Worker Framework but only the first two rows. Each of the remaining architectures focus on just a few columns and rows.

This chapter begins with a brief definition of Database Object Classes, and then provides the following information in support of their use as a fundamental enterprise architecture:

- Contrasting Database Object Class with other object classes.
- The business case for Database Object Classes.
- Database Object Class examples.
- Origin of Database Object Classes.
- DBMS technology need for Database Object Classes.
- DBMS encapsulation requirement.
- Four components of a Database Object Classes SQL DBMS alternative implementations of Database Object Classes.
- Database Object Class summary.

Included with this chapter are the Database Object Class work products, how they are interrelated, and how these work products fit with the work products of the other architectures.

Concisely stated, a Database Object Class is a structured collection of data about a person, place, or thing that has internal consistency, is identified and defined by the business, and is transformed from one recognized business state to another through well defined rules. The minimum value states are null and valued.

The internal behavior of a database object as it transforms from one state to another is immaterial to its user. Database Object Classes conform to the requirements of business rather than the converse. Database Object Classes are almost always complex. Only trivial Database Object Class data structures form a single two-dimensional table. Most database objects contain between 10-20 data structures.

## 5.1    Contrasting Database Object Class with Other Object Classes

There are generally considered to be three classes of objects: display objects, wholly contained process objects, and business objects. None of these, however are Database Object Classes. Display objects embrace buttons on a screen, a drop list of menu choices, a graphical user interface (GUI), or complete engineering drawings. Wholly contained process objects are for example, the COSINE function, a nautical distance function that when given two geographical coordinates returns the geographic distance between them, or a well-defined process that takes standard arguments and returns a specific value such as asking for the net asset value for a business given all assets and liabilities. Figure 5 illustrates a wholly contained process object. Finally, business objects encompass business components like an insurance policy that performs in a certain manner.

All three object classes have their proponents and detractors. What all three object classes have in common is that first and foremost they are self contained software in the form of an executable or embedded process that behaves according to certain fixed rules.

Database Object Classes share some common names and some common definitions as the other three object types. Because of common names and some common definitions, there may be confusion as to the nature of Database Object Classes. Not only are Database Object Classes not any of the three object classes described above, Database Object Classes are unique to database. They are identified, designed, implemented, operated through, evolved, or maintained through just one type of data processing facility, a database management system (DBMS). If the available DBMS is at least an ANSI SQL:1999 DBMS, most of the Database Object Class's definition and use can be direct. Otherwise, Database Object Classes can only be indirectly accomplished through proprietary facilities in one or more DBMSs.

Notwithstanding the availability of SQL:1999 or more recent ANSI SQL conformant DBMSs, Database Object Classes are absolutely essential to understand, specify, implement, and maintain world-wide heterogeneous database. Without adopting a Database Object Class approach enterprise database success is problematic.

Figure 5 is not a database object class for two reasons. First, it has a presentation layer. Second, it is not defined within a DBMS and operates solely there in.

## 5.2    The Business Case for Database Object Classes

The business case for Database Object Classes is straight forward. Distributed data and processes either through client/server or the Internet-based transactions, are here to stay, and rightly so. Not only are they empowering, they are essential because enterprises are highly distributed and world-wide. Enterprises must be able to respond to local needs, laws, customs and mores. But, if businesses are designed and tuned to respond to local situations, how can they act in concert within their world wide communities? How can you have world-wide consistency and semantics without suffocating local needs and practices? How can both ends of the information resource's spectrum be satisfied?

Business data needs far exceed today's DBMS's two dimensional table capabilities. Businesses cry out for semantically rich data management to meet business needs across world-wide, heterogeneous hardware and operating system environments. Business data management environments must behave consistently regardless of their host computing hardware environment and must be easy to specify, implement, use and maintain.

Businesses require hierarchies of complex data tables, collections of integrated rules for data integrity, well-defined procedure sets, and fixed transformations that move a business policy from one well-defined state to another. Examples of business needs include insurance policies and claims, court cases and documents, public safety incidents, sales and marketing databases that contain customers, sales organizations, forecasts, orders, deliveries, and product sales statistics, inventory control and deployment, and human resources. The business case for Database Object Classes is compelling:

> Two managers were trying to produce a three year marketing plan. One manager stated that the sales in the East were up. The other said they were flat. The first showed numbers to prove the point. The

second showed an equally impressive set of numbers that proved the counter point.

Finally, it was discovered that one manager was using "sales" based on sales organizations credited for specific sales, and the other was using "sales" based on addresses of product deliveries. In exasperation, they both exclaimed: "How can we plan when we're not working off the same *sheet of music*!"

What should be on the *sheet of music?* The notes for the oboe's part, the violins, or the orchestra director? The orchestra director's score not only contains a unified set of notes for all parts, but also the rhythm (cadence, meter, pulse), tempo (momentum and speed), articulation (clearness, distinctiveness), and expression (phraseology and style).

The marketing plan certainly required much more than just notes. To be effective, accurate, and able to respond to unforseen emergencies (first violinist's broken string), it requires both the static (sales numbers) and the dynamics (all the environmentals). With both, agreements (quality music) can be reached. Plans can be executed, tracked, and adjusted, just like a good symphony.

But, what forms the basis of a Database Object Class? Simply, it is a business' policies and procedures. While policies can exist without procedures, the converse is not true. This ontological priority dictates that procedure is dependent on policy. Not only do they go together like hand and glove, the glove (procedure) serves no useful purpose without the hand (policy).

As stated at the outset, a Database Object Class is a structured collection of data about a person, place, or thing that has internal consistency, is identified and defined by the business, and is transformed from one recognized business state to another through well defined rules. The minimum value states are null and valued.

The internal behavior of a database object as it transforms from one state to another is immaterial to its user. Database Object Classes conform to the requirements of business rather than the converse.

Policies and procedures, that is, Database Object Classes, bring order, consistency, and predictability. The larger the enterprise, the greater the dependence on policies and procedures. Data is the resulting evidence of policy's execution. An employee's personnel record is proof that the human resource's policies have been carried out. Procedures are the techniques, methods, or processes by which policies are carried out. If an enterprise has the policy to be profitable, then its balance statement, produced by processing all the general and subsidiary journals are the measure of adherence to the policy. If policy is met, the enterprise must be profitable.

Within an enterprise, policies, and in turn, data exist in two major areas: infrastructure and programmatic. Infrastructure areas address internal policy, such as human resource management, finance, and support services (e.g., plant security, business information systems, and facilities). Programmatic areas address external products that are designed, manufactured, marketed and sold. For a traditional business, this might be steel products, building products, automobiles, or houses. For an intellectual product business, these might be mortgages, insurance policies, courses, and students.

Policies and their associated data, address the well-bounded infrastructure and programmatic areas. The data takes on common everyday names such as employees, facility, mortgage, insurance policy, and student. The data representing these common names are complex, that is, whole multiple-level structures.

The procedures are named, and their data actions are associated with specific subsets of the named data structure. The names of the procedure sets represent data structure transformations from one recognizable state to another. Each state represents a determined value set within the business. Procedure examples include: establishing an employee requisition, accomplishing employee hiring, and performing employee assignment.

Enterprise database is a catch-phrase for an organization's operating condition in which there are both defined policy coherence and integrity as well as consistency in policy transformations throughout the enterprise irrespective of functional and organizational style and irrespective of policy transformation technology (that is, computers, operating systems, programming languages, and database management systems).

Organizations not pursuing database object specification, implementation, and business information system evolution through Database Object Classes will never achieve enterprise database. Rather, they will be left with complicated, redundant business information system specifications, expensive business information system implementation and inconsistent difficult business information system operation, evolution and maintenance.

Enterprise database is the expression, population, use, and manipulation of all Database Object Classes. Enterprise database contains not only all "real" Database Object Classes, but also all the policies and procedures surrounding their specification, implementation and evolution. Value is not only in the "data," but also in the specification of the data. The information technology assets of the enterprise are both its Database Object Classes and also its enterprise meta-objects. If only the former were valued, then only musical notes would be needed for a great symphonic score. Performances are differentiated however, from the grade-school band to a first-rate orchestra because of the musicians' talent that is coupled with the quality of the orchestra director's interpretation of the score's rhythms, tempo, articulation, and dynamics.

## 5.3    Database Object Class Examples

An example of a Database Object Class is an application for employment. Attachment 1 contains a sample application for employment that was obtained from:

http://www.quintcareers.com/employment_application.pdf

The idea of this four-page form is that it is really about one subject, is complete, and relatively intuitive as to what processes must be followed to complete the form. Left unsaid from this particular form are "completeness" statements. For example, whether the form would be considered complete if the education information was missing from page 1, or if the applicant's address was missing. There are many areas where this form could be improved, for example on page 1 it asks for the applicant's age rather than birthdate, and on the same page it asks for salary without asking whether it's for hour, day, week, month, or year.

The point of this example, however, is not its completeness but its fundamental components. It clearly has a data structure, and multiple data collections within the overall data structure. It has implicit processes for each data structure, and it likely has multiple states: Incomplete, complete, and Office Only (see page 2 of the form).

The data structures are for example: biographic, position applied for, work hours availability, education, criminal history, drivers license, office skills, references, military experience, and work experience. Some of these structures are single entry (e.g., name and address) while others allow multiple entry (e.g., education and work experience).

If there had been a detailed set of instructions with this Internet available form, it would likely have included instructions for each block of data. For an example, whether middle name is required or optional, what to put if the applicant does not have college level education, or what to enter if there is no previous work experience.

All of this data is about one single subject, an application for employment. It is also about one individual, the applicant. If the person is offered the job, takes it, and works for a period of time, there are likely to be other collections of data such as medical insurance and other benefits, leave records, job performance assessments, payroll deductions, and the like.

If all this data were analyzed and a database was created, there would be many database tables. All the rows of the tables are however related to one overall object, the employee. Because this is data intensive, it is appropriate to call this a data object. But since all of this is to be defined inside the scope of a DBMS it is called a Database Object Class.

As another example for needing Database Object Classes, consider the following Database Object Classes, which, while not through SQL, were validated 20 years ago through a large scale database project for the U.S. Army.

An Army General in 1985 wanted a DoD contractor located in Iowa, to develop 10 systems in one year when the contractor had previously developed two systems in three years; at less cost. By implementing the Whitemarsh methodology that is based on CASE, business information system generators, Database Object Classes and the Metabase, the mission was accomplished. The systems, instead of costing 1000% (10 times 100%) only cost 360%, a reduction of 64% per system.

In addition to tremendous short-term cost savings, there was also a long term benefit to the Enterprise. The Army General proposed a modification to the fundamental set of algorithms that governed Reliability, Availability and Maintainability (RAM). The 10 systems were already deployed. These systems were collecting data world-wide and producing the RAM studies the Army desperately needed to predict its materiel reorders. When the change request came down, the Metabase was immediately put to use to isolate the exact area of the specifications that had to change. The specifications led to the systems; the systems led to the programs; and the programs led to the modules. The changes were identified. When it was reported that all

> 10 systems could be changed and reassembled, all documentation
> changed, all user-manuals regenerated, reprinted, and redeployed in
> two weeks, the message came back down, "Stop! We merely wanted
> to give you six month notice!"

All this was possible because a highly engineered architecture of both data
and process specifications. The data specifications were effectively engineered
as 1980s versions of database object classes. The process specifications that
were not contained within the database object class were business objects. The
metadata for everything was in the Metabase. Since the Metabase was on the
critical path of all database and business information system engineering and
development, there was no question as to its correctness and authenticity.

## 5.4    Origin of Database Object Classes

Database Object Classes are not new. They were started in certain DBMS
types in the late 1960s. Relational DBMS, however, stopped the march to
Database Object Classes. It was not until the ANSI SQL:1999 data model
moved away from the relational model, and not until a whole programming
language was incorporated into ANSI SQL:1999 that the march toward
Database Object Classes was restarted. Even if the twenty-year delay had not
happened, computers, networks, languages and operating systems were just
not sophisticated enough to make Database Object Classes successful.

Database Object Classes are the foundation stones for enterprise
database. Organizations not pursuing their specification, implementation and
evolution are condemned to complicated, redundant specifications, expensive
implementation and difficult operation, evolution and maintenance.

The concepts behind Database Object Classes are also not new. They
were formulated almost 30 years ago by Matt Flavin. During the Seventies,
Matt who worked for Infodata of Rochester, NY and Fairfax, VA. Infodata
accomplished very early database management system research and
development. Infodata's DBMS, Inquire, was widely used in the U.S. Federal
Government. Matt represented Infodata to the ANSI Database Languages
committee, H2, in the late Seventies.

Matt clearly knew the difference between DBMS and database. The
former is a technology, and the latter is the application of quality planning,
organization, and management. When Matt joined Yourdon, Incorporated in
New York City, he began development of an information modeling discipline

based on Database Object Classes. As Matt would often say, "Database Object Classes are squarely based on an enterprise's policy." Matt insisted that fundamental business policy discovery and formulation was the very first step in discovery. Matt's Yourdon Monograph, *Fundamentals of Information Modeling*, set out the basic steps to identify and specify Database Object Classes. Matt's contribution to database was cut short with his untimely death in 1984.

An example of "nothing's new" is the use of SQL:1999 facilities to define 1972 data models. In 1971, the Council of Great City Schools created a whole series of database designs and supporting data load and retrieval systems to support what today would be called a data warehouse. The databases and supporting system was to support educational researchers and administrators develop and manage educational programs, student achievement, demographics, facilities, teachers, and the like within large urban school districts in the United States.

In 2000, this author recreated these 1971 database designs into SQL:1999 syntax. Each of the "tree structures" in the 1971 databases was re-cast into an SQL:1999 table. These SQL:1999 tables were then sent to an "August" member of the ANSI database languages committee for comment. His comment was, "Yes, now you see the real power of these brand new database objects." When he was told that this was already a capability of this 1967 DBMS, he fell silent. As the ageless expression goes, "The more things change the more they stay the same." Or was it put better by that classical philosopher, Yogi Berra when he said, "it's de je vu all over again?"

## 5.5   DBMS Technology Need for Database Object Classes

Database Object Classes are quite necessary in the overall set of architectures for the Knowledge Worker Framework. That is because almost every enterprise policy that is put into effect has a complex data structure and rigorously defined processes supporting it. Simple data structures for policies are naive, and separating data and process when they are intrinsically interlinked is absurd.

Additionally, these data-based policies proceed through business defined and engineered states. These states may be implemented through information technology, but they are defined from within the business and must conform to natural business rules and procedures.

As stated above, the DBMSs in the 1960s and 1970s were engineered to implement Database Object Classes. There were nested data structures to model Database Object Class complexity, and DBMS embedded processes that could be employed to transform these objects from one state to another.

The relational data model, starting in the early 1970s, and then becoming operational through DBMSs during the 1980s, stopped the march to quality Database Object Classes dead in its tracks. The fundamental engineering principle supporting the relational model is that there are two-dimensional tables. By two-dimensional, it is meant that there are rows of data and every column in each row be single valued. For example, if there was a person table then among the naturally existing columns would be PersonFirstName, PersonMiddleInitial, PersonLastName, Social SecurityNumber, BirthDate, TelehponeNumber, AddressLine1, AddressLine2, City, State, and Zip. But, what if there are multiple telephone numbers and multiple addresses? What happens further if there are multiple telephone numbers for a given address? In the relational model, the answer is always the same: add more tables. While that might be acceptable for trivial databases and for laboratory test cases, business is profoundly more complex and is in need of a more robust solution to its problems.

In real, large scale business databases, having to absorb the DBMS and technical bureaucracy for just simple tables of phone numbers and addresses, and having to deal with the computer processing inefficiencies associated with joining person tables of tens of thousands of rows with a telephone table of hundreds of thousands of rows to just get a person's set of telephone numbers is technologically ridiculous.

In short, the relational data model and DBMS can be seen as a great setback to business dominated and engineered database design. For a multiplicity of reasons, business objects have risen from the dead like the mythical phoenix and have now caused very significant changes to relational DBMSs. Gratefully, there are no more relational DBMSs.

Business requirements-based design has returned, and starting with the SQL:1999 standard, compliant DBMSs with this standard, or the SQL 2003 standard or even the upcoming SQL:2008 standard have now begun to restore to DBMS technology the data model capabilities of 30+ years ago. For all practical purposes, the relational model is dead, and that's great news.

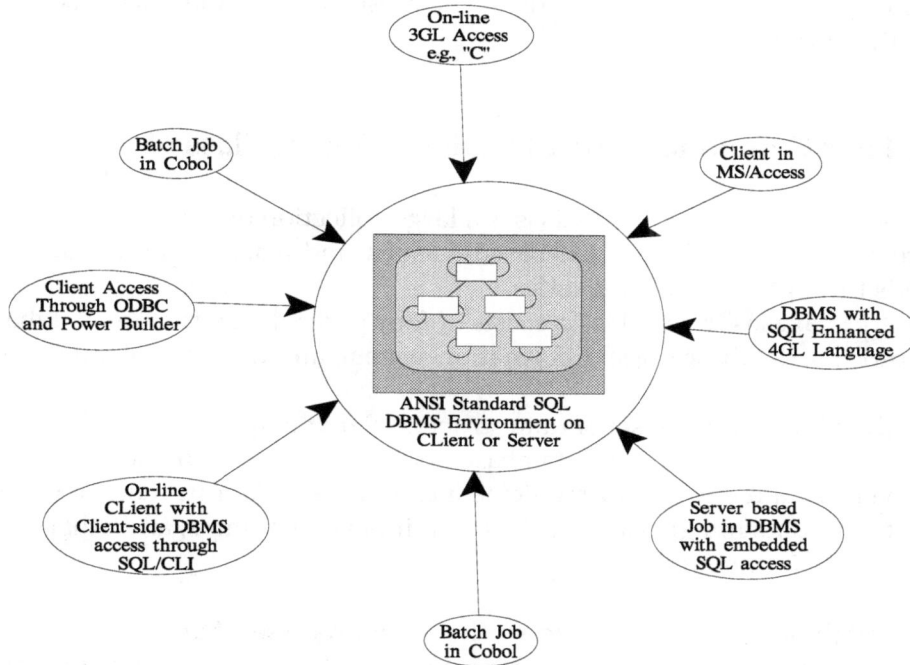

**Figure 11**. Methods and language alternatives to database update.

## 5.6    DBMS Encapsulation Requirement

A key characteristic of Database Object Classes is encapsulation. The outer most encapsulation agent of Database Object Classes is the DBMS.

The reason why the Database Object Class is to be fully defined inside the scope of the DBMS is because there are so many different methods and procedures of interacting with a database. Figure 11 illustrates all the different methods and languages that cause updates to a database. If any of these methods were employed then each would have to have 100% of the data valuation rules. Without 100% uniformity of rules inside the language's application program, one entry program may reject a name without a middle name another might accept. One might allow no education and other might reject it. Since accomplishing 100% conformity across all languages and methods of update is close to impossible, the only safe technique is to then encapsulate all the business rules inside the most common software processor, that is, the DBMS.

## 5.7    Four Components of a Database Object Class

From above, a Database Object Class is a large collection of data and processes that are tied together for business-based reasons, and when instantiated, proceeds through well defined states.

A Database Object Class consists of four parts: data structure, database object process, database object information system, and database object state.

- Data Structure: the set of data structures[8] that map onto the different value sets for real world database objects such as an auto accident[9], vehicle and emergency medicine incident. Each data structure contains fields, data integrity constraints, and if tables, columns, and other types of constraints.

- Database Object Table Process: the set of processes that enforce the integrity of data structure fields, references between Database Object Classes and actions among contained data structure segments, the proper computer-based rules governing data structure segment

---

[8]    A database object data structure has an identifier to isolate its instances from all others and fields which represent single values, arrays, groups, repeating groups, and nested repeating groups. When a data structure only contains single valued fields, it is termed a simple data structure database object. If the data structure contains arrays though nested repeating groups, it is termed a complex data structure database object.

[9]    One of the standard Whitemarsh examples for database objects is based on a state public safety agency that was establishing a state-wide system that embraced a multi-tiered set of client-server systems. Each agency (e.g. state and local police, roads, licencing, inspections, and emergency medicine) had their own client-server systems. The state maintained the large scale agency-state client-server system that coalesced data, regulated valid values, created state wide statistics, etc.

insertion, modification, and deletion. An example would be the proper and complete storage of an auto accident.

- Database Object Information System: the set of specifications that control, sequence, and iterate the execution of various collections of database object table processes that cause changes in database object states to achieve specific value-based states in conformance to the requirements of business policies. For example, the reception and database posting of data from business information system activities (screens, data edits, storage, interim reports, etc.) that accomplish entry of the auto accident information.

- Database Object State: The value states of a database object that represent the after-state of the successful accomplishment of one or more recognizable business events. Examples of business events are auto accident initiation, involved vehicle entry, involved person entry, and auto accident DUI involvement. Database object state changes are initiated through named business events that are contained in business functions. The business function, auto accident investigation includes the business event, auto-accident-incident initiation, which in turn causes the incident initiation database object information system to execute, which in turn causes several database object processes to cause the auto accident incident to be materialized in the database.

Database Object Classes are identified in the Database Object Classes column at the System row and are fully specified in the Technology row as they are created in concert with Implemented Data Models.

Figure 12 displays a graphic that depicts the composition of a Database Object Class. In this figure there are rectangles. These represent the database object tables that are the data structure of the Database Object Class. There are five database object class tables, and they are all related by primary and foreign keys. In SQL:1999 or SQL:2003 these structures would all be contained inside complex columns.

Connected to each data structure rectangle are processes (i.e., the circles) that are invoked automatically to check in the quality of the data that is being inserted or changed. These processes might be column constraints, insertions, triggers or some other form of stored procedure.

Surrounding the entire set of data structures and processes is the curved corner rectangle that signifies the database object information system

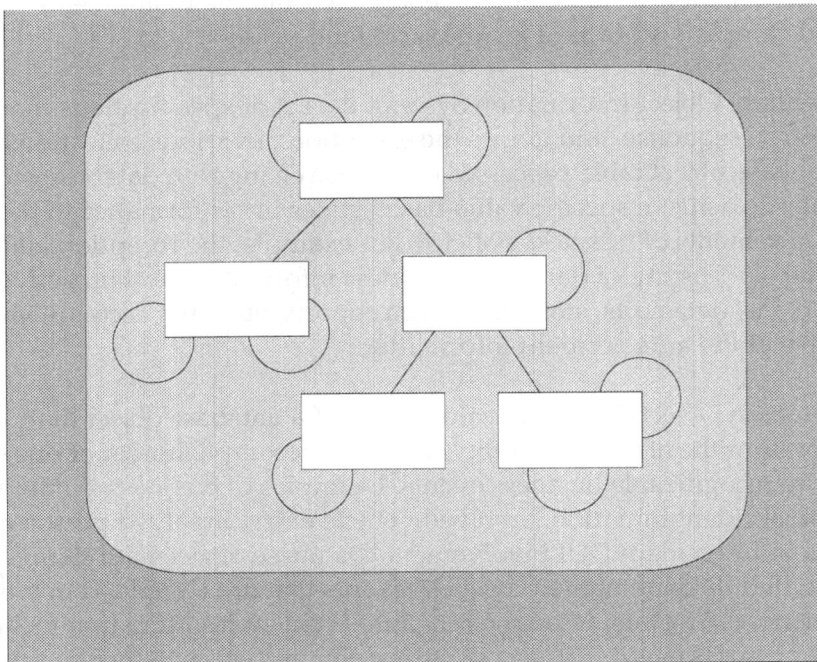

**Figure 12**. Graphic displaying the composition of a database object.

that would, in a predetermined sequence, execute the database object table processes. The result of the execution of the database object information system is binary. Either it is entirely successful, meaning that all the contained database object table processes have executed correctly, or they have not. If not, the database object is returned to its prior state. Else, the achieved state remains.

Database is state based. When the database is entirely devoid of data, it is in a state of integrity. As rows of data are added to tables individually or as collections of rows of data are added to collections of tables, the state of the database must always be one of integrity. By integrity, it means that all value-based constraints test true. A value-based constraint might be a referential integrity statement, a column constraint, an insertion, trigger, or some invoked stored procedure. If an action occurs that causes a constraint to fail, the action must be rolled back to some prior state of integrity.

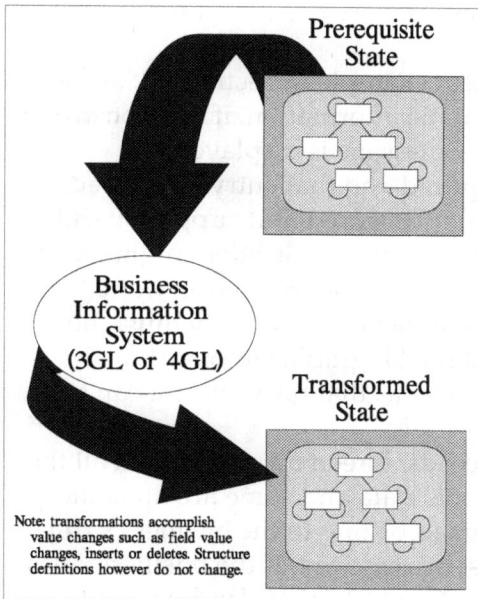

Prerequisite State

Business Information System (3GL or 4GL)

Transformed State

Note: transformations accomplish value changes such as field value changes, inserts or deletes. Structure definitions however do not change.

**Execution Sequence (effectively)**

1. Data is obtained through 3GL and 4GL

2. Database object requested state is invoked through Business Information System. (Outside Square)

3. Data is passed to the database object information system (Rounded Edge Square)

4. Database object processes are passed data and they perform their actions (Circles to rear of white squares

5. Database object data structure is modified through inserts, changes, and deletes (connected collection of white squares)

6. If success, then commit, otherwise rollback.

**Figure 13**. Database object transformation from one state to the next.

Figure 13 illustrates this process. The top of Figure 13 contains a database object in some state. A database object information system executes. If it is successful, the transformed state is achieved. Otherwise, all the updates are reversed through a DBMS facility called rollback. In this particular example, the data is obtained through some business information system's presentation layer. This data is sent to the DBMS through the activation of a series of SQL commands that ultimately invoke the Database Object Information System and through a previously defined set of database object table processes.

If all the constraints are satisfied, the new state is accepted. From the Employee Application in Attachment 1, there might be a business information system that takes in all the data from the paper-based application all at once. In such a case, there is only two states: Null and entirely acceptable. Thus, if all the data is acceptable, the entire application is stored. Else, it is removed from any kind of temporary storage and the database exists as if the application was never acted upon.

Using the application for employment example in Section 5.3, as the data is entered, say starting with the biographic information, if any constraint fails, the entire transaction fails and an error message is displayed.

For example, if Middle Name is required and that entry is skipped, that screen would fail and the data would not be stored. But suppose it did pass and the biographic information was stored, the application might go on to taking in the education information. If a highschool graduation was a minimum requirement and the entry of that data failed, not only must the education data be removed but so too must the biographic information. It must be removed because the "business rule" was that no applicant can be accepted without a High School diploma.

As the application's data entry proceeds, screen by screen until all the data are entered, some screens are for optional data and some are mandatory data. If any of the mandatory data fails then according to the business's rules, the entire application for employment must be removed. If the business rules change, then so too would be the Database Object Class's rules for accepting and rejecting data.

An alternative to the all or nothing approach is to have a series of database object states that allow increasing quantities of data in a building block fashion. At each database object state success, the named state of the database object changes. That way, a query can be launched to list the current state, and/or all the states that the database object has completed.

## 5.8    Database Object Class Components

Figure 14 shows a high-level data model for Database Object Classes. This general model is contained entirely in the Database Object Classes column of the System and Technology rows. The Technology row is required because the tables that the Database Object Class uses are those from Implemented Data Models. From Column there's a connection to an ISO 11179 data element that is in the Business row. From Column there's also a connection to Attribute that would be in the Specified Data Model of the Business Row. Finally, there's a connection between Database Object Information Systems and Business Information Systems.

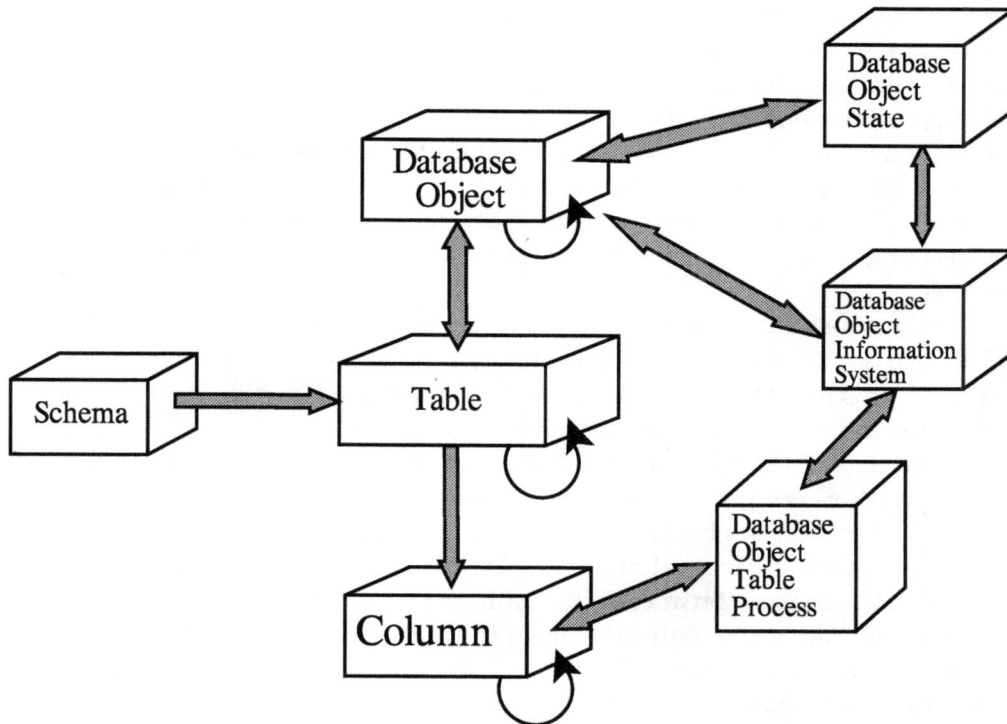

**Figure 14**. High level data model for database object classes.

The point of all this "who begat who"is to show that the metadata from all the columns and rows must be integrated and non-redundant. Otherwise it's just a bunch of metadata stove-pipes, each in its own specialized metadata tool. That's the whole point of the Metabase: it embraces the entirety of the Knowledge Worker Framework.

The enumeration and definitions of the Database Object Class components are provided in Table 9.

The relationship between the database object components and the Knowledge Worker Framework is this: Missions, and their lower level noun-intensive database domain descriptions are employed in the definition of databases.

If, however, all the discovered data classes across all the database domains are two-dimensional tables, there would be a blizzard of tables to understand. The data model diagrams at this point will be far larger than mere mortals comprehend.

Not only must these 6 x 10 foot diagrams be simplified to be understood, but their complexity thwarts seeing the forest because of the trees, and the trees because of the blades of grass (i.e., the tables). Well-formed collections of entities will emerge if there's a database domain by database domain analysis. What emerges are Database Object Classes as each well-portioned database domain suggests them. Since database domains may naturally reference the same database object class, the metabase stores the database object classes in a many-to-many relationship with database domains.

When just the Database Object Classes are merged across the collection of database domains, the entire enterprise-level data model is greatly simplified. It is more valid, easier to present, and management can finally see the trees from the grass, and the forest from the trees.

Database Object Classes are thus a key element in the layered (i.e., Knowledge Worker Framework rows) understanding of the enterprise. Database Object Classes become a natural integrating mechanism between missions and their database domains and the various database designs.

Finally, because business information systems are fundamentally engineered to mirror the requirements of the business, Database Object Classes, because of their natural data structures, are naturally existing data models for the business information systems to employ as they value, manipulate, evolve, and eventually dissolve proof of enterprise policy.

| Database Object Class Components | |
|---|---|
| Name | Description |
| Column | Columns are the manifestation of the semantics of a data element within a table of a schema. Additionally, a column is a deployment of the semantics of an attribute. Columns may have additional semantics that further refine the column within the context of either the attribute or the data element. The order of processing these additional semantics is that the column must first be a subset of the attribute, which in turn must be a subset of the data element. Not all the columns of a table must map to attributes from a single entity. |
| Database Object Information System | A Database Object Information System is a collection of processes defined within the domain of the DBMS usually as a stored procedure that transforms one or more rows of a database object from one valid state to another. A database object information system accomplishes one or more database object table processes. |

| Database Object Class Components | |
|---|---|
| Name | Description |
| Database Object Class | A Database Object Class is a large collection of data and processes that are tied together for business-based reasons, and when instantiated, proceeds through well defined states. A database object can exist in two forms: a collection of interrelated database tables, or the set of a column-based nested structures within a table. The rows that comprise an object are transformed from one valid state to another via database object table processes and database object information systems. Database objects are related to one or more database domains. |
| Database Object Class State | A Database Object State is a well-defined value state of a database object. States occur in a particular sequence, typically from the null state through a set of value states and returning to a null state. A database object state is accomplished through one or more database object information systems. |
| Database Object Class table process | A Database Object Table Process is a process such as insert, change, or delete that executes against one row of a single table within a database object. A table owns (and is thus acted upon by) one or more database object table processes. A database object table process may be invoked by one or more database object information systems. |
| Schema | A schema is a database structure that encapsulates all its contained tables as well as containing other classes of schema objects such as data types, procedures, constraints, including the interrelationships of the various schema objects.<br><br>Implemented Data Models are cast within the domain of a schema. The set of all tables within a schema is not required to be taken from a single set of entities within a subject area. |
| Table | A Table is intended to be a well-defined expression of one policy within a schema. Ideally, the collection of all the tables within a schema area should define a coherent collection policy. Although unlikely, some tables and even some schemas may never be represented within Operational Data Models. Additionally, some columns within a table may never be employed. A table may contain columns that map to attributes from multiple entities. Tables can be sub-typed.<br><br>A table represents a collection of columns, which when bound to a particular DBMS and valued, represents a set of rows of data for those columns. Tables have precise specifications including constraints, primary and foreign keys, and other table centered features. Within the scope of the Implemented Data Model generalization level for data |

| Database Object Class Components | |
|---|---|
| Name | Description |
| | architectures, these table specifications do not represent actual rows of data because this level is not bound to a particular DBMS and is not related to any specific business information systems. These tables, and the entire Implemented Data Model is intended to be a data architecture design layer.<br><br>Tables can be subtyped to represent collections of columns that have a common set and then several non-intersecting sets. |

**Table 9.** Database Object Class components.

## 5.9    SQL DBMS Alternative Implementations of Database Object Classes

The external specifications of a database object are independent of its SQL DBMS implementation. SQL DBMSs have either created SQL:1999 facilities or not. If the SQL DBMS has not created these facilities, the Database Object Class data structure can only be implemented as a collection of tables that are all related through primary and foreign key relationships.

If an SQL DBMS has created SQL:1999 facilities, it can directly create the necessary database object data structures by having the SQL tables become the Database Object Class and declare column-based substructures. The top level of single-valued columns become the Database Object Class's root table, and the column-based nested structures become the Database Object Class contained data structures.

Database Object Classes range from the trivial to the complex. A *trivial* database object is: 1) is a simple data structure (a set of single value fields), 2) is instantiated through simple databases processes (INSERT, MODIFY, DELETE) that are 3) part of one encapsulating business information system, and 4) takes on a minimum of two values states: null and valued.

A complex database object has the following characteristics:

- It is a complex data structure with multiple segments containing single, multi-valued, groups, repeating groups, and nested repeating groups of fields,

- It is instantiated through collections of database processes that are.

- It is part of one or more collections of complex business information systems, and

- It takes on a whole series of discrete business policy recognizable states from null to any number of discrete valued states back to a null state.

In short, the full life cycle of a business resource (employee, contract, asset, etc.).


## 5.10   Database Object Class Summary

This chapter defined what a Database Object Class is, how it contrasts with other types of object classes, and the unique role Database Object Classes play in a database environment.

This chapter presented the business case for database objects and shows several examples. This chapter also presented how Database Object Classes can be implemented in SQL DBMSs that are not object-oriented, and how these classes can be implemented in SQL:1999 or more DBMS that are object-oriented.

This chapter finally described the Database Object Class work products, how they are interrelated, and how these work products fit with the work products of the other architectures.

Chapter 6, Data Architecture, starts with a presentation of the various classes of the database architectures that most commonly exist with enterprises, be they small or large. The chapter proceeds to fully define each of the five data generalization levels, that is, data elements, Specified Data Models, Implemented Data Models, Operational Data Models, and View Data Models. The chapter sets out the work products that must be created for each model, and how all these work products are thoroughly integrated one with the other.

## 5.11 Questions and Exercises

1. Are database object classes anything really new, or just something we've been trying to do within areas of a database's design with stored procedures, triggers, and business information system segmentation and engineering? Do the four parts of the database object class make good architecture and engineering sense?

2. How does having database object classes defined and deployed in your databases assist in understanding enterprise-wide database and business information system architectures?

3. Doesn't it make good sense to centrally define business rules based processes?

4. Doesn't it make good data management sense to factor common processes and embed them into the DBMS for unavoidable processing?

5. How have you been implementing, and maintaining your database object classes? Is there value in triggers and stored procedures?

6. Do you find that your business information system often revolve around just a few database object classes?

7. How would you manage ad hoc updates to databases through all different languages if you don't have integrity-enforcement centralized in the DBMS?

8. How do database object classes compare and contrast with the other object classes?

9. How do you compare and contrast business objects with database object classes? Should business object classes call database object classes? What is the benefit from factoring database object classes from within business objects?

10. Does your organization employ SQL DBMSs that have object-oriented facilities as defined in SQL:1999?

# 6

# Data Architecture

---

Chapter 5, Database Object Classes, set out the highest level specifications of the major policy-based data groupings in the enterprise. These data groupings are created, manipulated, and ultimately dissolved in the enterprise as its mission is carried out.

This chapter, Data Architecture, provides an overall approach to managing the enterprise's data models. One of these data models, the Implemented Data Model, is the data model class within which database object data structures are defined.

This chapter starts with a presentation of the various classes of the database architectures, which commonly exist across enterprise organizations be they large or small.

The chapter proceeds to fully define each of the five data model generalization levels, that is, Data Elements, Specified Data Models, Implemented Data Models, Operational Data Models, and View Data Models. The chapter sets out the work products that must be created for each model, and how all these work products are thoroughly integrated one with the other.

Data architectures relate only to the metadata about the data, not the real data itself. There are two dimensions to data architectures: Dataase architectures, and data model generalization levels.

The first data architecture dimension, database architecture class, represents the class of database that a given data model addresses. If an analogy helps, a database architecture class is like an automotive vehicle class, that is, truck, minivan, or car. Each has some similar functions, but they are for really different purposes.

The second data architecture dimension, data model classes, relates to the named levels of generalization that exist independent of any database architecture class. Again, if an analogy helps, one such class might be the class of all vehicle parts within major categories, e.g., power-trains, steering, exhaust, body, and frame. Another, but "lower" generalization class might be the engine assemblies, transmission assemblies, exhaust assemblies. These

---

would be specific examples of component assemblies of a power-train. Each such assembly is complete and engineered and might be used in multiple vehicle types within a particular vehicle class. Further, different assemblies might employ parts from a power train collection, and/or an exhaust collection.

At an even lower generalization class might be the Ford F150 truck, or the Volvo XC90. Each of these vehicle classes uses an engine assembly, and a transmission assembly.

The most specific generalization level would be a specifically built Ford F150 that has just come off the assembly line and is ready to operate. That specific Ford truck has a drive train assembly that is composed of part assemblies from drive train, transmission, and exhaust, which in turn, consists of parts from the categories, power train, steering, exhaust, and the like. At this lowest level, "real parts" exist.

Analogous to the automotive example above, there are five data model generalization levels that span from enterprise data elements and data models of concepts through to the models of the databases that actually execute on physical computers under specific operating systems. Each level is complete in its own right but is more detailed and/or specific at the next lower level, and finally enables a given lower level to be subseted and grouped by the higher level.

## 6.1   Database Architecture Classes

Figure 15 provides a diagram that shows the general topology across all the database architecture classes. The classes of database architecture are:

- Original data capture.
- TDSA, that is, transaction data staging area.
- Subject area databases.
- Data warehouses (wholesale and retail).
- Reference data.

A more detailed description of these database architecture classes is contained in Attachment 2, Database Architecture Class Descriptions.

Data generally progresses from left to right. As data is created and stored in Original Data Capture databases, it should proceed through a

## Reference Data

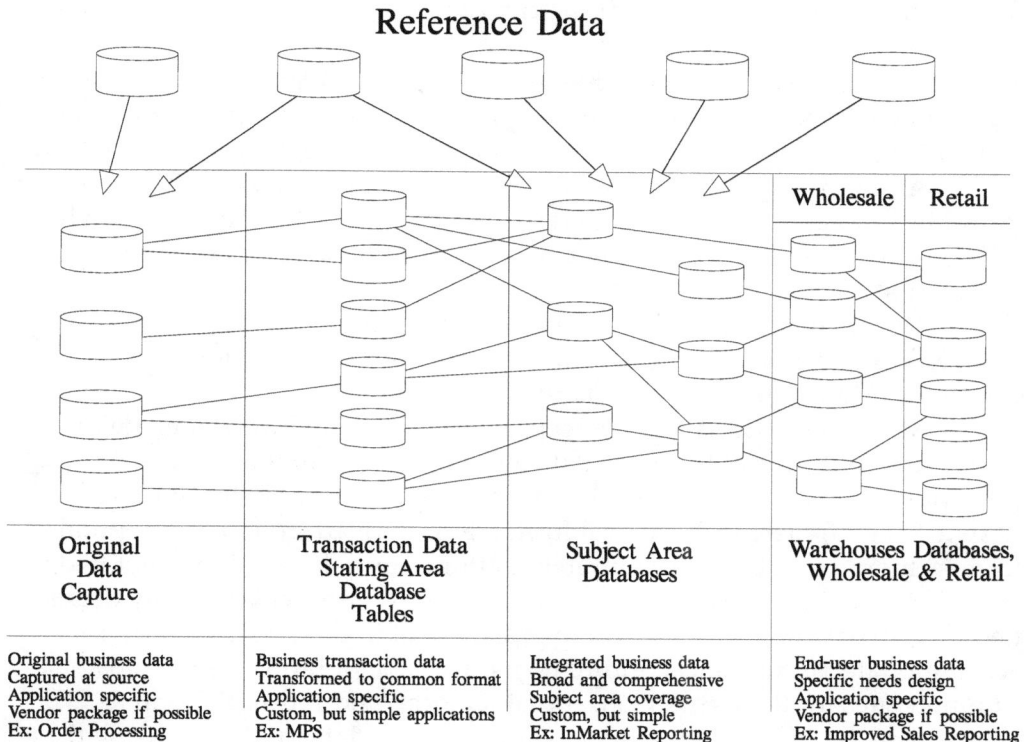

|  |  |  | Wholesale | Retail |
|---|---|---|---|---|
| Original Data Capture | Transaction Data Stating Area Database Tables | Subject Area Databases | Warehouses Databases, Wholesale & Retail | |

| Original business data | Business transaction data | Integrated business data | End-user business data |
|---|---|---|---|
| Captured at source | Transformed to common format | Broad and comprehensive | Specific needs design |
| Application specific | Application specific | Subject area coverage | Application specific |
| Vendor package if possible | Custom, but simple applications | Custom, but simple | Vendor package if possible |
| Ex: Order Processing | Ex: MPS | Ex: InMarket Reporting | Ex: Improved Sales Reporting |

**Figure 15**. Database architecture classes.

process of standardizing granularity, precision, temporal aspects,and semantics. Once the data is standardized, it can proceed onwards to the other database architecture classes such as the subject area databases (sometimes called Operational Data Stores), and to the various classes of data warehouses.

The final class of database architecture, Reference Data, is the sets of data that represent things like gender codes, city-state-zip triples, and the like. There may be specific databases within the Subject Area class that are the definitive sets of values, for example, the definitive sets of employee names, product names and descriptions, and the like. This class of database architecture has been called Golden Source, Strategic Data, or most recently, Master Data.

## 6.2    Data Model Generalization Levels

The second dimension for data architectures is the data model generalization levels that exist across all classes of database architectures. The data model generalization levels and a brief description for each are provided in Table 10.

A common question to Whitemarsh is "What's this Data Element thing? Isn't it just a column of a table, or an attribute of an entity? And, why call the levels Specified, Implemented, and Operational as opposed to Conceptual, Logical, and Physical?"

The answer to all these questions is quite simple: To benefit the users, and because the names of the levels, while somewhat analogous to Conceptual, Logical, and Physical are quite different.

Most often, the names, Conceptual, Logical, and Physical relate to three different forms of the *same* data model. First, there is a database's conceptual form, that is sort of a fuzzy and not a completely thought out design. Second, there is the logical form that is derived from its conceptual form, is more precise, and is definitely in third normal form, but is not tied to any particular DBMS. Third, there is the physical form, which is fully detailed, tied to a particular DBMS, and quite possibly not in third normal form to accommodate performance requirements. These definitions are the most common ones for the terms, Conceptual, Logical, and Physical. Because Whitemarsh has a different scope and purpose for data modeling, using these terms would greatly shortchange the data model management capabilities provided by Whitemarsh.

| Data Model Generalization Classes | |
|---|---|
| **Name** | **Description** |
| Enterprise Data Elements | Data elements are enterprise-level business fact definitions independent of use within specific databases. Data elements are defined according to the requirements of ISO 11179 for data element metadata. Additionally, data elements include semantic and data use modifiers so as to enable automatic name construction, automatic definitions, and automatic abbreviations. There is a one-to-many relationship between data elements and Specified Data Models. |

| Data Model Generalization Classes | |
|---|---|
| **Name** | **Description** |
| Specified Data Models | Specified Data Models are data models of concepts that are independent of use within specific databases. These Specified Data Models of concepts are defined as entities, attributes and relationships within specific subjects. Entities can be related across subjects. There is a many-to-many relationship between the Specified Data Model and the Implemented Data Model. |
| Implemented Data Models | Implemented Data Models are models of databases that are independent of any particular DBMS such as Oracle or DB2. The Implemented Data Models obtain their data structures from one or more Specified Data Models, and in turn, provide these database data structures for use in the construction of data models of databases that actually operate under specific DBMS, and run on computers. These Implemented Data Models are defined as tables, columns and relationships within schemas. Tables cannot be related across schemas. All the tables in this data model generalization level are in at least third normal form so as to ensure data model clarity and quality design. There is a many-to-many relationship between an Implemented Data Model and an Operational Data Model. |
| Operational Data Models | Operational Data Models are models of databases that conform to the requirements of a particular DBMS such as Oracle or DB2. Additionally, the database's design must conform to the expected processing requirements of the particular set of database applications supported by the particular database. Operational Data Model designs may vary because of many factors such as transaction volume, the host operating system, and the computer hardware size and throughput capabilities. Regardless, every variation of a given Operational Data Model database is related back to their source Implemented Data Models. These Operational Data Models are defined as DBMS tables, DBMS columns and relationships within DBMS schemas. "DBMS" is employed here to signify that these data model components are tied to a specific DBMS. There is a one-to-many relationship between an Operational Data Model and a View Data Model. |

| Data Model Generalization Classes | |
|---|---|
| **Name** | **Description** |
| View Data Models | View data models are the Business Information System and Operational Data Model intersection mechanisms. View data models consist of views and view columns. They are also related to the business information systems that are the sources or targets of the database data. Views are specifically tied to specific DBMSs and view columns from a source view may be mapped to the view columns of a target view. Finally, view columns may be computed or derived. |

**Table 10.** Data model generalization levels.

Figure 16 shows the general relationships among the five models: Data Element, Specified, Implemented, Operational, and View. This diagram shows high level versions of the key metadata tables involved in all these data models. A more detailed but still a high-level version of each data model is shown in subsequent sections.

Figure 16 shows that the relationships among the models is at the data element to an attribute to a column to a DBMS column to a view column. This type of relationship enables all the facilities described above. If these models were traditionally related then there would be relationship lines between entity to table to DBMS table. Even more strictly, there would be relationship lines between Subject to Schema to DBMS Schema. If either of these two relationships existed then these models would be transforming one into the other. But because the relationship lines are data element to attribute to column to DBMS column to view column these models are all able to be independently defined and mapped one to the other.

Each of the data model generalization levels is described in sections that follow. Within each section is a general description, and then there is a table that identifies and describes the key components of the data model generalization level.

**ISO 11179 Data Element Model**

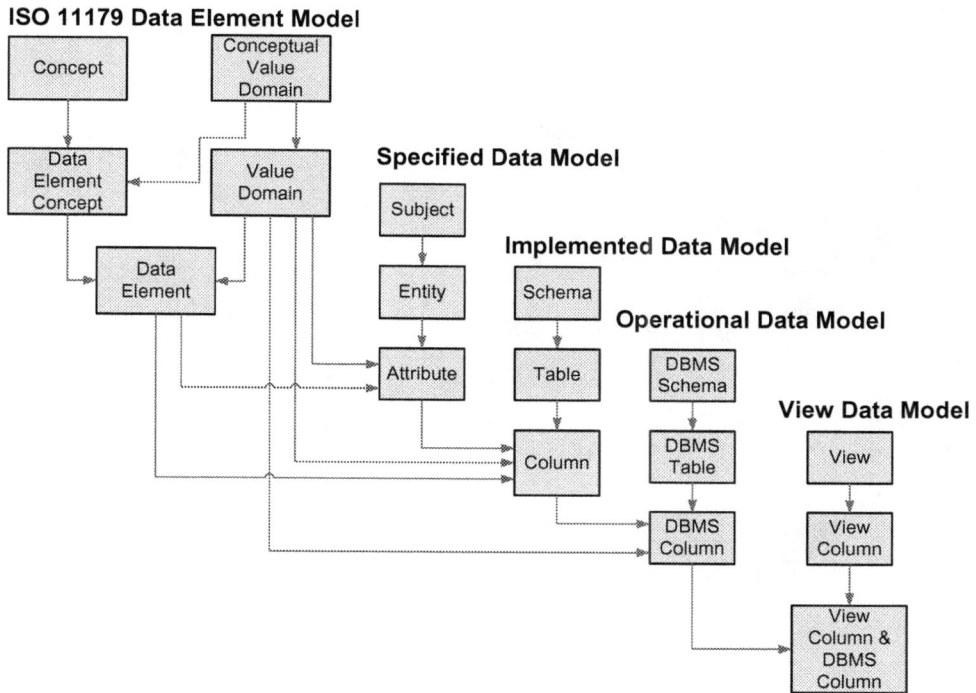

**Figure 16**. Relationships among Data Element through View Data Models.

## 6.2.1   Data Element Models

Data elements are key to understanding and administering data across the enterprise. It is common for a business fact, regardless of what it is called, to be reused between 30 and 100 times across a collection of database data models. It would clearly be a waste to require that each and every reuse be redefined. Data elements are thus both integral and critical to the proper management of enterprise data. Data element metadata is defined according to the ISO 11179 standard. Figure 17 shows a high level diagram of the key components of the Data Element Model. Included in a comprehensive ISO 11179 Data Element Modeling effort are the creation of classes of data element metadata found in Table 11.

Data types for data elements are defined from the ISO standard for language independent data types. A data element can be assigned both

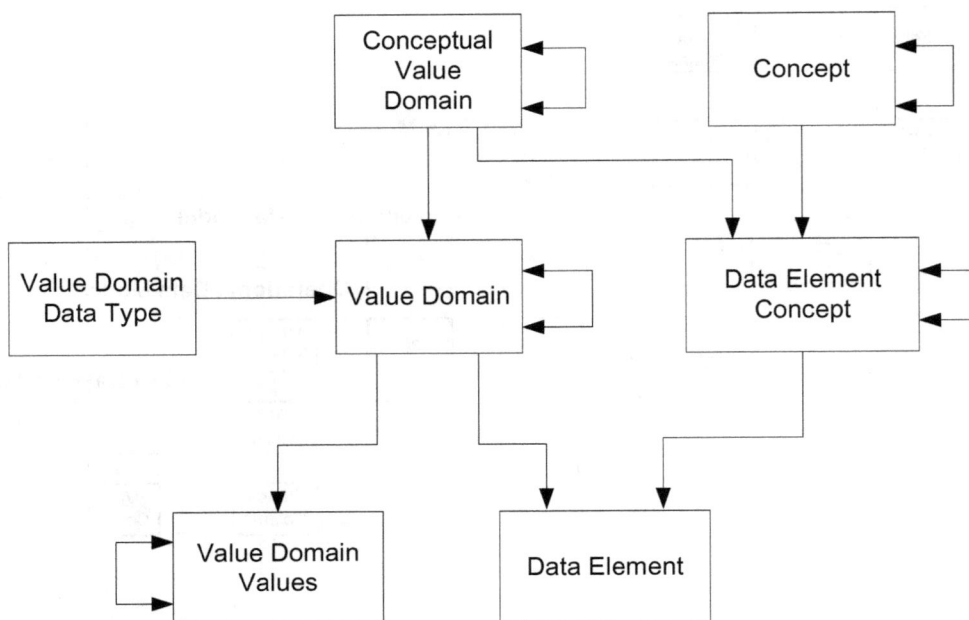

**Figure 17**. Key components of the Data Element model.

semantic and data use modifiers as can attributes of Specified Data Models and columns from tables. Data elements can also be assigned a value domain.

As with the Implemented and Specified Data Models, if an attempt is made to assign a semantic that is either the same, or that is not a proper subset of the already assigned semantic, the assignment is disallowed. There is thus a proper hierarchy of semantic modifiers, data use modifiers, and value domains enforced across the Data Element Model and the specified, implemented and operational models.

| Data Element Model Components | |
|---|---|
| **Component** | **Description** |
| Data Element Concepts | Data element concepts are identified, described, and interrelated. Data element concepts are the conceptual forms of data elements.<br><br>A Data Element Concept is the joining of a Concept and a Conceptual Value Domain that, in turn, is a generalized representation of a collection of data elements. An example of a Data Element Concepts is real property characteristics. The Data Element Concept contained Data Elements that would result would be a real property name, description, dimensions, valuations, and the like. Data Element Concepts can be either simple, or complex. If complex, they can be networks or hierarchies.<br><br>Data element concepts are able to be assigned semantic and data use modifiers to specialize their general nature. Together, these enable automatic data naming, definitions, and abbreviations. |
| Concepts | Concepts are identified, described, and interrelated. Concepts are the root-semantic source for all data elements. These concepts may be similar to the concepts named in the subjects of the Specified Data Models, but that is merely a coincidence. Concepts may be complex in their relationships with other concepts forming either, hierarchies, networks, or both. An example might be resources, of which an example might be a materiel resource such as equipment, or supplies. There also then might be a non-material resource such as intellectual property or intelligence. |
| Conceptual Value Domains | Conceptual value domains are identified, described, and interrelated. Conceptual value domains are the concepts behind value domains from which both data element concepts and value domains are derived. An example of a concept behind a value domain might be numbers, and within that, integers, floating point. Another might be descriptions, text and codes. Conceptual value domains can be either simple, or complex. If complex, they can be networks or hierarchies. |
| Data Elements | Data elements are defined within the context of their data element concepts and their assigned value domain. Data elements are the semantic-laden business facts that are used to create either attributes of entities from subjects within Specified Data Models or columns of tables from schemas within Implemented Data Models.<br><br>Data elements are able to be assigned semantic and data use modifiers to specialize their general nature. Together, these enable automatic data naming, definitions, and abbreviations. All semantic, data use, and value domains that are assigned to a data element must be a subset of any previously assigned to a data element concept. |

| Data Element Model Components | |
|---|---|
| **Component** | **Description** |
| Data Element Classifications | Data element classifications (not shown on Figure 16) are a way to assign data elements to certain classification schemes. A data element may be assigned to more than one classification scheme. |
| Meta category values | Meta category values are words or phrases that have a specific and controlled meaning in the enterprise. These words/phrases are either prefixed to the common business name of a data element concept, data element, attribute, or column, or are suffixed to the common business name. In the case of the former, these are semantic modifiers, and in the case of the later they are data use modifiers. An example of semantic modifiers is geography such as United States, New England, Rhode Island, and Providence. There can be other classes of semantic modifiers including for example, temporal, or precision. Only one semantic modifier of each class can be assigned. Data use modifiers are for example, data type or role. Only one data use modifiers of each class can be assigned. Assignments are always checked to ensure that proper semantic nesting is enforced. |
| Value Domains | Value domains, along with their value domain values and relationships among value domain values, are identified, defined, described, and if appropriate, enumerated. Value domains are also associated with their parent conceptual value domains. Value domains are able to be assigned to data elements, attributes of entities of Specified Data Model subjects, columns of tables of Implemented Data Models schemas, and DBMS columns of DBMS tables of Operational Data Model schemas. |

**Table 11.** Data element model components.

This kind of semantic management is generally impossible with traditional ER modelers because their foundation is the diagram, not the repository.

## 6.2.2 Specified Data Models.

The Specified Data Model is a collection of data models of concepts. The triple for the Specified Data Model is: Subject, entity and attribute. Each concept, represented as a subject, can have multiple entities and attributes. Examples of subject might include location, address, telephone numbers, education information, part's information, and the like.

Figure 18 shows a high level diagram of the key components of the Specified Data Model. Included in a Specified Data Modeling effort are the metadata components found in Table 12.

Subjects can be hierarchically constructed. For example, Human Resources might contain persons, evaluations, hiring, and the like. Each contained subject, for example, person might then have a collection of entities for the person, skill sets, education, and benefits.

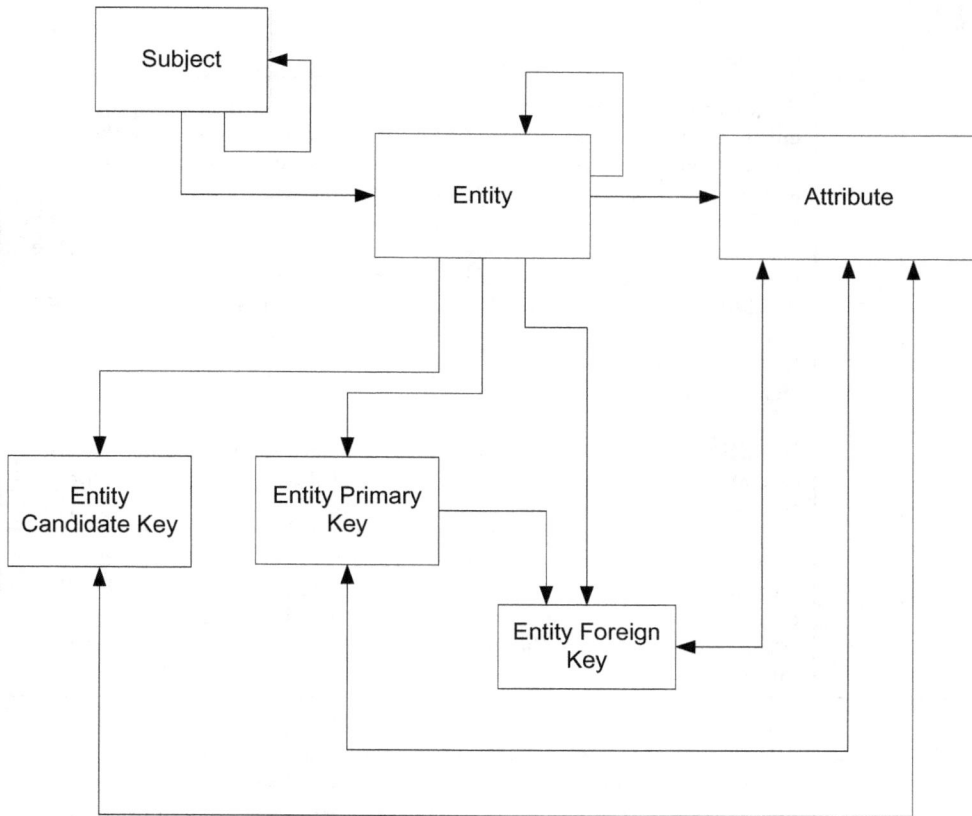

**Figure 18**. Key components of the Specified Data Model.

| Specified Data Model Components | |
|---|---|
| **Component** | **Description** |
| Attribute Assigned Value Domain | An assigned value domain is a value-based constraint on the attribute. The assigned value domain cannot be the same as that assigned the data element. Nor can a value domain be more expansive than that assigned the data element. |
| Attribute Assigned Meta Category Values | An assigned meta category value, whether a semantic or data use modifier is a "meaning" constraint on the attribute. The assigned meta category value cannot be the same as that assigned the data element. Nor can a meta category value be more expansive than that assigned the data element. |
| Attribute | An attribute is intended to be a data-value based partial descriptor of an entity. There are three classes of attributes. Those that represent the entity's content, for example, if the entity is address then the content attributes would be Street-1, Street-2, City, State, and Zip. There are attributes related to the instance of the entity. For example, the set of attributes which have a combined value such that only one row from the entity is found. This is commonly called the entity's primary key. The third set of attributes represent infrastructure needs such as who created or updated an entity's instance; what project caused the entity's instance to be added or changed; and finally, what was the date of the creation or change of the entity's instance.<br><br>Note: Specified Data Models are never database models and thus, there can never be "instances" of data. This third set of attributes is just for completeness of the entity's definition. |
| Entity | An entity is a collection of business facts that are commonly called attributes. Every entity should relate back to a specific policy within the domain of the entity's subject. Entities can be subtyped to represent collections of attributes that have a common set and then several non-intersecting sets. |
| Specified Data Model Relationship | A relationship is a defined mechanism to relate one instance of one entity to a set of instances of another entity. While there are eight classes of relationships, the most common are the one-to-many, and one-to-one. In the case of one-to-many, the relationship mechanism is the primary key attributes of one entity related to the foreign key attributes of the related-to entity. The term, foreign key, comes from the fact that it's really a "transplant" of the "related-from" entity's primary key. Relationships should always be named and defined to the extent that the real purpose of the relationship is clear. |

| Specified Data Model Components | |
|---|---|
| **Component** | **Description** |
| Subject | A subject is a area of interest from within the enterprise that is to be represented through structures of data values. Examples can include address structures, person name structures, contracts, purchase orders, and the like. Subjects can be hierarchical. Commonly, the subjects are related to policies accomplished by knowledge workers that require "proof of execution." Subjects are not databases, however. Nor are subjects the concepts from within the Data Element Model. |

**Table 12.** Specified Data Model components.

Entities can have subtypes to any depth. An example might be for education which might have a common set of attributes for all classes of education, and then subtypes for each different education class such as high school, college, or trade school. Attributes are the use of the semantics of data elements. Because of this one-to-many relationship between data element and attribute, users can see which attributes employ a data element's semantics regardless of the entity or subject.

Attributes can also be assigned various modifier semantics and data use semantics. This enables automatic name construction for attributes. Automatic definitions and abbreviations are also enabled because there is a persistent relationship between the assigned semantic and the attribute. This too enables finding and reporting attributes regardless of entity and subject on the basis of either a semantic or data use modifier.

There can also be relationships among the entities within one subject, and there can be relationships between entities from multiple subjects. If this were just a conceptual data model then there could not be relationships across different subject-based data models. Each would be a stove-pipe that can only be transformed into a logical and then physical form.

Specified Data Models are not conceptual forms of a data model. Rather, they are well developed data models in their own right. Each Specified Data Model should be in third normal form. Specified Data Models are persistent. Their form remains as defined. Its structures, that is, the data models of the concepts, are available as templates for the construction of one or more Implemented Data Models.

Almost all of the above is not possible with traditional ER modeling tools because they are fundamentally diagram-based with a supporting repository rather than repository-based with the ability to generate ER diagrams.

## 6.2.3  Implemented Data Models.

The Implemented Data Model is a collection of data models of databases. Each Implemented Data Model is composed of the triple: Schema, table, and column. Figure 19 shows a high level diagram of the key components of the Implemented Data Model. Included in an Implemented Data Modeling effort are the metadata components found in Table 13.

There can be relationships among the tables within one schema as well as data types, assigned value domains and other appropriate metadata for complete data models. There can also be assigned semantic modifiers, data use modifiers, and value domains assigned just in the Specified Data Model. Thus, as with the Specified Data Model there can be automatic name, definition, and abbreviation construction. But because the Implemented Data Model comes from a repository, any semantic assignment conflicts between the specified and Implemented Data Models are immediately discovered and prevented.

Each table may be constructed through the use of a collection of attributes from a single Specified Data Model entity, or collections of attributes from multiple Specified Data Model entities within one or more subjects. An entity or sub-collection of attributes from one entity can be used to form the data structure in multiple tables. The relationship between the Specified Data Model and the Implemented Data Model is thus, many-to-many, as it exists in real-world data modeling environments.

Tables in the Implemented Data Model can be subtyped. Columns can also be complex to support nested structures of arbitrary depth. The data types assigned to an Implemented Data Model are those allowed by the ANSI SQL standard.

Finally, because the Implemented Data Model is built from a foundation of the data models of concepts from the Specified Data Model, a complete cross reference between the two classes of models is easily reported.

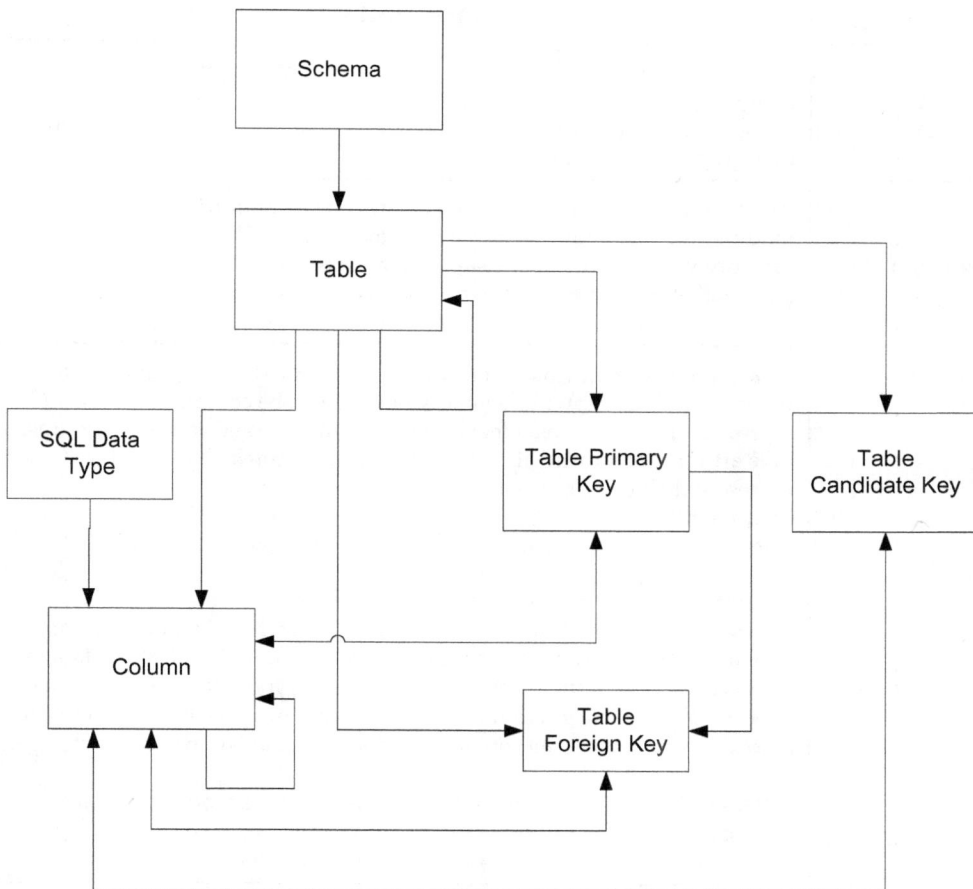

**Figure 19**. Key components of the Implemented Data Model.

| Implemented Data Model Components | |
|---|---|
| **Component** | **Description** |
| Column Assigned Value Domain | An assigned value domain is a value-based constraint on the column. The assigned value domain cannot be the same as that assigned the data element or the attribute. Nor can a value domain be more expansive than that assigned the data element or column. |
| Column Assigned Meta Category Values | An assigned meta category value, whether a semantic or data use modifier is a "meaning" constraint on the column. The assigned meta category value cannot be the same as that assigned the data element or an attribute. Nor can a meta category value be more expansive than that assigned the data element or the column. |
| Column | A column, like an attribute of an entity, is intended to be a data-value based partial descriptor of a table. Columns can be complex, and thus represent arrays, groups, repeating groups, and nested repeating groups. Like attributes there are also three classes of columns. Those that represent the table's content. For example, if the table is CustomerAddress then the content attributes would be CustomerStreet-1, CustomerStreet-2, CustomerCity, CustomerState, and CustomerZip.

There are columns also related to the instance of the table. For example the set of columns which have a combined value such that only one row from the table is found. This is commonly called the table's primary key. The third set of columns represent infrastructure needs such as who did the table's creation or update; what project caused the table to be added or changed; and finally, what was the date of the add or change.

Note: Implemented Data Models are never database models and thus, there can never be "instances" of data. This third set of columns is therefore just for completeness of the table's definition. |
| Implemented Data Model Relationship | A relationship is a defined mechanism to relate one instance of table to another. As with the Specified Data Model, the most common are the one-to-many, and one-to-one. The keys are almost always primary and foreign keys. Relationships cannot exist between tables in different schemas. |
| Schema | A schema is a database structure that encapsulates all its contained tables as well as containing other classes of schema objects such as data types, procedures, constraints, including the interrelationships of the various schema objects.

Implemented Data Models are cast within the domain of a schema. The set of all tables within a schema is not required to be taken from a single set of entities within a subject area. |

| Implemented Data Model Components | |
|---|---|
| **Component** | **Description** |
| Table | A Table is intended to be a well-defined expression of one policy within a schema. Ideally, the collection of all the tables within a schema area should define a coherent collection policy. Although unlikely, some tables and even some schemas may never be represented within Operational Data Models. Additionally, some columns within a table may never be employed. A table may contain columns that map to attributes from multiple entities. Tables can be sub-typed. |
| | A table represents a collection of columns, which when bound to a particular DBMS and valued, represents a set of rows of data for those columns. Tables have precise specifications including constraints, primary and foreign keys, and other table centered features. Within the scope of the Implemented Data Model generalization level for data architectures, these table specifications do not represent actual rows of data because this level is not bound to a particular DBMS and is not related to any specific business information systems. These tables, and the entire Implemented Data Model is intended to be a data architecture design layer. |
| | Tables can be subtyped to represent collections of columns that have a common set and then several non-intersecting sets. |

**Table 13.** Implemented Data Model components.

Again, almost all of the above is not possible with traditional ER modeling tools because they are fundamentally diagram-based with a supporting repository rather than repository-based with the ability to generate ER diagrams. Traditional data modeling tools are for modeling databases as separate independent metadata stove-pipes. For enterprise-wide data management this is entirely unacceptable.

## 6.2.4 Operational Data Models.

The Operational Data Model is similar to the Implemented Data Model in its capabilities. The triple for the Operational Data Model is DBMS Schema, DBMS table, and DBMS column. Figure 20 shows a high level diagram of the key components of the Implemented Data Model. Included in a Specified Data Modeling effort are the metadata components found in Table 14.

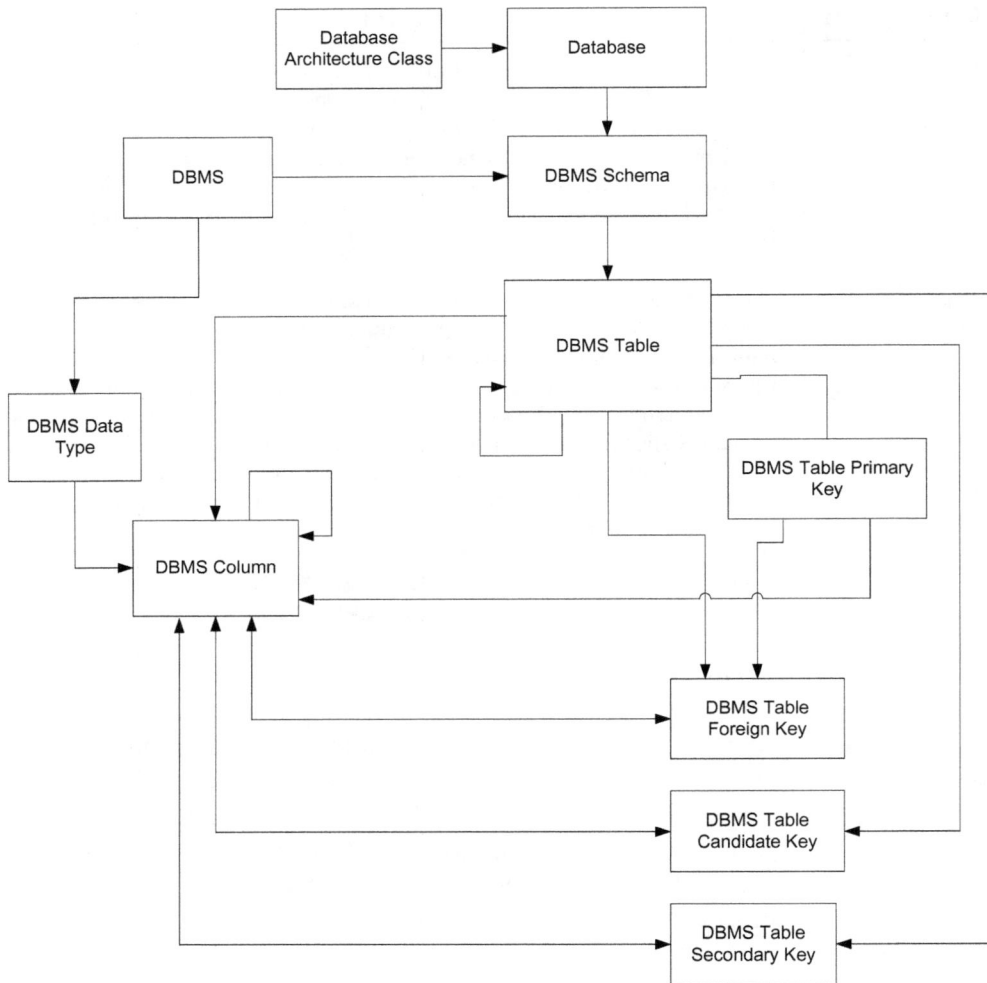

**Figure 20**. Key components of the Operational Data Model.

A key difference in the Operational Data Model from the Implemented Data Model is that it represents the data structures that result in SQL DDL that feeds the DBMS to actually make the databases.

There may be multiple Operational Data Models for a given Implemented Data Model. Each may be a different subset of the Implemented Data Model's tables and columns, or in some cases, it's all the tables and columns, but some tables may be brought up under a parent table. For example, there might have been an Implemented Data Model table for telephone numbers that in the Operational Data Model are transformed into TelephoneNumber-1 through TelephoneNumber-5. This is a kind of denormalization created to improve performance.

There may also have been multiple implemented data models for a given operational data model. This commonly occurs in data warehouse data model designs where the data model for the data warehouse is sourced from multiple implemented data models.

The string, "DBMS" prefixes these three terms because this data model is directly tied to a specific DBMS. The Operational Data Model can contain subtyped DBMS tables, and substructures in DBMS Columns. It can also have an assigned value domain and the data types reflect that of the containing DBMS.

Each DBMS table may be constructed through the use of a collection of columns from an Implemented Data Model table, or collections of columns from multiple Implemented Data Model tables within one or more Implemented Data Model schemas. A table or sub-collection of columns from one Implemented Data Model table can be used to form the data structure in multiple DBMS tables. The relationship between the Implemented Data Model and the Operational Data Model is thus, many-to-many as it is in real data modeling environments.

| Operational Data Model Components | |
|---|---|
| **Component** | **Description** |
| DBMS Column Assigned Meta Category Values | There are no assigned meta category values because at this data model generalization level there should be no additional modification of semantic and data use modifiers. |
| DBMS Column Assigned | An assigned value domain is a value-based constraint on the DBMS column. The assigned value domain cannot be the same as that assigned |

| Operational Data Model Components | |
|---|---|
| **Component** | **Description** |
| Value Domain | the data element, attribute, or column. Nor can a value domain be more expansive than that assigned the data element attribute, or column. |
| DBMS Column | A DBMS column, like an attribute of an entity is intended to be a data-value based partial descriptor of a DBMS table. DBMS Columns can be complex, and thus represent arrays, groups, repeating groups, and nested repeating groups. Like columns, there are also three classes of DBMS columns, and those definitions are not be repeated again. |
| DBMS Table | A DBMS table is a database construct that exists within a DBMS schema to represent a collection of DBMS columns that are bound to a particular DBMS and represent a set of rows of data across those DBMS columns. DBMS Tables have precise specifications including constraints, primary and foreign keys, and other table centered features. Within the scope of the Operational Data Model generalization level for data architectures, these DBMS table specifications represent actual rows of data because this level is bound to a particular DBMS and is related to any specific business information systems.<br><br>Every DBMS table should relate back to a specific policy within the domain of the DBMS table's schema. DBMS Tables can be subtyped to represent collections of DBMS columns that have a common set and then several non-intersecting sets. |
| DBMS Schema | A DBMS schema is a DBMS structure that encapsulates all its contained DBMS tables as well as containing other classes of DBMS schema objects such as data types, procedures, constraints, including the interrelationships of the various DBMS schema objects. The string, "DBMS" is attached to these components because at this data architecture level, these components are directly representative of the real and operating databases under the control of a specific DBMS. |
| Operational Data Model Relationship | A relationship is a defined mechanism to relate one instance of one DBMS table to another. As with the Implemented Data Model, the most common are the one-to-many, and one-to-one. The keys are almost always primary and foreign keys. Because the Operational Data Model supports the SQL DDL for an actually operating database, a fourth key type, Secondary, is supported. This key type consists of one or more DBMSs columns such that when the values are supplied, a subset of rows is materialized from the table. |

**Table 14.** Operational Data Model components.

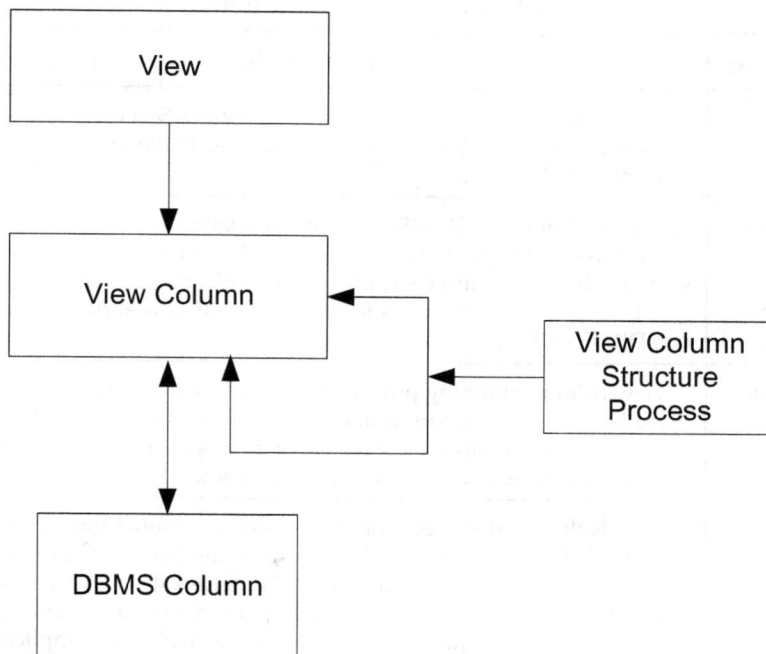

**Figure 21**. Key components of the View Data Model.

## 6.2.5  View Data Models.

View data models and its high level components are shown in Figure 21. Views, which represent the interface between Operational Data Models and Business Information Systems, consist of views and view columns with the associated hierarchies of joins and selects to give applications a flat "record set" for processing.

Included in the views can be rename clauses and on-the-fly calculations. View elements map to DBMS columns and as appropriate compound data elements and derived data elements. Included in a View Data Model effort are the metadata components found in Table 15.

| View Data Model Components | |
|---|---|
| **Component** | **Description** |
| View Column | A view column is a "data" component of a view. Some view columns are the result of a computation that "goes on" inside the view involving multiple DBMS columns. |
| View Column and DBMS Column | A View Column and DBMS Column is a relationship between a view column and the Operational Data Model. This enables a given view to be specified in the Metabase such that it is applicable to multiple DBMSs and multiple databases. An executing view, of course, is applicable to only one DBMS and one database. |
| View Column Process mapping | A view column mapping process is a process-specific mechanism that maps between view columns of different views. This enables the specification of an input view from one database to an output view to another database, or even to several databases. |
| View | A view is the interface between the Operational Data Model and the Business Information System. Views are defined within the scope of the Operational Data Model for a specific database within a specific DBMS. A key component of a retrieval view is that it can contain complex selection logic and also multi-table normalization logic that enable application programs to not have to know about the database's structure or to navigate the database. An update view can also contain constraint clauses that check the quality of the data prior to it being sent to the DBMS that in turn updated the database. |

**Table 15.** View data model components

## 6.3    Data Model Integration and Reuse

The next three figures illustrate the integration and reuse of metadata across the Data Element, Specified, Implemented, and Operational Data Models. The first figure, Figure 22, shows the definition and reuse of Data Element metadata (right side) within the Specified Data model (left side). Figure 23 shows the definition and reuse of Specified Data Model (left side) metadata within the Implemented Data Model (right side). Figure 24 shows the definition and reuse of Implemented Data Model (left side) metadata within the Operational Data Model.

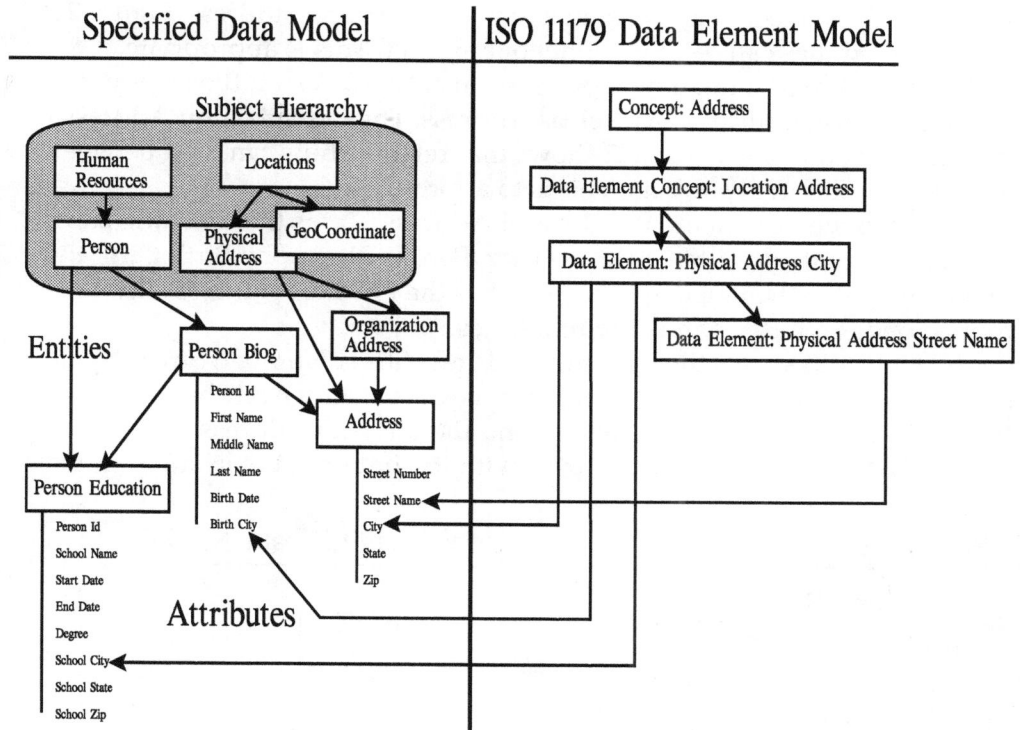

**Figure 22**. Integration and reuse of Data Element to Specified Data Model.

In Figure 22, the right side of the figure shows the concept, Address, a data element concept related to Address, that is, Location Address, and two data element example uses, Physical Address City, and Physical Street Name. There could be many other Data Element Concept uses of Address such as Email address, Receiving Address, and the like. For the Data Element Concept, Physical Address, the data element, Physical Address City is an example of a component of the Physical Address. Other components could be Physical Address State, Postal Address Zip Code, and the various parts of the actual street address. Included could also be P.O. Box number.

On the left side of Figure 22, there are two main subjects. The first is Human Resources. It has a Person subordinate subject and then two entities, Person Biog[raphy], and Person Education. The relationships between the subject, Person, and the entities Person Biography, and Person Education are shown. Similarly, there is the Physical Address subject, and it has two relationships between it and Organization Address and Address. Figure 22 shows that entities can belong to only one subject. This is appropriate.

There are also relationships between entities. Person Biography is the parent of Person Education as well as Address. The Organization Address is the parent of Address. Figure 22 shows that relationships can exist between entities from different subjects. This is to appropriate.

As to the data elements, Physical Address City is the semantic parent to three different attributes, Address City, Person Biography Birth City, and Person Education School City. This case has the Physical Address City defined once and used three different times.

Figure 23 shows the use of the Address Street Number, Street Name, and City each being used two different times. These three attributes are defined within the Location's subject, and the Physical Address subordinate subject. The Human Resources subject with its contains Person subordinate

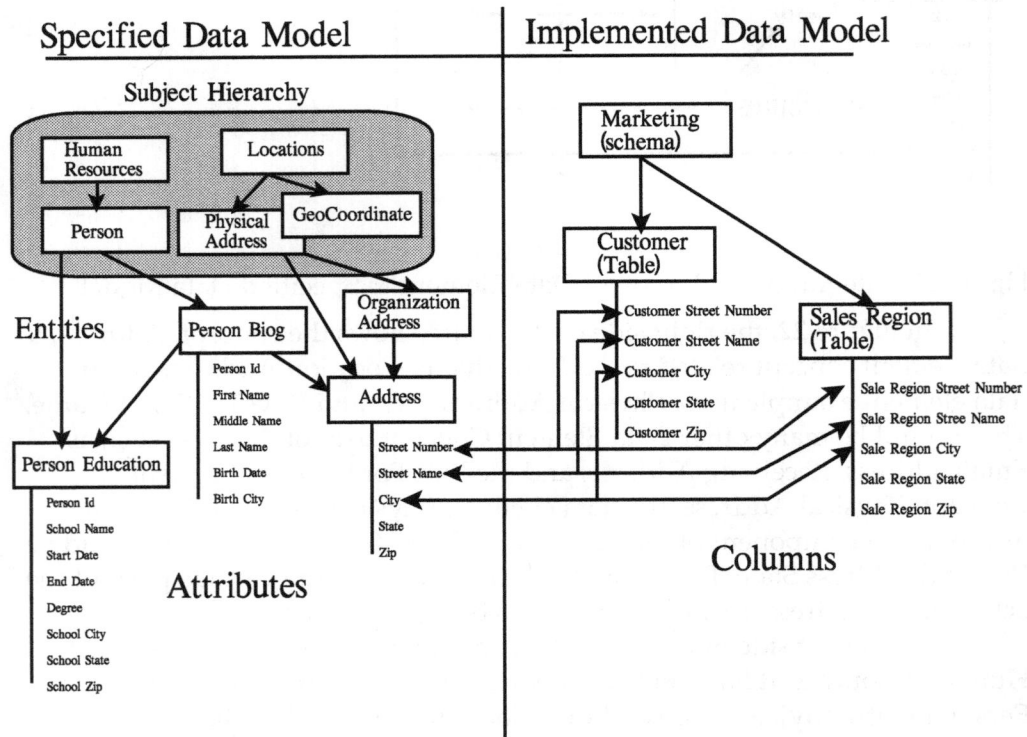

**Figure 23**. Integration and reuse of Specified Data Model to Implemented Data Model metadata.

subject shows two entities. The Address entity is related to the Person Biography entity. This allows multiple address for a given person. Within the Address entity there are the two attributes, Street Number, and Street Name.

On the right side of Figure 23 is the use of the three left side attributes. Each set is used twice. The first use is with the Customer table and provides the semantics for the Customer Street Number, Customer Street Name, and Customer City for the Customer's address. The second use is for the Sales Region table and provides Sales Region Street Number, Sales Region Street Name, and Sales Region City for the address of the Sales Region. This again is an example of the define-once, use many times principle of database.

Given the initial definition of the Data Element, Physical Address City, it now has been defined once and its semantics have been used three different times in the Specified Data Model, and one of the uses in the Specified Data Model has been used twice in the Implemented Data model.

The final integration and reuse example is presented in Figure 24. In this example, the left side shows a Marketing Schema with three tables. The right side shows four tables. In this example, all four tables are resident in four different schemas, Customer Management, Sales Region Management, Sales Management, and Product Management. These four schemas are not shown to keep the example simpler. Each of these four tables makes use of different columns from the Implemented Data Model. Customer Id from the Customer Table is used as the in the Customer table from the Customer Management schema. This column is also used in the Sales data warehouse table, Sales as part of a primary key and as a dimension. Similarly, Region Id is used from the Sales Region table for the same named table in the operational data model. Sales Region Id is used from the Sales table into the data warehouse table, Sales Region as both part of the primary key and as a dimension. Not shown in this example would be the use of City. It would be appropriately used in the Customer, Sales Region, and Sales tables.

## 6.4     Top-down versus Bottom-up Modeling

Data models across these five levels of generalization can be built either top-down or bottom-up. It makes no sense to presume that data modeling can only be accomplished top-down. If that were the case then all organizations with existing database inventories (which means close to 100% of all

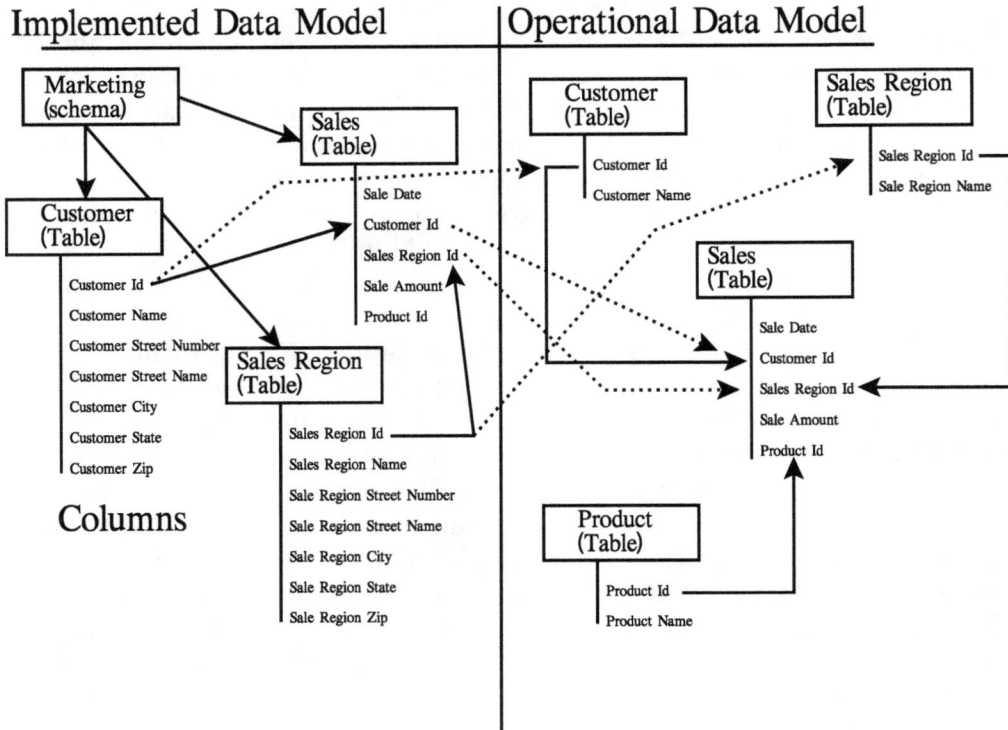

**Figure 24**. Integration and reuse of Implemented Data Model and Operational Data Model metadata.

organizations) would have to blow up all their Operational Data Model inventories and start over to re-engineer their entire data model environment.

Since "top-down-only" is a non-starter suggestion, there has to be a process of importing existing data models at the Operational Data Model level, inductively arriving at "union" data models on a functional grouping basis at the Implemented Data Model level, and then by induction once more, distilling out all the data models of the concepts and creating the Specified Data Model level.

While starting top-down might appear to be simpler and quicker, actually it actually takes longer. That is because proceeding from theory to reality always involves many iterations of evolving the theory until it reflects reality. By starting at reality and moving up to theory, the process is faster, and certainly has immediate payout.

The top-down approach requires the creation and exposition of all enterprise-wide data elements first, then all data models of concepts, then all Implemented Data Models, and then through some unknown magic mapping process, the mapping of the Implemented Data Models to the existing Operational Data Models. Simply put, it takes too long, costs too much, produces too little, and always results in significant culture classes.

By starting bottom-up, as illustrated in Figure 25, a collection of data models in a given functional area can be identified and loaded into the repository through an SQL DDL import. An examination of these models will likely produce one that is the "least worst" or the "most comprehensive." That model is promoted up to the Implemented Data Model level. Then, the remaining models in the functional area are mapped, or they result in more tables or more columns. Either way, there quickly evolves a "union" model across the entire functional area. That, in turn, enables immediate "where-used" reporting.

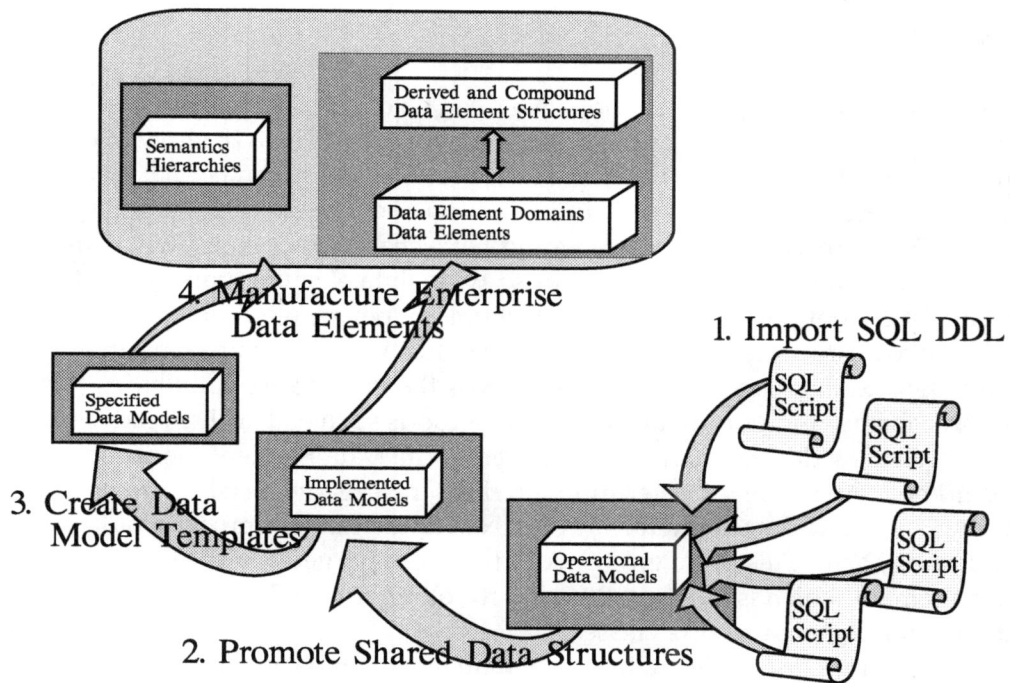

**Figure 25**. Reverse engineering approach to data architecture management.

115

If value domains are available, they can be entered into the Data Element Model and mapped to the appropriate columns of the Operational Data Model. If there are two different value domains for DBMS columns that are, in turn, mapped to the same Implemented Data Model column then there's a data interoperability mis-match at the operational level. Knowing that produces immediate value.

This bottom-up approach can then proceed to discovering columns that are used multiple times (same meaning but different name) and then making them data elements. Finally, there could be quick discoveries of commonly used concepts about which little data models could be constructed.

This bottom-up approach is a bit messy, but is clearly faster, and never suffers from the "when will this ever be done and be of value" syndrom. The information technology graveyard is full of top-down enterprise data models. No more are needed, ever.

## 6.5    Division of Effort

The five data model generalization levels can be divided across three functionally different groups of knowledge workers. Figure 26 shows the three general functional categories: Data Administration, Functional Data Administration, and Database Administration and Systems Development.

These three environments would have charge over their own areas of data model management. The enterprise-wide data element management group, likely not part of information technology per se, would be charged with discovering enterprise-wide data elements, value domains, and the semantic and data use modifiers from across the inventory of databases, reports, forms, and non-database access methods such as Excel spreadsheets.

As new data elements are uncovered, the Data Element managers would be responsible for determining if they are already exist but are just hiding, or if new data elements need to exist and what the impact would be by adding them. This same group would also be charged with value domain management which is a critical function for all reference data use within any of the database architecture classes.

The functional area data model managers, almost always not directly associated with information technology would be charged with the creation and management of all the Specified Data Models of concepts such as facilities, money, persons, and the like, regardless of how these data models of

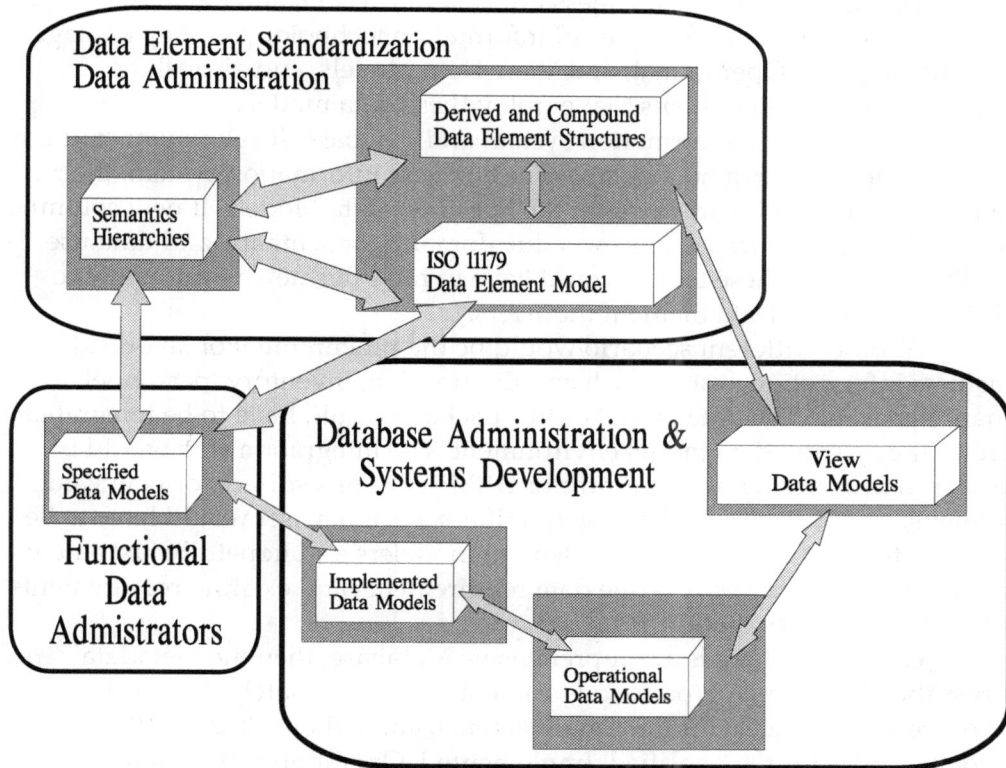

**Figure 26**. Functional distribution of data architecture efforts.

concepts are deployed in Implemented Data Model database designs. Each data model of a concept would employ only enterprise-wide data elements, and only subsets of value domains or semantic and data use modifiers.

As with the data element management, if new concept data models cause new data elements, value domains, or semantic and data use modifiers, these new work products would be surfaced to the Data Element managers for review and possible adoption. The goal here is managing enterprise-wide semantics. These two functional groups have different understandings, responsibilities and duties within the enterprise. The functional data modelers are primarily concerned with the functionally correct data structures required by policy, and in a supporting way, all the value domains and the semantic and data use modifiers that are appropriate.

117

The final group, the business information system and database development staff are clearly part of information technology as they manage the Implemented, Operational, and View Data Models, and also all the business information systems that employ these data models.

If the business information system and database development staff are instructed to develop a new database or business information system, their data models would be drawn from the Specified Data Models. If new columns or DBMS columns surface, or new value domains, or semantic and data use modifiers surface, these teams would have to raise this new requirement to the functional and Data Element modelers.

Another different scenario would be the procurement of an outside business information system such as a distribution, inventory, personnel, or finance package. The data model of this package would have to be integrated within the existing data model environment. The integration step would be similar to discovering new columns or DBMS columns surface, or new value domains, or semantic and data use modifiers. Each new set would have to be raised to the functional and Data Element modelers and hopefully just a new mapping between these package data requirements and existing requirements would have to be created.

Given that there is a comprehensive Metabase, then the metadata across these functional groups can be managed appropriately. If however there are spread sheets for the Data Elements, and either different ER modeling tools for the Specified, Implemented, Operational and View Data Models there will be no enterprise integration. There will only be minimal reuse and maximal semantic dis-integration. In short, these three groups will just be producing large quantities of metadata stove-pipes that must thereafter be disambiguated, reused, and integrated.

Soon, budgets will be consumed and there will be not be anything of value to show for all the expended resources. This is not good. It is the inverse of what should be achieved. To accomplish value, there must be metadata integration and non-redundancy across the enterprise. Value will then be created. Expanded roles and responsibilities will be in the offing instead of "pink slips."

## 6.6    Data Architecture Summary

This chapter started with the explanation of the two data architecture dimensions: Database architecture classes, and Data Model Generalization levels. The database architecture classes are:

- Original data capture.
- Transaction data staging area.
- Subject area databases.
- Data warehouses (wholesale and retail).
- Reference data.

The original data capture database architecture classes represent the actual databases that reside within organizations within an enterprise and may provide data to other database classes. These database types are often called OLTP databases because they support on-line transaction processing.

The transaction data staging area database architecture class represents the data extracts from the original data capture databases that, if necessary, are modified to the required semantics for other database architecture classes. Any interface between any database architecture class may proceed through a transaction data staging area.

The subject area database architecture class represents the subject-based integrated databases of data that, in turn, support some measure of analyses and reports, analysis results retention, and supports the generation of other classes of databases, that is, data warehouses.

The data warehouse (wholesale and retail) database architecture represents the transformed and likely redundant sets of data that serve special reports and analyses. The key set of differences between wholesale data warehouses and retail data warehouse is one of volume, duration and specialization. Data mart data warehouse designs are commonly created along the lines of "star schemas" or "snow-flake schemas," and when compared to wholesale data warehouses have smaller volumes, shorter durations, and are more specialized.

The reference data database architecture class represents data that form the critical characterization and discrimination characteristics of data from within the entire set of business facts. Included, for example are genders, city names, state names, all codes, and like. Ideally, all reference data would be exactly the same across all the other four data architecture classes.

Realistically, however, different agencies and providers have different reference data value versions for the same reference data and different data value versions across time. All reference data must be managed centrally and then distributed in so far as it is possible to all databases of the other data architecture classes.

Every one of these databases employs and/or proceeds through the following data model generalization levels:

- [11179] Data elements.
- Specified Data Models.
- Implemented Data Models.
- Operational Data Models.
- View data models.

Database Object Classes, the subject of Chapter 5, are defined within the Implemented Data Model and made operational during the Operational Data Model.

The Data Element level provides the ability to have enterprise-wide business facts combined with semantic, data use modifiers, and language independent data types.

Specified Data Models are value based representations of the various concepts included in databases throughout the enterprise. These Specified Data Models can be employed in the development of databases that are used throughout the enterprise such that these databases are integrated and non-redundant.

Implemented Data Models are models of specific databases of one or more classes such as original data capture, transaction data staging area, subject area databases, warehouses, and reference data. Some of the subject area databases, also called Operational Data Stores (ODS) may contain data that is classified as master data, which is also known as strategic data, golden source data, and authoritative data sources.

Data warehouses are a class of database that contain enterprise data in various organizational configurations such as time, organizations, products, and the like.

The final database architecture class, Reference Data, contains the enterprise determined value sets for key facts such as genders, zip codes, countries, products, financial classifications, and the like.

Operational Data Models are the database models of the databases that are actually govern the structures and data value domains of enterprise data.

In general, an enterprise-wide effort can be made to discover data elements through an analysis of any number of enterprise documents including database schemas, manual and computer generated reports, policy and procedure manuals, and forms. This type of effort can largely proceed independently of any functional data modeling effort, or any database and/or business information system effort.

Similarly, functional data administrators can begin efforts to create subject-based data models of common seen data structures within their functional area.

The various data model generalization layers are interrelated within the Database Object Classes column, and for the Operational Data Model level, there are relationships with other Knowledge Worker Framework columns such as the Business Information Systems.

The data model generalization layers are interrelated with the enterprise's architecture as the data architectures are derived from database domains that are created from missions. The Implemented Data Model layer contains all the database tables defined within Database Object Classes. These database objects are directly related to the Resource Life Cycle Analysis architecture that is addressed in Chapter 7, and Business Information Systems Plan in Chapter 8.

Finally, this chapter set out the work products that must be created for each data model generalization layer, and then how all these work products are thoroughly integrated one with the other.

Chapter 7, Resource Life Cycles, defines enterprise resources and Resource Life Cycles, what business objectives are fulfilled by their employment, where these fit within all the other architectures. While valuable in their own right, Resource Life Cycles also serve as a key linking mechanism between the Enterprise's Architecture, Database Object Classes, and Data Architectures on the one hand and Business Information Systems Plans on the other hand.

## 6.7 Questions and Exercises

1. Do you agree with the types of database architecture classes? Which ones are missing? How would you characterize yours? Are the various database architecture classes interrelated similar to that depicted in Figure 15? If not, how are they interrelated?

2. Does an ERP package contain more than one database architecture class? How do you accommodate and/or integrate ERP package databases into your existing set of databases?

3. Do you have a Transaction Data Staging Area (TDSA) database architecture class? What do you call it? What value does it serve?

4. Could you see using a TDSA database architecture class as a way to integrate ERP packages? Have you done that? What's been your experience?

5. What value would there be to your enterprise if granularity, precision, temporal aspects, and value domains were synchronized across your databases and business information systems? How would TDSA and reference data help?

6. Master data is a hot new phrase. Is this really anything new? Shouldn't we have been doing "master data" all along? What have you called your "master data." How has it been managed?

7. Do you agree with the characterization of the five data model generalization levels? Do you have more or fewer levels? Which of the book's levels missing in your organization? What has been the effect on your enterprise-wide data standardization efforts as a consequence of missing these layers?

8. The terms, Specified, Implemented, and Operational are used instead of Conceptual, Logical, and Physical. Are the book's definitions for these terms clear? Have the roles been clearly set out. Did the Figures 22, 23, and 24 help make the case for having persistent and different data models in each of these layers?

9. How can you integrate data model metadata across the enterprise? Is it of value to do that? If so, why? If not, why not?

10. How would enterprise-level data management integration help with business information system design, implementation, integration, and maintenance?

11. Do you see value in having data management development across the enterprise as shown in Figure 25?

12. If you had the ability to automate names, abbreviations, and definitions, would that help? If so, how? How much money and time would be saved? Would management have a better and more understandable data?

# 7

# Resource Life Cycle Analysis

Chapter 6, Data Architectures, set out the two data architecture dimensions, that is, the database architecture classes, and the data model generalization levels. This does not however answer the question, where are these databases used within the overall operational scope of the enterprise? That's what this chapter addresses.

This chapter, Resource Life Cycles Analysis, defines enterprise resources and the life cycles of these resources. The chapter also sets out the business objectives fulfilled by Resource Life Cycle employment, where the Resource Life Cycles fit within all the other architectures. While valuable in their own right, Resource Life Cycles also serve as a key linking mechanism between Enterprise's Architecture, Database Object Classes, and Data Architectures on the one hand and Business Information Systems Plans on the other hand.

Ron Ross, a well known "data" consultant formalized his ideas about corporate resources and their life cycles in a 1992 monograph, *Resource Life Cycle Analysis a Business Modeling Technique for IS Planning*. Resource Life Cycle Analysis (RLCA) uses a form of business modeling to perform information strategic planning. Ross identifies the need for this type of planning because:

> ...It is therefore unreasonable to attempt to satisfy both dimensions of scope---i.e. "process vs. data"---in a single type of project. I believe strategic planning should produce two types of projects — one for "data" and one for "process". . . Scoping for each type of project is orthogonal---no attempt is made to satisfy both dimensions at once---so that the result is like weaving a fabric. . . .Creating such a data-based infrastructure clearly requires early attention to data architecture for at least some of the "data" projects before any "process" project kicks off. That means pursuing high-level or "framework" entity modeling for at least some of the individual data projects. . . during or in parallel with the strategic planning phase.

In Ross's parlance, "data" projects refer to those that exist under the Knowledge Worker Framework column, Database Object Class, while "process" projects are those that fit under the Business Information System column.

Resources too live in the Database Object Classes column. That is because they are state-oriented and are often configured as subject area databases. Resources are however not subject area databases. Rather it's merely that the domain of data for a given resource may be the same domain of the subject area database.

Resources and their life cycles are different from an Enterprise's Architecture, Database Object Classes, Data Architectures, and Business Information Systems architectures in the following ways. The enterprise's architecture is the overall specification of "what the enterprise is," and what are its main missions, functions, organizations, and database domains.

Resources and their life cycles are what the enterprise employs within its infrastructure to accomplish its mission. For example, the enterprise employs people, money, assets, facilities, products, inventory, distribution, sales, marketing, and finance to accomplish its mission, which might be "building, selling, and servicing automotive vehicles to the world." Each of the people, etc. are the resources, while the mission is automotive quality and world dominance. In short, resources are not missions, but are the enabling components of mission accomplishment.

Resources are also not Database Object Classes. That should almost be intuitively obvious as the data domain of some resource maps most often to an entire subject area database. In contrast, Database Object Classes are also somewhat small, and highly engineered. Database Object Classes are exclusively data oriented as even their encapsulated processes exist solely to successfully achieve a data object state. In contrast, resources are much broader and may involve many different Database Object Classes and database object achieved states, which in turn, demonstrate that the resource has moved from one Resource Life Cycle state to the next.

Resources are also not data models because, a resource is not only different from a data model, it also may be much broader or possibly narrower than a data model. Clearly, a resource cannot be any of the data model generalization levels (i.e., Data Element Model through to View Data Models) because any one data model, or less than one data model, or even multiple of these data models can be employed in the full definition of a resource. An Operational Data Model's realized actual data may contribute achieved state evidence to multiple nodes of different Resource Life Cycles.

Finally, a Resource and its Resource Life Cycles are not Business Information Systems Plans (Chapter 8). However, the set of resources and also the collection of Resource Life Cycles for those resources are a critical ingredient in accomplishing a quality, malleable, and cost effective Business Information Systems Plan.

When a Business Information Systems Plan is accomplished, the objective is to create and/or evolve various databases business information systems in a business-requirements-based sequence. Resources and Resource Life Cycles are a key ingredient in identifying that sequence.

Once the business information systems are created and begin to execute, the various resources of the enterprise begin to march through their Resource Life Cycles, one-achieved node state at a time. As the resources march, database objects, as proofs of accomplishment, are created, modified, or deleted. Database objects, set within data architectures, enable knowledge workers to view the state and progress of the enterprise including all the business transactions that produce evidence of the achieved states.

## 7.1   Resource Life Cycle Analysis Objectives

The goal of Resource Life Cycle Analysis is to build a bridge between the operational level needs of information technology organizations and the strategic level organization business process needs required by upper management. The main goal of the strategic level is to identify and describe the major resources essential to the enterprise's survival, while the main goal of the business information systems organization is to plan, develop, deliver, and maintain the various business information systems projects required to implement the enterprise resources in the most effective manner possible. Resource Life Cycle Analysis builds this bridge goal by determining:

- The Resource Life Cycle networks.

- The Database Object Class projects and Business Information System projects, and establishing their proper sequence for analysis, design, and implementation.

- A strategic view of the ongoing business information systems development and major maintenance work.

Resource Life Cycle Analysis determines three components of the Resource Life Cycle networks, that is, the resource, the resource's life cycle chain and the precedence vectors between Resource Life Cycles. A resource is an enduring asset with value to the enterprise. The life cycle is a linear identification of the major states that must exist within life of the resource. The life cycle of a resource represents the resources' "cradle to grave" set of the most-critical state changes. The precedence is a vector that may occur between nodes on different resources life cycles, and thus indicates which Resource Life Cycle node enables another Resource's Life Cycle node.

## 7.2    Building Resource Life Cycles

Resource Life Cycles are a key component in the planning, development, and evolution of the enterprise. Resource Life Cycles are properly identified subsequent to mission and Database Object Class analysis, and once created serve as a framework for understanding how they work and how the databases and business information systems support the enterprise's processes.

## 7.2.1  Resource Identification

Once mission analysis and database object identification has been completed, the resources of the enterprise quickly surface. For example, a state-wide judicial court system environment's resources include: Cases, Documents, Court Personnel, Calendars, Court Facilities, and the Law. While there are not lower or upper limits to the quantity of resources, 15 to 20 are common. A resource is necessary if the business is incomplete without it. Similarly, a resource is unnecessary if the business is complete without it.

In the Courts example, an essential resource is Cases. How could the court operate without cases? An unnecessary resource would be public outreach programs. These, while nice and of public benefit, they are not critical to the court's existence.

## 7.2.2 Resource Life Cycles

Each resource has a life cycle of state changes. The resource (at a minimum) is created, maintained, and terminated. Each resource state change represents a value-added accomplishment of a significant set of business activities. Further, each accomplishment is significant with respect to the previous Resource Life Cycle node in some way. The total sum of the implied processes for a resource is a "value chain" that comprises the life cycle of the resource. Figures 27, 28, and 29 illustrate the life cycles for Case, Court Person, and Document.

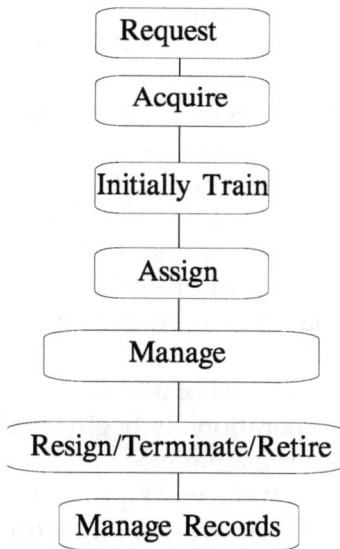

| Court Person | Case | Document |
|---|---|---|
| Request | File | Identify |
| Acquire | Classify | Classify |
| Initially Train | Assign | Store |
| Assign | Schedule | Act Upon |
| Manage | Process | Schedule Follow-up |
| Resign/Terminate/Retire | Dispose | Finally Determine |
| Manage Records | Archive Records | Archive |

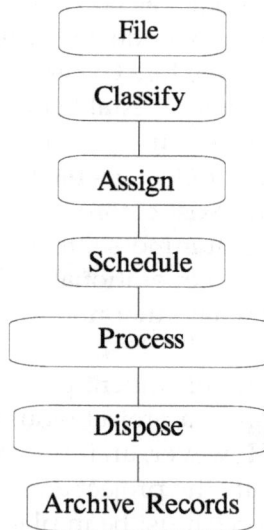

**Figure 27**. Court Person.     **Figure 28**. Case.     **Figure 29**. Document.

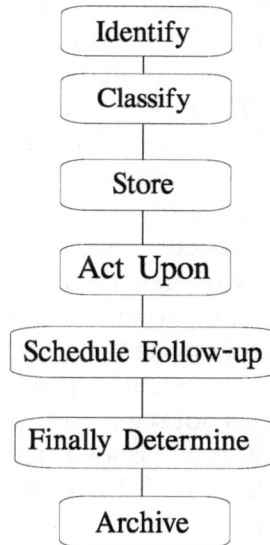

### 7.2.3  Resource Life Cycle Networks

After the resources and life cycles are complete, precedence vectors are established. There are actually two types of precedence vectors: Within the value chain and between resources. Precedence vectors *within* the value chain are established during the life cycle analysis. These are the lines that connect one node to the next. Any of the lines within Figures 27, 28, and 29 are such vectors.

A precedence between two different resources, that is, between the Document and Case resources, is created when a specific Resource Life Cycle node's state cannot be effective or correctly accomplished until the state of a different Resource Life Cycle node has been established or completed. A precedence vector is drawn from a node on the enabling Resource Life Cycle to a node on the enabled Resource Life Cycle.

The most difficult problem in establishing the precedence is the mind set of the analyst. The interdependence of nodes between life cycles is not to reflect operational order, but to reflect enablement order: that is, what Resource Life Cycle state must exist before the next Resource Life Cycle state is able to occur. This is a difficult mind-set to accept, as there is a natural tendency to view the life cycle in operational order. The test of precedence becomes: what node enables what other node, and what node is enabled by what other node?

For example, project establishment precedes the award of a contract. This does not seem natural, since a project would not operationally begin until after a contract is awarded. However, an infrastructure must have been previously established to create the project and to perform the work prior to the contract award. A workforce must be in place to perform work along with the ability to assign work to the employee on the contract, and the ability to invoice the customer.

Therefore, the project enables the contract. Here are three possible reasons for enablement.

- The accomplishment of the preceding Resource Life Cycle state saves money.

- The Resource Life Cycle state leads to rapid development of another Resource Life Cycle state

- The Resource Life Cycle state permits faster, more convenient accomplishment of another Resource Life Cycle state.

If one or more indicators exist, then a precedence vector should be created. Two alternatives exist relative to the existence of the enterprise: newly established or existing. Experience shows the preferred perspective is that of an already-existing enterprise.

RLC states may or may not occur during a life cycle, or events may occur in parallel. For example, an employee may receive an award, but then again, may never receive an award. An employee may work before and after a security clearance is granted. The strategy to deal with parallel or optional Resource Life Cycle states is to create a single stream of Resource Life Cycle states in which none are parallel or optional by "pushing down" the parallel or optional Resource Life Cycle states to a lower level.

Figure 30 presents the Resource Life Cycle network for documents, cases, and court personnel. What this diagram is "saying" is that court personnel must be assigned before a case can be classified. Then, once a case is processed, a particular document can be acted upon.

When these interrelationships are brought into the development or evolution of the collection of business information systems and databases, those which are associated with the first three nodes of a Court Personnel Resource Life Cycle must be in place and operational before any Court Personnel can be Assigned. Similarly, the databases and business information systems associated with the File node of the Case Resource Life Cycle must be in place before a Case can be classified. The databases and business information systems up to and including the Process Resource Life Cycle node of the Case Resource Life Cycle must be in place before any document can be Acted Upon. Finally, the database and business information systems up to and including the Act Upon Resource Life Cycle node of the Document Resource Life Cycle must be in place before a document can be acted upon.

## 7.3    Resource Life Cycles as an Architecture

Resource Life Cycle Analysis is an important architecture within the enterprise. Resource Life Cycle Analysis is however distinct from but complementary with business functions, databases, business information systems, and Database Objects Classes.

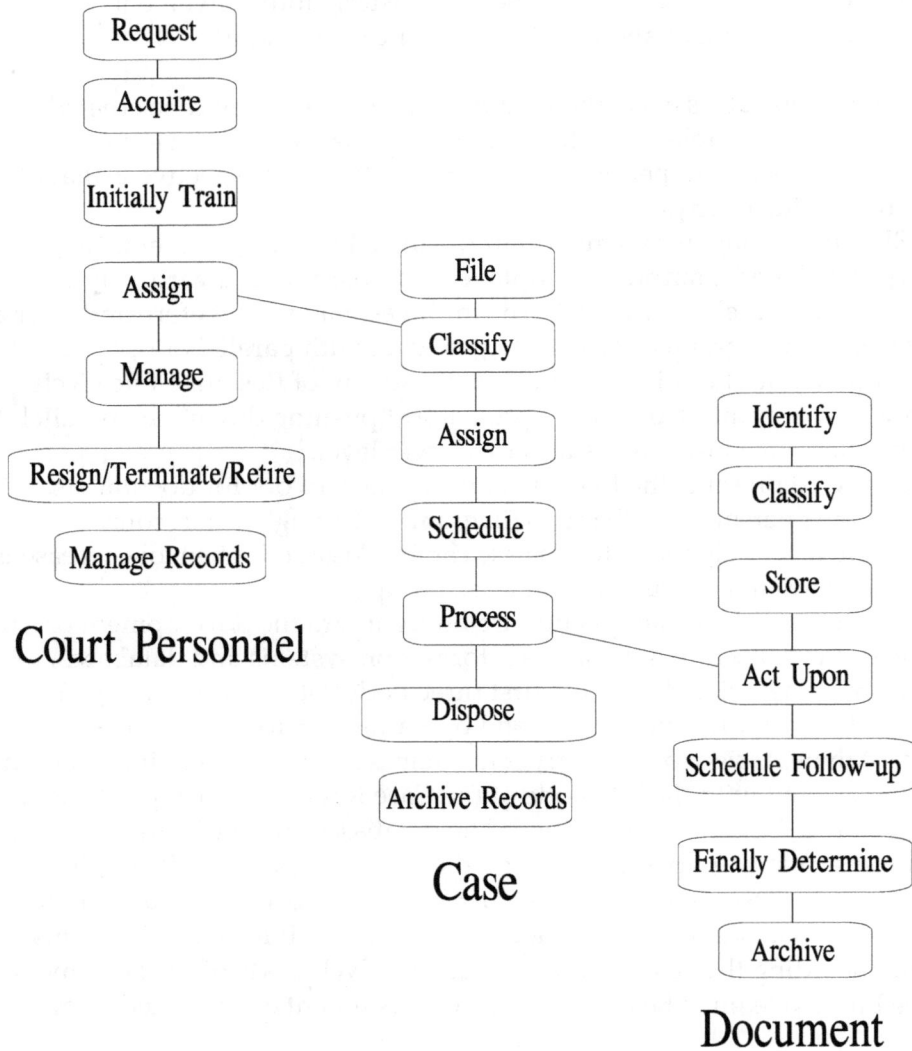

**Figure 30**. Precedence vectors among court persons, case, and document.

Resource Life Cycle Analysis acts as a framework upon which to attach and thus interrelate key components of an enterprise database. Through Resource Life Cycles, the following can be interrelated in a non-redundant fashion:

- Mission, Organizations, Functions, Positions and their Management Levels.

- Information Needs of these Missions, Organizations, Functions, Persons and their Management Levels.

- Business information systems.

- Databases (and in turn, database objects and data models).

Figure 31 illustrates these interrelationships at a high level. In this figure, the first box is essentially the material gathered during the first row of the Knowledge Worker Framework. While not addressed in this book, Information Needs are then determined across the various positions that are performing organization-based functions in the accomplishment of one or more missions. These Information Needs are then allocated to the various Resource Life Cycle nodes.

What that essentially means is that these information needs have to be satisfied to then accomplish the Resource Life Cycle node. The information for the Resource Life Cycle node is provided by the business information systems and databases. The databases are of course defined through the data models and database objects.


## 7.4    Employing Resource Life Cycle Networks

The Resource Life Cycle network represents the enterprises' need for information in an enablement order. Because there is a network, similar to a project management system's PERT network, information technology projects can be staged in Resource Life Cycle network order. The Resource Life Cycle network thus represents a natural network for accomplishing projects.

The Resource Life Cycle networks serves as a very useful framework for allocating existing databases and business information systems. The

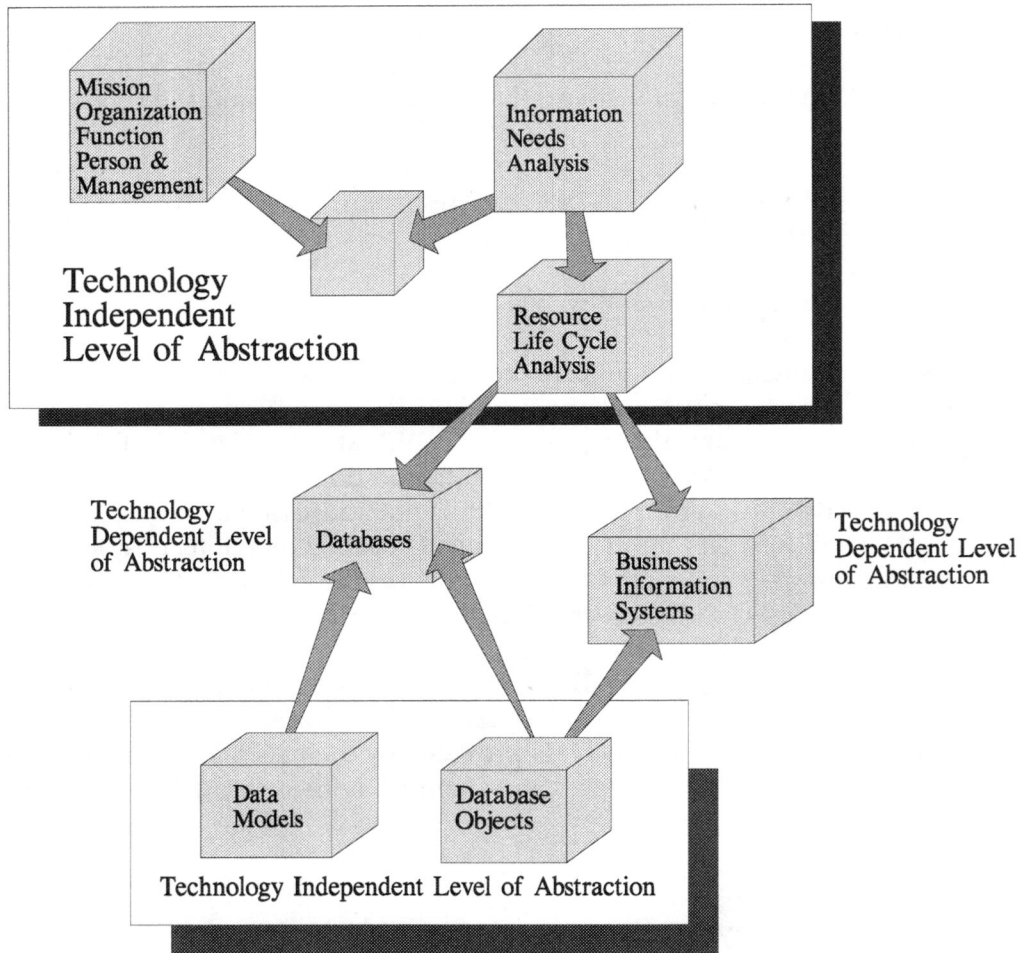

**Figure 31.** Interrelationships Between Key Components of Enterprise Database and Resource Life Cycles.

Resource Life Cycle network gives information technology organizations the ability to answer questions such as:

- What information technology projects address a particular segment of the enterprise?

- What business resource is served/enabled?

- When can one project be started and completed before another?

- What information technology projects are largely redundant one with another?

- Which segments of the Resource Life Cycle networks are either under or over served by IT?

Figure 29, as an example, shows that there are multiple systems allocated to several of the Resource Life Cycle nodes. There are three systems assigned to the Store node. Analysis should be performed to ensure that the semantics of these systems are neither at cross purposes nor completely redundant. If redundant, then elimination should be considered.

As information technology projects are proposed, the required resources (i.e., staff, time, hardware and software) of a project can be quantified in terms of the difference between the existing and proposed state of information technology assets allocated to the Resource Life Cycle node. Project estimating for technology improvement projects can be greatly improved when standardized project methodology templates are associated with these proposed projects. Finally, if metrics have been kept on past efforts, realistic estimates of efforts can be quickly determined.

When all the information technology improvement projects have been identified and estimated, the very fact that they are allocated against the Resource Life Cycle network enables them to be scheduled through a project management system, en mass.

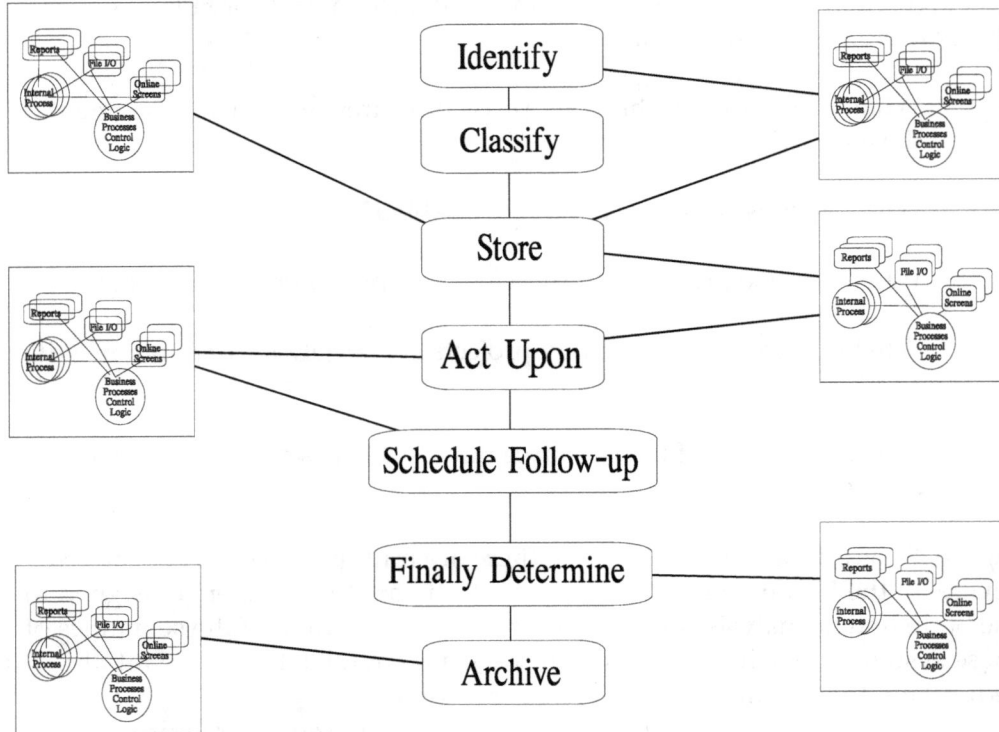

**Figure 32**. Allocated Information Systems to RLC, Case.

## 7.5    Real Benefit from Resource Life Cycle Analysis

Under the presumption that the result of the en mass scheduling is normal, that is, a requirement for an infinite amount of time coupled with infinite resources, a key value of Resource Life Cycle Analysis comes into play.

Because the Resource Life Cycle network is a reflection of the essential business resources, their life cycles, and the interactions among the life cycles, business analysts and managers can quickly grasp its significance. It represents the business. Playing secondary and supporting roles are all the databases and business information systems, as they should. So, when infinite corporate resources are not available, the Resource Life Cycle networks enable the "problem" to be put back where it belongs: squarely on enterprise management, who cannot then avoid answering three critical questions:

- What needs to be done? (That's expressed as the allocated databases and business information systems against the Resource Life Cycle nodes.).

- When is it appropriate to do it? (That's expressed through the precedence vectors.)

- Why does it benefit the enterprise? (That's expressed as the resources and their life cycle nodes.)

The only question left for the information technology staff is, "How will it be done?" This question is commonly answered through packages, custom development, and business information system generators, or not at all. As each "how" is answered and/or refined, the effects of the answer should be expressed as changes in resource requirements for the information technology projects allocated to the nodes. Once changed, the entire enterprise-wide Resource Life Cycle Analysis based information technology project set can be re-estimated. This process is iterated until a least-unobjectionable solution is found.

Once the Business Information Systems Plan has been agreed-to and signed-off by business management, the plan can be quickly and easily revisited whenever technology changes, packages are discovered, or business information system generators, repositories and CASE tools are obtained.

## 7.6    Resource Life Cycle Analysis Components

Figure 33 provides a high level model of the data that is collected to support Resource Life Cycles. The information need is related to the Resource Life Cycle Node of the Resource. Different Resource Life Cycle Nodes from different Resource Life Cycles are interrelated as shows in Figure 32. Database Object Classes and Business Information Systems are then interrelated with the various Resource Life Cycle Nodes. Included in a Resource Life Cycle modeling effort are the metadata components found in Table 16.

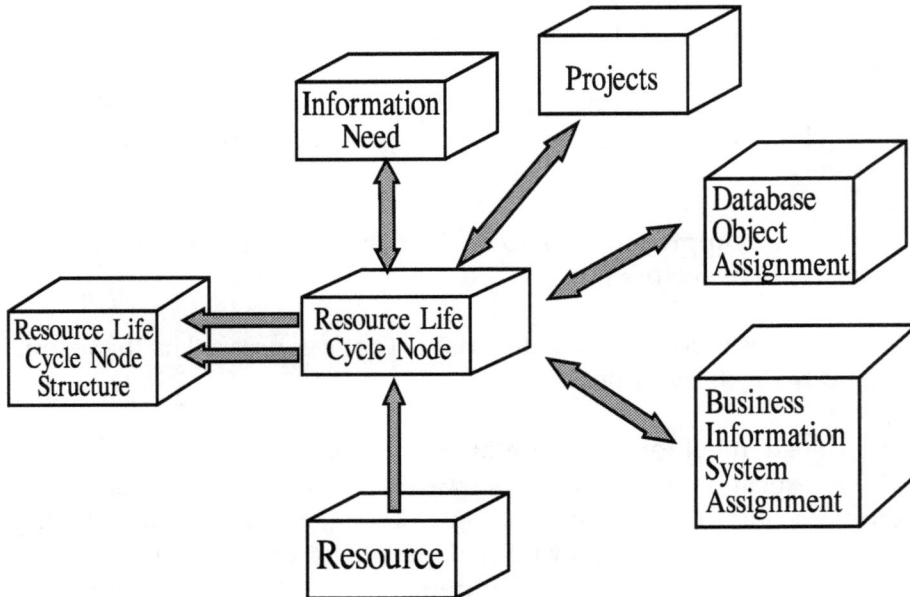

**Figure 33**. Key components of the resource life cycle analysis model.

| Resource Life Cycle Components | |
|---|---|
| **Component** | **Description** |
| Business information system Assignment | The Business information system Assignment is an association between the business information system with one or more Resource Life Cycle nodes. |
| Database Object Assignment | A Database Object Assignment is an association between a Resource Life Cycle node and a database object. A database object may be assigned to one or more Resource Life Cycle nodes and a Resource Life Cycle node may be related to one or more database objects. |
| Resource Life Cycle Node Structure | The Resource Life Cycle Node Structure is the association of one Resource Life Cycle Node and another. The association represents a relationship between the two resources for some purpose. |

| Resource Life Cycle Components | |
|---|---|
| **Component** | **Description** |
| Resource Life Cycle Node | A Resource Life Cycle Node is a life cycle state within the Resource. If the resource is employee, the life cycle node may be employee requisition, employee candidate, employee new hire, assigned employee, reviewed employee, and separated employee. |
| Resource | A Resource is an enduring asset of value to the enterprise. Included for example are facilities, assets, staffs, money, even abstract concepts like reputation. If a resource is missing then the enterprise is incomplete. |

**Table 16.** Resource Life Cycle Analysis model components.

## 7.7    Resource Life Cycle Analysis Summary

Resource Life Cycle Analysis enables business mangers to participate in the identification of the resources, their life cycles, and then precedence vectors among the life cycles. The information technology staff then has a business management defined network against which management can allocate the existing business information systems and databases. Once allocated, information technology can root out the conflicting and redundant systems and databases. Information technology projects that represent advances in the sophistication of its support to the business can be identified and resource-estimated through standardized methodologies and metrics. Once the set of information technology projects are estimated, the entire enterprise-network of information technology projects can be scheduled through project management software. At that point, management re-enters the picture and makes the hard choices, what, when, and why. Information technology is left with the How. That's as it should be.

To that end, this chapter defined enterprise resources and the life cycles of these resources. The chapter also set out the business objectives fulfilled by Resource Life Cycle employment, where the Resource Life Cycles fit within all the other architectures.

It is again important to note that while valuable in their own right, Resource Life Cycles also serve as a key linking mechanism between Enterprise's, Database Object Classes, and Data Architectures on the one hand and Business Information Systems Plans on the other hand.

Chapter 8, Business Information Systems Plans, are explained with respect to their necessary characteristics. These characteristics have been glaringly unfilled by other Business Information Systems Plan development methodologies. This explained methodology is the next logical building step from the prior architectures and employs all their work products. The Business Information Systems Planning methodology then leverages the large quantity of project methodology and metrics' templates to produce Business Information Systems Plans that are reliable and repeatable, and are malleable as new technologies unfold.

## 7.8    Questions and Exercises

1.      Across your databases and business information systems do you know how they are all linked, interlinked, and enforce the accomplishment of enterprise missions?

2.      How many resources does your enterprise have? Show how the Resource Life Cycles embrace all aspects of your enterprise?

3.      How are your Resource Life Cycle nodes interlinked between different Resource Life Cycles in you enterprise?

4.      How can the enterprise's inventory of databases and business information systems be allocated to the various Resource Life Cycle nodes? Has this helped you discover over-coverage and under-coverage?

5.      When you examine your Resource Life Cycle node network and allocated inventory of databases and business information systems, does that network reflect a natural build sequence? Is that what you're following? If yes, has it helped? If no, what have you done? Explain.

6.      Does the Resource Life Cycle node network and allocated inventory of databases and business information systems enable you to see the entire set of information technology efforts in a new way? Explain the old and new way?

7.      Does this network based sequence give business management a new way to see the what, where, and why of information technology projects?

# 8

# Business Information Systems Plans Architecture

Chapter 7, Resource Life Cycle Analysis, represented a business analysis chapter. That is, what resources the business contains, the life cycles of the resources, and the relationships that exist between different resource life cycles. This analysis and configuration is necessary to have a lattice work upon which to allocate all the enterprise's databases and business information systems. Once allocated, it becomes clear which Resource Life Cycle Analysis nodes have too many and likely conflicting databases and business information systems, and which Resource Life Cycle Analysis nodes are too sparse. While all this is valuable in its own right, an additional key value is that it enables Business Information System Plans.

This chapter sets out the necessary characteristics for Business Information Systems Plans to be successful, efficient and effective. Not only are these characteristics not accomplished by other Business Information Systems Plan development methodologies, these other methodologies are 10x more expensive to accomplish. The methodology in this chapter is the next logical building step from the prior architectures and employs all their work products.

The set out Business Information Systems Planning methodology leverages a large quantity of project methodology and metrics' templates to produce Business Information Systems Plans that are reliable and repeatable, and are malleable as new technologies unfold.

## 8.1   Are Business Information Systems Plans Really Needed?

Every year, $300-700 million dollar corporations spend about 5% of their gross income on business information systems and their supports. That's from about $15,000,000 to $35,000,000! A significant part of those funds support enterprise database, a philosophy of databases and business information systems that enable corporations to research the past, control the present, and plan for the future.

Even though a business information system costs from $1,000,000 to $10,000,000, and even through most chief information officers (CIOs) can specify exactly how much money is being spent for hardware, software, and staff, CIOs cannot however state with any degree of certainty why one system is being done this year versus next, why it is being done ahead of another, or finally, why it is being done at all.

Many enterprises do not have model-based business information systems development environments that allow system designers to see the benefits of rearranging a business information systems development schedule. Consequently, the questions that cannot be answered include:

- What effect will there be on the overall schedule if a business information system is purchased versus developed?

- At what point does it pay to hire an abnormal quantity of contract staff to advance a schedule?

- What is the long term benefit from 4GL versus 3GL?

- Is it better to generate 3GL than to generate/use a 4GL?

- What are the real costs of distributed software development over centralized development?

If these questions were transformed and applied to any other component of a business (e.g., accounting, manufacturing, distribution and marketing), and remained unanswered, that unit's manager would surely be fired!

We not only need answers to these questions NOW!, we also need them quickly, cost effectively, and in a form that they can be modeled and changed in response to unfolding realities. This chapter provides a brief review of a successful 10-step strategy that answers these questions.

Too many half-billion dollar organizations have only a vague notion of the names and interactions of the existing and under development business information systems. Whenever they need to know, a meeting is held among the critical *few*, an inventory is taken, interactions confirmed, and accomplishment schedules are updated.

This ad hoc Business Information Systems Plan was possible only because all design and development was centralized, the only computer was a main-frame, and the past was an acceptable prologue because budgets were ever increasing, schedules always slipping, and information was not yet part of the corporation's critical edge.

Well, today is different, really different! Budgets are under real pressure, and slipped schedules are being cited as preventing business alternatives. Confounding the computing environment is different operating systems, DBMSs, development tools, telecommunications (LAN, WAN, Intra-, Inter-, and Extra-net), and distributed hard- and software.

Rather than having centralized, long-range planning and management activities that address these problems, today's business units are using readily available tools to design and build ad hoc stop-gap solutions. These ad hoc systems not only do not interconnect, support common semantics, or provide synchronized views of critical corporate policy, they are soon to form the almost impossible to comprehend confusion of systems and data from which systems order and semantic harmony must spring.

Not only has the computing landscape become profoundly different and more difficult to comprehend, the need for just the right--and correct--information at just the right time is escalating. Late or wrong information is worse than no information.

Business information systems managers need a model of their business information systems environment: A model that is malleable. As new requirements are discovered, budgets are modified, new hardware/software is introduced, this model must be such that it can reconstitute the Business Information Systems Plan in a timely and efficient manner.

## 8.2    Characteristics of a Quality Business Information Systems Plan

A quality Business Information Systems Plan must exhibit five distinct characteristics before it is useful. These five are presented in Table 17.

| Business Information Systems Plan Components | |
|---|---|
| **Characteristic** | **Description** |
| Maintainable | The Business Information Systems Plan must be maintainable. New business opportunities, new computers, business mergers, etc. all affect the Business Information Systems Plan. The Business Information Systems Plan must support quick changes to the estimates, technologies employed, and possibly even to the fundamental project sequences. Once these changes are accomplished, the new Business Information Systems Plan should be just a few computer program executions, at most, a few days away. |
| Quality | While the Business Information Systems Plan must be a quality product, no Business Information Systems Plan is ever perfect on the first try. As the Business Information Systems Plan is executed, the metrics employed to derive the individual project estimates become refined as a consequence of new hardware technologies, business information system generators, techniques, or faster working staff. As these changes occur, their effects should be installable into the data that supports Business Information Systems Plan computation. In short, the Business Information Systems Plan is a living document. It should be updated with every technology event, and certainly no less often than quarterly. |
| Reproducible | The Business Information Systems Plan must be reproducible. That is, when its development activities are performed by any other staff, the Business Information Systems Plan produced should essentially be the same. The Business Information Systems Plan should not significantly vary by staff assigned. |
| Timely | The Business Information Systems Plan must be timely. A Business Information Systems Plan that is created long after it is needed is useless. In almost all cases, it makes no sense to take longer to plan work than to perform the work planned. |
| Useable | The Business Information Systems Plan must be useable. It must be so for all the projects as well as for each project. The Business Information Systems Plan should exist in sections that once adopted can be parceled out to project managers and immediately started. |

**Table 17.** Characteristics of a quality of a Business Information Systems Plan.

Whenever a proposal for the development of a Business Information Systems Plan is created, it must be assessed against the characteristics in Table 17. If a proposal fails to meet these characteristics, or not to address them in an optimum way, the entire set of funds for the development of a Business Information Systems Plan is risked.

## 8.3    Business Information Systems Plans within the Context of the Metadata Environment

The Business Information Systems Plan is the plan by which databases and business information systems of the enterprise are accomplished in a timely manner. A key facility through which the Business Information Systems Plan obtains its "data" is the Metabase.

The domain of the Metabase is set forth in Figure 34, and, through this figure, persons through their role within an organization perform functions in the accomplishment of enterprise missions, they have information needs. These information needs reflect the state of certain enterprise resources such as finance, people, and products that are known to the enterprises. The states are created through business information systems and databases.

The majority of the metadata employed to develop the Business Information Systems Plan resides in the meta entities supporting the Enterprise's Architecture, the Resource Life Cycles, the databases and business information systems, and project management. All these meta entities are depicted within the Metabase meta model in Figure 35.

## 8.4    The Business Information Systems Plan Steps

The Business Information Systems Plan project determines the sequence for implementing specific business information systems. The goal of the strategy is to deliver the most valuable business information at the earliest time possible in the most cost-effective manner.

The end product of the Business Information Systems Plan project is the plan itself. The plan sets out the staging of the database and business information system projects such that they can be tracked and ultimately evaluated.

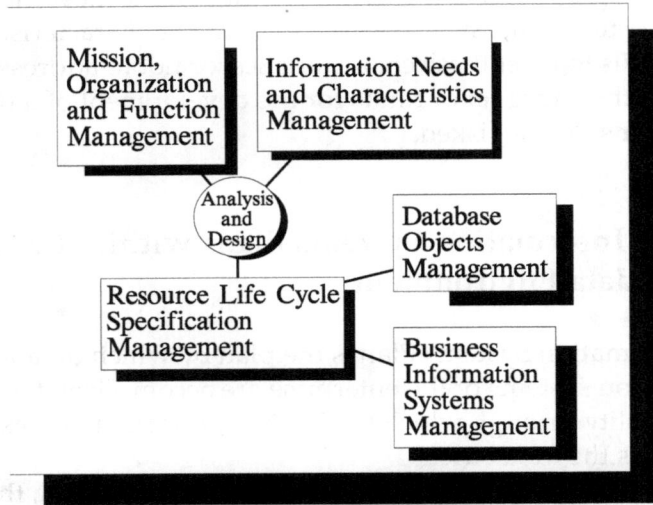

**Figure 34**. Knowledge worker framework and metadata domain.

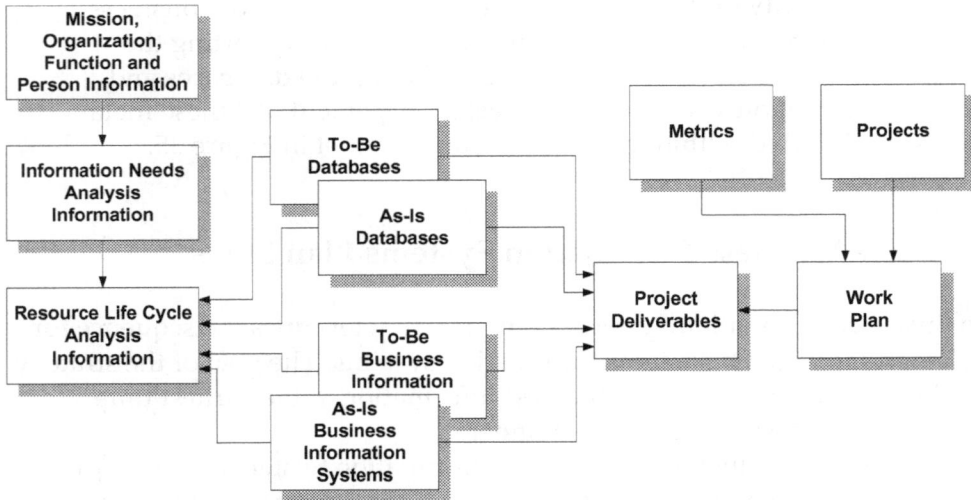

**Figure 35**. Refined view of metadata involved in information systems plan.

148

Once deployed, the business information systems department can implement the plan with confidence that they are doing the correct business information systems project at the right time and in the right sequence. The focus of the Business Information Systems Plan is not one business information system but the entire suite of business information systems for the enterprise. Once developed, each identified business information system is seen in context with all other business information systems within the enterprise.

The steps for the development of a Business Information Systems Plan are set out in Table 18. Steps 1 through 5 of this effort should have already been accomplished.

| Business Information Systems Plan Development Steps | | |
|---|---|---|
| **Step** | **Name** | **Description** |
| 1. | Create the mission model | The mission model, generally shorter than 30 pages presents end-result characterizations of the essential raison d'etre of the enterprise. Missions are strategic, long range, and apolitical because they are stripped of the "who," "how, " and "technology." |
| 2. | Develop a high-level data model | The high-level data model is an entity relationship diagram created to meet the data needs of the mission descriptions. No attributes or keys are created. |
| 3. | Create the Resource Life Cycles (RLC) and their nodes | Resources are drawn from both the mission descriptions and the high-level data model. Resources and their life cycles are the names, descriptions and life cycles of the critical assets of the enterprise, which, when exercised achieve one or more aspect of the missions. Each enterprise resource "lives" through its Resource Life Cycle. |
| 4. | Allocate precedence vectors among Resource Life Cycle nodes | Tied together into an enablement network, the resulting Resource Life Cycle network forms a framework of enterprise's assets that represent an order and set of inter-resource relationships. The enterprise "lives" through its Resource Life Cycle network. |

| Business Information Systems Plan Development Steps | | |
|---|---|---|
| **Step** | **Name** | **Description** |
| 5. | Allocate existing business information systems and databases to the Resource Life Cycle nodes | The Resource Life Cycle network presents a "lattice-work" onto which the "as is" business information systems and databases can be "attached." See for example, the meta model in Figure 35. The "to-be" databases and business information systems are similarly attached. "Difference projects" between the "as-is" and the "to-be" are then formulated. Achievement of all the difference projects is the achievement of the Business Information Systems Plan. |
| 6. | Allocate standard work break down structures to each Resource Life Cycle node | Detailed planning of the "difference projects" entails allocating the appropriate canned work breakdown structures and metrics. Employing work breakdown structure and metrics from a comprehensive methodology supports project management standardization, repeatability, and self-learning. |
| 7. | Load resources into each Work breakdown structure node | Once the resources are determined, these are loaded into the project management meta entities of the Metabase, that is, metrics, project, work plan and deliverables. The meta entities are those inferred by Figure 35. |
| 8. | Schedule the Resource Life Cycle nodes through a project management package facilities. | The entire suite of projects is then scheduled on an enterprise-wide basis. The PERT (Program Evaluation and Review Technique) chart used by project management is the PERT chart represented by the Resource Life Cycle enablement network. |
| 9. | Produce and review the Business Information Systems Plans | The scheduled result is predicable: Too long, too costly, and too ambitious. At that point, the real work starts: paring down the suite of projects to a realistic set within time and budget. Because of the metadata environment (see Figure 34), the integrated project management metadata (see Figure 35), and because all projects are configured against fundamental business-rationale based designs, the results of the inevitable trade-offs can be set against business basics. Although the process is painful, the results can be justified and rationalized. |

| Business Information Systems Plan Development Steps | | |
|---|---|---|
| **Step** | **Name** | **Description** |
| 10. | Execute and adjust the Business Information Systems Plan through time. | As the Business Information Systems Plan is set into execution, technology changes occur that affect resource loadings. Only steps 6-9 need to be repeated. As work progresses, the underlying metadata built or used in steps 1-5 will also change. Because a quality Business Information Systems Plan is "automated" the recasting of the Business Information Systems Plan should only take a week or less. |

**Table 18.** Steps for Business Information Systems Plan.

Collectively, the first nine steps take about 5,000 staff hours, or about $500,000. Compared to an information technology budget $15-35 million, that's only about 3.0% to 1.0%.

If the pundits are to be believed, that is, that the right information at the right time is the competitive edge, then paying for a Business Information Systems Plan that is accurate, repeatable, and reliable is a small price indeed.

## 8.5 Executing and Adjusting the Business Information Systems Plan Through Time

Business Information System projects are accomplished within distinct development environments. The two most common are: discrete project and release. The discrete project environment is typified by completely encapsulated projects accomplished through a water-fall methodology.

In release environments, there are a number of different projects underway by different organizations and staff of varying skill levels. Once a large number of projects are underway, the ability of the enterprise to know about and manage all the different projects degrades rapidly. That is because the project management environment has been transformed from discrete encapsulated projects into a continuous flow process of product or functionality improvements that are released on a set time schedule. Figure 36 illustrates the continuous flow process environment that supports releases.

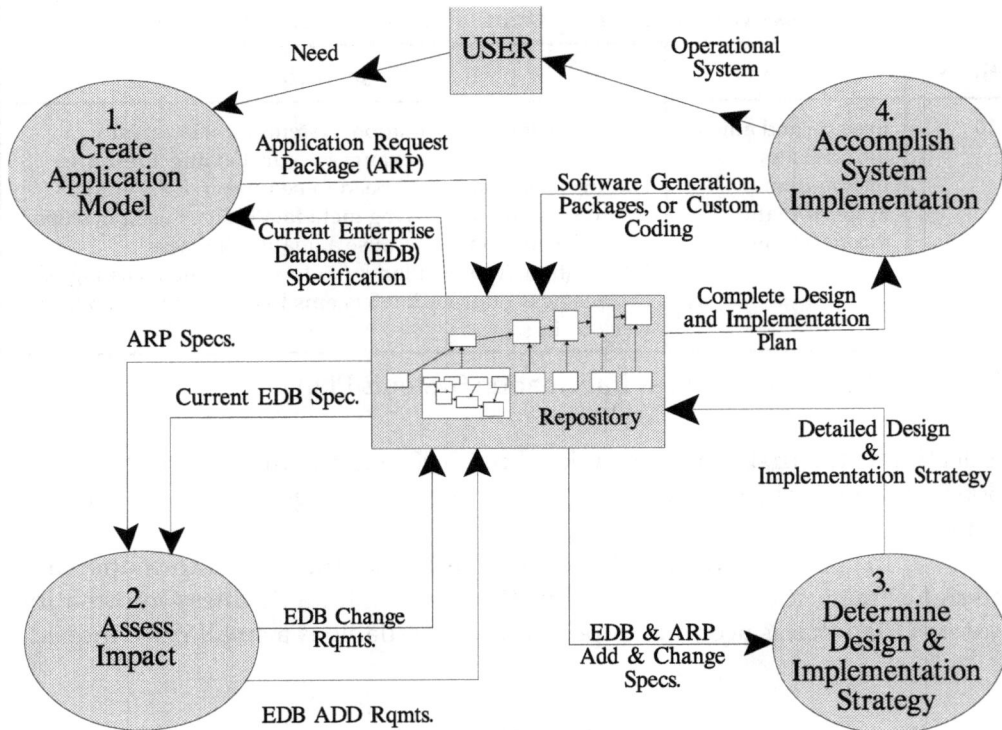

**Figure 36**. Continuous flow process.

.

The continuous flow process environment is characterized by:

- Multiple, concurrent, but differently scheduled projects against the same enterprise resource.

- Single projects that affect multiple enterprise resources.

- Projects that develop completely new capabilities, or changes to existing capabilities within enterprise resources.

It is precisely because enterprise's have transformed themselves from a project environment to a release environment that Business Information

Systems Plans that can be created, evolved, and maintained on an enterprise-wide basis are essential.

There are four major sets of activities within the continuous flow process environment. The user/client is represented at the top in the small rectangular box. Each of the ellipses represents an activity targeted to a specific need. The four basic needs are:

- Create Application Model.
- Assess Impact.
- Determine Design and Implementation Strategy.
- Accomplish System Implementation.

The box in the center is the meta data repository. This is an iconic representation of Figure 9 which are the columns of the Knowledge Worker Framework. The metadata represented are from the Enterprise's Architecture, Database Object Classes, Data Model Generalization levels, and Resource Life Cycle architectures presented in Chapters 4 through 7. In short, this is all the metadata that can be inferred from the Knowledge Worker Framework in Table 3.

Specification and impact analysis is represented through the left two processes. Implementation design and accomplishment are represented by the right two processes. Two key characteristics should be immediately apparent. First, unlike the water-fall approach, the activities do not flow one to the other. They are disjoint. In fact, they may be done by different teams, on different time schedules, and involve different quantities of products under management. In short, these four activities are independent one from the other. Their only interdependence is through the Metabase.

The second characteristic flows from the first. Because these four activities are independent one from the other, the enterprise evolves by means of releases rather than through whole systems. If it evolved through whole systems, the four activities would be connected either in a waterfall or a spiral approach, and the enterprise would be evolving through major upgrades to encapsulated functionality within specific business resources. In contrast, the release approach causes coordinated sets of changes to multiple business resources to be placed into production. This causes simultaneous, enterprise-wide capability upgrades across multiple business resources.

Through this continuous-flow process, several unique features are present:

- All four processes are concurrently executing.

- Changes to enterprise resources occur in unison, periodically, and in a very controlled manner.

- The Metabase always contains the enterprise resource specifications: current or planned. Simply put, if enterprise resource semantics are not within the Metabase, they cannot be considered part of enterprise policy.

- All changes are planned, scheduled, measured, and subject to auditing, accounting, and traceability.

- All documentation of all types is generated from the Metabase.

## 8.6    Business Information Systems Plan Summary

In summary, any technique employed to achieve a Business Information Systems Plan must be accomplishable with less than 3% of the information technology budget funds. Additionally, it must be timely, useable, maintainable, able to be iterated into a quality product, and reproducible.

Information technology organizations, once they have completed their initial set of databases and business information systems will find themselves transformed from a project to a release environment. That necessitates a transformation from either of two standard development life cycles, waterfall and/or spiral to one of continuous flow.

The continuous flow environment becomes the only viable alternative for moving the enterprise forward. It is precisely because of the release environment that enterprise-wide Business Information Systems Plans that can be created, evolved, and maintained are essential.

This 10-step strategy is described in greater detail in the Whitemarsh Business Information Systems Plan book. The strategy is supported by the Whitemarsh database project methodology, the Business Information Systems Plan course, the Whitemarsh Metabase (its Metabase), and the Whitemarsh project management software.

This chapter set out the necessary characteristics for Business Information Systems Plans to be successful, efficient and effective. These characteristics have been glaringly unfilled by other Business Information Systems Plan development methodologies. The methodology in this chapter is the next logical step from the prior architectures and employs all their work products.

Finally, the very process of configuring a final Business Information Systems Plan involves intense database and business information system project planning. This process can be largely automated through the use of sophisticated project planning software where the PERT chart is the Resource Life Cycle Node network, and the individual projects associated with the nodes are easily estimated because of a large quantity of project plan and metric templates.

If project plan and metric templates are subsequently refined over time, the ability to automatically generate new Business Information Systems Plans becomes quite easy. Further, these generated plans will be reliable, repeatable, and are malleable as new technologies unfold.

The next chapter, Chapter 9, The Role of the Metabase, shows how the Metabase is employed to store all the work products from these architectures. Metadata repositories that store just operational or technical metadata miss about 99% of their true value to the enterprise. Clearly, if we focus solely on the optimization of the past we will never be able to plan, see, and accomplish the future. It is through the exposition, optimization, and recasting of our missions, organizations, functions, database objects, databases and business information systems that the future will be unfolding in ever better forms.

## 8.7    Questions and Exercises

1.      Has there been a Business Information System Planning experience within your organization? Were the results worth the effort? If yes, why? If not, why not?

2.      What is the value from having the Business Information System Planning component metadata integrated with all the other four architectures' metadata?

3.      How can standalone Business Information System Plans be seen as anything other than more stove-pipes?

4.    How would a Business Information System Plan that has Resource Life Cycle Analysis as the network infrastructure for planning help? Would it save time and money? How much and by whom?

5.    Should there be a requirement that the Business Information System Plans bet automatically updated as new databases and business information systems are created, implemented, and maintained?

6.    Should it be a requirement that the metadata that supports Business Information System Plans be automatically updated as new databases and business information systems are created, implemented, and maintained? Should the Business Information System Plan be static or dynamic? Compare and contrast the contents and value from a static or dynamic approach.

7.    Should a database or business information system inclusion in the current Business Information System Plan be considered a pre-requisite for any information technology project approval? If yes, why? If not, why?

8.    Should the use of project management templates for deliverables, tasks, and metrics be an essential component of any Business Information System Planning effort?

9.    What process should be initiated to allow emergency database and business information system projects that lie outside a current Business Information System Plan? Once such a project is started should there be an update to the Business Information System Plan? Should the new project have an effect on existing projects?

# 9

# Role of the Metabase

Chapter 8, Business Information Systems Plan, presented the use of many of the work products from four of the architectures. This and other features makes the creation of Business Information System Plans reliable, repeatable, and fast.

Chapter 3 through 8 all described classes of work products that are the "data" of the Metabase. Metabase data represent the specifications of an enterprise's memory. If there is no highly engineered Metabase system and metadata databases, the enterprise will almost always be running blind and crash into every pillar and post that comes along. Staff and virtually all enterprise resources will be suboptimized and under performing. Policy and procedure will seemingly be ad hoc, conflicting, and chaotic. Use of the Metabase must not be exceptional in the enterprise; it must be commonplace.

A metadata database, simply put, is just a database encapsulated in a metadata oriented business information system that has as its sole purpose the capture, manipulation, and reporting of metadata. Since it's a metadata database, the term, Metabase, which Whitemarsh has been using since the early 1980s for just this purpose is appropriate. The objectives of a Metabase system are these:

- Capture requirements and design work products set out in the Knowledge Worker Framework.

- Support the extraction of design work products to feed down-stream business information system generators and schemas for database management systems.

- Capture operational metadata, sometimes also called technical metadata, that is generated as consequence of the operational aspects of databases and business information systems.

This chapter focuses on the first objective. The second object is simple to achieve through creation of the SQL data definition language representations of the Operational Data Models. Spending any part of this book on that objective would not be productive. Figure 37 illustrates such an environment.

This second objective environment is divided into UpperCASE and LowerCASE. UpperCASE focuses on Requirements Analysis and Design. LowerCASE focuses on the remaining stages of business information systems development, that is, Detailed Design, Code, Unit Test, and System Test. In this environment, the data model generalization levels are shown on the left panel of Figure 37. What is generated and sent to the right panel of the diagram are the data definition language statements that enable the creation of the databases and the SQL data definition language that create the SQL database on the server. The right panel of Figure 37 imports these statements and through the business information system generator creates the actual business information system. The right panel also shows the creation of the SQL database via the SQL scripts that are also imported from the UpperCASE side.

The third objective, capturing operational or technical metadata, is addressed by many different metadata repository environments that have been around for many years. This chapter does not address that objective either.

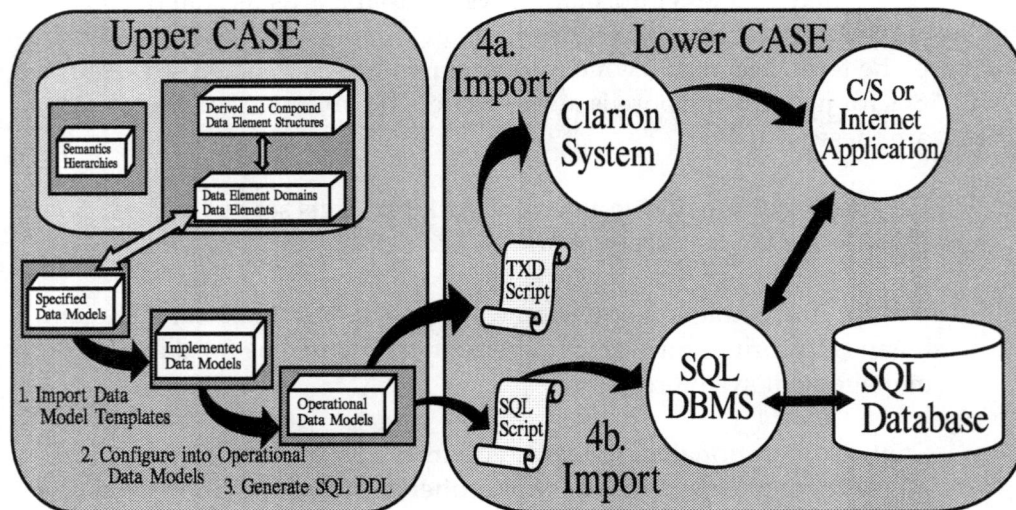

**Figure 37**. Interrelationship between Metabase and Clarion.

The reason the first objective, capturing requirements and design work products, is so important is clearly established the enumeration of the reasons for failure that are set out in the GAO analyses of the many multi-hundred million dollar information technology failures. The summary percentages are presented in Table 5. Again:

- 41% of the reasons for failure exist if there's a failure in the enterprise architecture, that is, the metadata set out in Chapter 4.

- 50% of the reasons for failure exist if organizations and functions are not reconfigured to take advantage of new databases and business information systems. This is addressed in Chapter 3 on the Knowledge Worker Framework.

- 8% of the reasons for failure exist if the Business Information Systems Plan is not engineered correctly. This is addressed in Chapter 8.

- 5% of the reasons for failure exist if the databases and business information systems are not properly configured. The metadata for these are addressed in Chapters 5, 6, and 7.

Since all these failure percents relate to the first objective, it just makes common sense to focus on the first objective. From this, the reason for focusing on the first Metabase objective should be beyond question.

This chapter, The Role of the Metabase, asserts that 100% of all metadata should be entered into a Metabase during – not after – enterprise architecture work is accomplished. This applies to all 36 cells of the Knowledge Worker Framework. As the metadata is created during analysis and design, so too should it be captured.

Metadata repositories that store just operational or technical metadata, that is, the metadata of the third objective miss a high percent of their true value of enterprise metadata. That is because if we focus solely on operations we will never be able to plan, see, and accomplish the future. It is through the exposition, optimization, and recasting of our missions, organizations, functions, database objects, databases and business information systems that the future will be unfolding in ever better forms.

## 9.1 Structural Basis for the Metabase

The structural basis for a Metabase's database design was set out in prior Chapters. Chapter 2 presented the overall requirements for architecture components, and also set out the framework for the Knowledge Worker. Chapter 3 presented the Knowledge Worker Framework row by row and column by column. Chapters 4 through 7 presented high level descriptions and diagrams of the key Metabase data model structures necessary for success. The high-level diagrams include Figures 10, 14, and 17 through 21.

In addition to the rows and column explanation of the Knowledge Worker Framework, there are relationships among cells, an overall relationship across all the columns, the interrelationships between the framework cells and a Metabase, and finally, how the "data" from within each of the cells are brought together within a Metabase and are employed through a methodology to achieve an integrated whole. As with the other topics from this book, there are extensive materials about the Metabase from the Whitemarsh website including a fully functional demo-version of the Metabase that can be downloaded and put to immediate use.

Prior to discussing inter-cell relationships, the overall business case for a Metabase is be established.

## 9.2 Business Rationale for the Metabase

*No one would ever question why a business needs its finance books. Well, the Metabase is the business's business information systems' books. If you cannot run a good business without the former, you cannot run good databases and Business Information Systems environment without the latter.*

A significant portion of the time and costs associated with resolving the Year 2000 problem was directly attributed to a lack of a quality metadata environment within business information systems organizations. The fact that one business information system organization within an enterprise had virtually no Year 2000 problem while another organization within that same enterprise was running their business information systems shop "24x7" was no accident. The former had a long history of metadata management and the later thought that metadata was a wasted overhead expense.

Vital to database and business information system success is control over semantics. The controls are mainly in the area of the definitions that form the basis of the interfaces to standard processes (e.g., computing net profit) and the standard data definitions (e.g., what does profit *mean?*).

It is not necessary, however, to control the interfaces to the *end user*. Just how a data entry screen or report looks to different people is largely immaterial so long as the enforced semantics (rules of meaning and usage) are the same.

In the development of large information technology projects dealing with enterprise-wide, indispensable business functions, the documentation of the design requirements and resulting business information system specifications is seldom accomplished such that it is timely, accurate, or complete. That is disastrous for the following three reasons:

- Only the momentous facts that are remembered are recorded.

- As systems are specified, the lower-level design details are redundantly developed, often in conflicting manners.

- As system components are maintained, the efforts are crippled because of the undocumented business knowledge that is essential to understanding the component.

Amelioration of these three important problems starts with organizations adopting formal methods for performing analysis and design. Formal methods are only measurably productive and repeatable if they are very detailed and proceduralized. Such detail, however, dehumanizes knowledge workers, who, in turn, are certain to generate protests about being production workers on an assembly line, which, by the way, is worthwhile only when all of the products are the same. In contrast, to the production line, business information system designs are unique assemblies of large sets of components, many of which are similar in design.

Designing business information systems is not an activity for the production worker; rather, it is an activity for a knowledge worker. While there is clearly procedure to both activities, designing a business information system requires individualized applications of creativity, human factors techniques, and rule making. Accordingly, requiring the robot-like use of a fully detailed methodology cannot result in responsive business information system designs. Work plans must be drawn from proven techniques against which metrics have been captured and honed over the years.

Building a business information system, once it is designed in sufficient detail, is largely a rote application of computer language coding. There are a number of quality and robust business information system generators such as Clarion, that can use the metadata for a business information system design to produce computer code that is competitive in performance to a human coded application. There is, of course, no comparison between human coding costs and business information system generator costs.

To fully respond to the three problems cited above, knowledge workers should have the freedom to create their own analysis and design work products for data and processes within strictures dealing with format, time, quality, and resources. These work products must be placed into a Metabase. This is UpperCASE work and is depicted in the left panel of Figure 37.

The Metabase, containing these products in fixed formats and sequences, can be accessed by business information system generators (both human and computerized) to build the business information system. This is LowerCASE work as shown in the right panel of Figure 37.

If the generator is quick enough, a fully functional version of the business information system design can be live-tested a short time later. As design flaws are found, the Metabase's metadata can be changed and the business information system regenerated. *In short, an interactive design process, in which the Metabase is the empowering component.*

Traditionally, it is common to expend 20 percent of a total systems development lifecycle on requirements and design. The remaining 80 percent is expended on building, testing, and documentation. Six staff months of analysis and design thus requires an additional 24 staff months for the first cycle of implementation. This is a 30-staff month total.

Once implemented, 5x more is spent over a system's life cycle for changes, fixes, and evolutions, also in a 20/80 ratio. The overall total is thus 30 staff months for the first cycle plus 150 staff months for the evolution and maintenance efforts, for a total of 180 staff months. If, with business information system generators, the 80 percent is reduced to just 20%, there must also be a profound reduction in the overall systems life cycle cost. The first cycle is reduced to 12 months, and the remaining cycles are reduced to 60 staff months. The overall reduction is from 180 to 72 staff months. That's a 60% reduction. In short, the business case for the Metabase is compelling. The

Metabase as UpperCASE, and the business information system generator as LowerCASE comprises Integrated-CASE. I-CASE, a goal of Information Technology in the late 1980s is now here.

## 9.3     Metabase Model Relationships

There is a large quantity of relationships among the various metadata models. The combined set of meta models set out in Chapters 4 through 8 for the five architectures are both interrelated and non-redundant. Table 3 is an indispensable aid in following the subsections that follow.

The main points of the subsections below serve to illustrate that the metadata across the entire Knowledge Worker Framework's architectures are interrelated. It logically follows that it must be integrated and non-redundant. Otherwise, these metadata collections are just another set of stove-pipes. This time, however, metadata stove-pipes.

A key reason why there are stove-pipe databases and business information systems is because they are founded on stove-pipes of the metadata. Because of this pari of stove-pipes any integrated and non-redundant metadata would be accidental. The approach espoused in this book provides an opportunity to eliminate metadata stove-pipes, and thus, start down the road of eliminating database and business information system stove-pipes.

The key "take away" from these sections is that while the cells of the Knowledge Worker Framework are depicted left-to-right and top-to-down that is not how the work is accomplished. Rather, the work is accomplished accordingly to a methodology that results in metadata work products that are, in turn, stored in a Metabase. Sometimes the work will be accomplished top-down, other times bottom-up, and finally, sometimes inside-out. The metadata represented by the Knowledge Worker Framework cells are retrievable such that the enterprise can be seen as a Left-to-right and Top-down Knowledge Worker Framework fashion in addition to retrieval in a "doing" fashion. This is all possible if and only if:

- There is an integrated and non-redundant Metabase.

- The Metabase is commonly accessible for all who need to accomplish Knowledge Worker Framework efforts and/or see and approve knowledge worker work products.

## 9.3.1 Knowledge Worker Framework Relationships

The Knowledge Worker Framework products are clearly related both to each other and to the tables that exist in the Metabase. Figure 38 illustrates this in a suggestive way. The cell comes from some interrelated set of frameworks wherein the cell represents a common set of work products across three frameworks shown in Figure 7. Each of the cell's products results in the metadata that is either depicted on the right side of Figure 38, or are related to

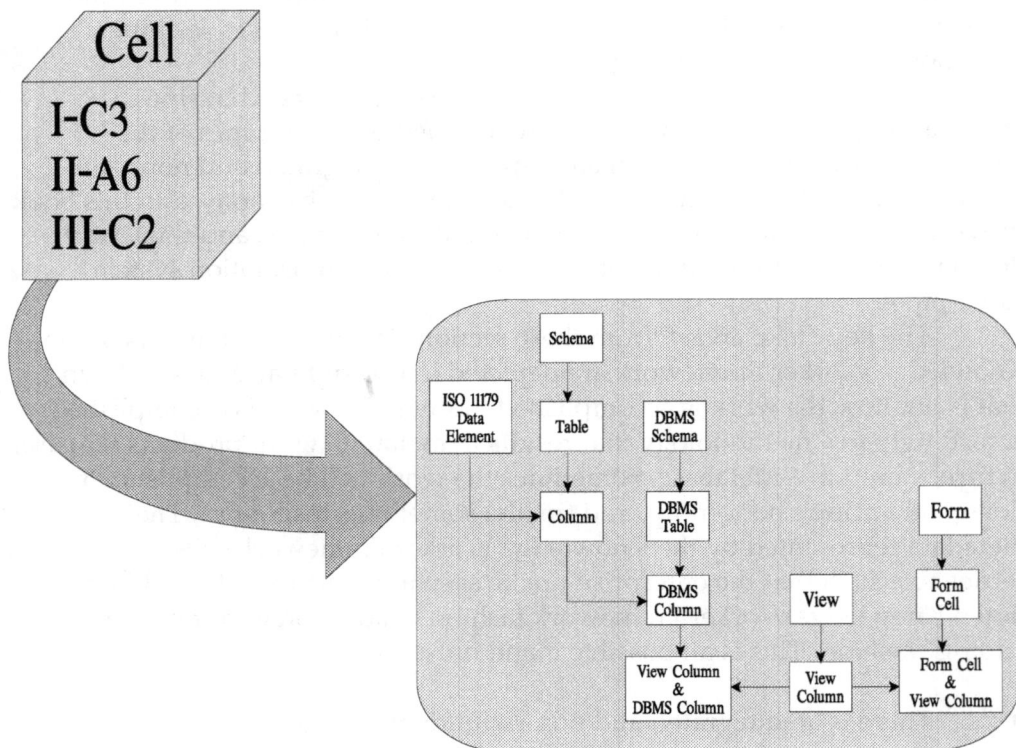

**Figure 38**. Relationship between framework cell and a metadata database.

some other metadata.

Suppose for example, the cell was the "Deployment (R-7) - Database Object Class (C-2)" intersection cell. The key product shown in Table 3 for that cell is the Operational Data Model. In Figure 38, the key meta entities from the Metabase for that cell are DBMS Schema, DBMS Table, and DBMS Column. Note: There are many other meta entities in the Operational Data Model and these are set out in the complete Metabase documentation of the Operational Data Model.

Figure 38 figure also shows the "upstream" and "downstream" relationships to other metadata. Specifically, the Operational Data Model meta entity DBMS column has an upstream "parent," Column, from the Implemented Data Model. There are also "downstream" meta entities from the View model, and from the View data model to the Form meta model, which are all shown in different cells from Table 3.

The Metabase's meta model is thus the integrating mechanism across all the products contained in the Knowledge Worker Framework and by implication, the integrating mechanism across all the architectures.

## 9.3.2 Enterprise's Architecture Relationships

The enterprise's architecture relationships are not only across all the cells from the scope and business rows, but also downward to the systems row. The main sets of relationships among the components across the enterprise's architecture model that occupies the first two rows of the Knowledge Worker Framework is illustrated in Figure 10 and defined in Table 8.

From Figure 10, Database Object Classes are in an interrelationship with the System row, and the Business Information Systems are from the Business information systems column.

An example of a hierarchical relationship is missions related to missions. This keeps all the missions within the mission's column at the scope and business rows tightly organized.

An example of inter-product relations is missions and organizations as mission-organizations. Not only is this a Knowledge Worker Framework Column 1 to Column 6 relationship, this is a many-to-many relationship that is represented as two one-to-many relationships. If the relationship between mission and organization was purely hierarchical, it would be an organization within a mission, and, if an organization was involved in multiple missions, the organization data would have to be repeated. Under the many-to-many relationship, the various organizations supporting missions, and missions supported by organization reports can be shown.

### 9.3.3  Database Object Relationships

The components in Database Object Classes are depicted in Figure 14 and defined in Table 9. Database objects proceed from database domains which are created within the Business row of the Mission column. Database object data structures are created in the Technology row by means of the tables from the Implemented Data Model, which, in turn, get their column semantics from attributes from the Specified Data Model, and their value domains from the Data Element Model.

Database Object Classes are also related to Resource Life Cycle Nodes, and to Business information systems.

### 9.3.4  Data Model Generalization Level Relationships

The components of the five data model generalization levels are presented in Figures 17 through 21, and are defined in Tables 11 through 15.

The first generalization level, ISO 11179 data elements, are identified in the Business Row - Database Objects column cell. These Data Elements, however can surface during either the forward engineering process of building Specified, Implemented, or Operational Data Models, or can surface as a consequence of reverse engineering from SQL data definition language streams to the Operational Data Model DBMS schemas, tables, and columns, and then upwards to Implemented and Specified Data Models.

Data elements from the Data Element Model are normally not compound nor derived. Data elements may be mapped to compound or derived versions of the data elements, which, in turn can be mapped to the View Data Model. This kind of relationship goes between the business row directly to the operations row rather than to just adjacent cells. To require and/or force immediate cell adjacency, as in this case, is not just sensible.

Specified Data Models are initially defined within the Business row, but may be fully defined in the System row. These work products are mainly related to data elements, value domains, and to columns within tables of the Implemented Data Model.

The Implemented Data Model interrelationships are to work products in Database Object Classes, to attributes of entities from the Specified Data Model, and to DBMS columns of DBMS tables within the Operational Data Model. Implemented Data Model columns may also be related to data elements and value domains.

The Operational Data Model relationships are to work products in the View Data Model and to work products in the Implemented Data Model.

Finally, the view model may be related to the Data Element Model, the Business Information System model, and the Operational Data Model.

### 9.3.5 Resource Life Cycle Analysis Relationships

The components of Resource Life Cycle Analysis are depicted in Figure 33 and Table 16. Components from the Resource Life Cycle Analysis model are related to Database Object Classes, Business Information Systems, and Missions. Resource Life Cycle Analysis components are also related to the identified and defined information needs, which are in turn related to the functions performed by organizations accomplishing missions.

### 9.3.6 Generated Metadata Relationships

It is not enough to just have all the metadata for one class of database and business information system interrelated with different sets of missions, organizations, functions, and the like. That is just horizontal and vertical integration. There must also be depth integration as well. That means that there has to be integration across missions, across functions, and the like.

Figure 36 illustrates this. In this environment, Figure 36 shows business functions, business information systems, database objects, and resource life cycles. All these relate to the Courts. It is just not sufficient to have each of these architectures defined. They must be integrated and non-redundant. If the enterprise operates best when it's integrated and non-redundant, so also must the metadata models of the enterprise operate best when they are integrated and non-redundant. It is pure accident to have integrated and non-redundant databases and business information system given metadata stove-pipes.

Figure 40 illustrates the illusion of integration and non-redundancy. In this case, the metadata repository that was engineered did not really have integration. This diagram is shown in three parts. The top part is a set of icons that relate to the major phases of a business information system development. In this case there are three different projects.

The middle part of Figure 40 shows the metadata repository as merely collections of deliverables. The bottom part shows the deliverables for each of the three projects. Note, that these are separate, unintegrated, and very likely redundant.

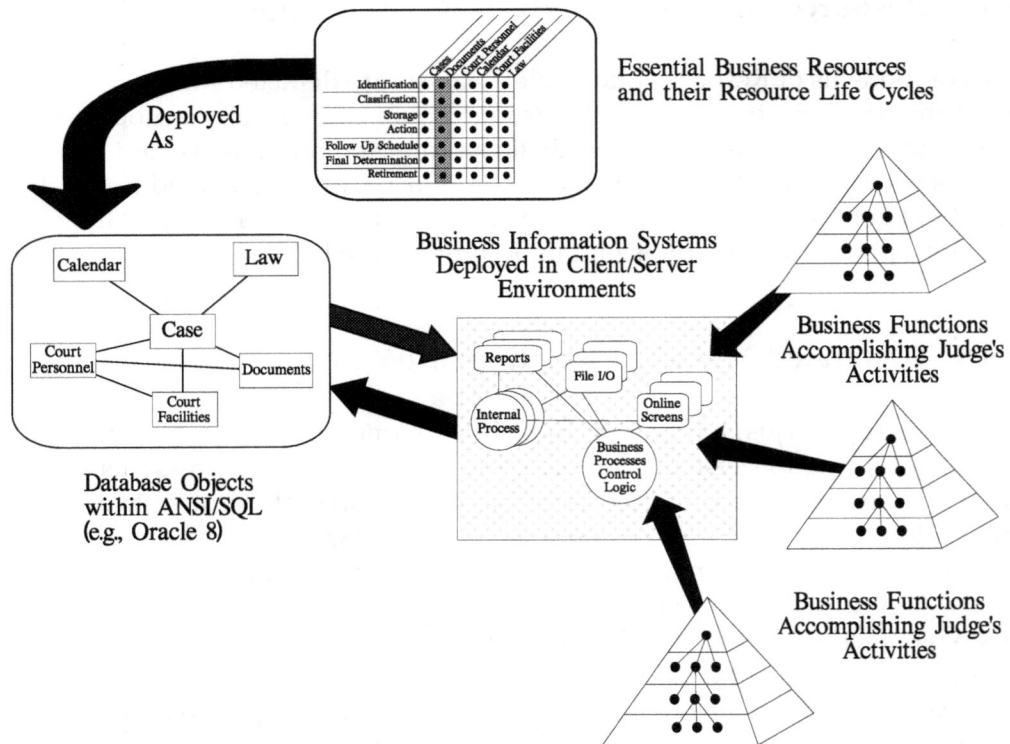

**Figure 39**. Metadata integration across multiple enterprise architecture models.

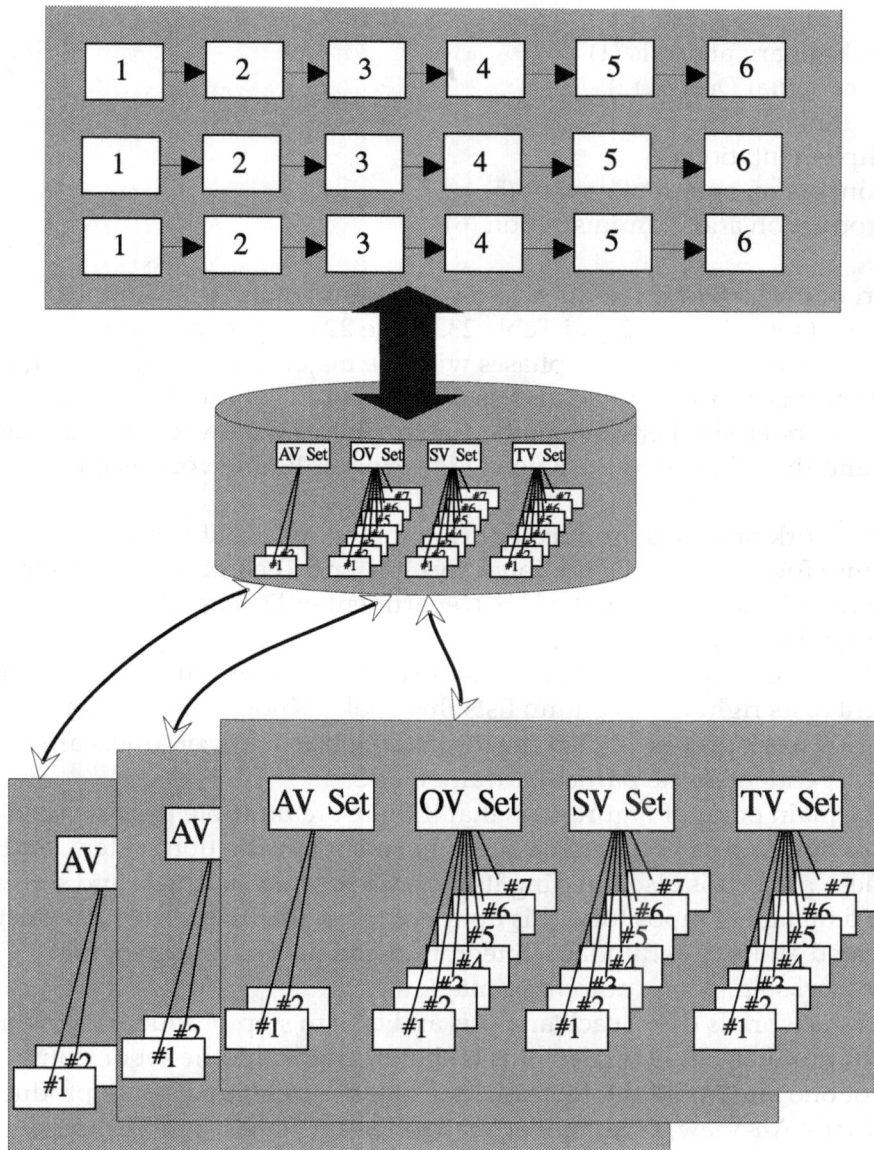

**Figure 40**. Illusion of metadata integration and non redundancy.

The phases are:

- Preliminary analysis (1)
- Conceptual Design (2)
- Binding (3)
- Implementation (4)
- Conversion and deployment (5)
- Production and Administration (6)

In support of the goal of integration and non-redundancy, Attachment 4 contains two tables, Table 22 and Table 23. Table 22 is a general cross reference between methodology phases with the major work products as the rows and the enterprise architectures as the compared columns. Table 23 shows a cross reference between methodology phases with work products as the rows and the columns of the Knowledge Worker Framework as the columns.

The work products produced during this six-phase life cycle are grouped into four sets: All, Operational, System, and Technical. These four work product classes are from the U.S. Department of Defense Architecture Framework (DoDAF).

Attachment 3 provides a table that lists the work products by class. In Attachment 3, its right most column lists this book's Knowledge Worker Framework's work products. That means that the true work products are largely independent of the particular framework.

The main point of Figure 40 is that if there are multiple projects such that each is building its own database and business information system, and each of these projects is also building its own set of work products and stores them into a metadata repository, this does not mean that these work products are integrated and non-redundant. Integration and non-redundancy is a necessary workstep, not an automatic magic step.

As the work is done, each analysis and design step produces its own set of work products. In Figure 40, this is shown by the middle set of icons. There's not one integrated set. Instead, there are the individual work product sets within the All-View, Operational Views, System Views, and Technical View classes. Each deliverable is its own document that is likely a combination of graphics, text, and tables. While this is a deliverable, it's certainly not a "report" from a Metabase.

Each of the work products, as shown in Figure 40 are stored in the metadata repository. Each is stored separately, and the whole collection from one project is stored separately from the collection of another project. The repository in this case just becomes a metadata work products' warehouse. Or, as some have said, a metadata landfill.

From Figure 40, it should be clear in this situation that if three different teams use the same methodology and the same metadata repository, there will be no integration and non-redundancy because the teams, their management, and the metadata repository did not enable it, demand it, and enforce it. First, of course, the metadata repository must enable integration and non-redundancy.

Thereafter, a simple way to demand and enforce integration and non-redundancy is to place such a clause in Statements of Work or contracts, and to withhold monies until it is achieved. As the old saying goes, "When you grab them by their wallet, their hearts and minds soon follows."

From Figure 40, it is clear that the integration and non-redundancy steps were not taken because there are three sets of work products. So, where's the metadata integration and non-redundancy? Nowhere.

In contrast to Figure 40, there's Figure 41. This diagram shows in contrast that there is only one set of work products. How did this happen? Was there some sort of magic? No, of course not. What is different is that integration and non-redundancy was declared to be an essential success factor right from the start. Thus, all the work products had to be built in an integrated manner, not as separate independent deliverables. The difference is in the middle part of the figure. The middle part is an "icon" version of Figure 9. Figure 9, in turn, is a generalized version of Figures 10, 14, and 17 through 21.      There's a Metabase, not just a metadata repository. All the deliverables are parts within one integrated whole just as is described in the Sections above.

Finally, in the bottom of Figure 41, there is just one set of deliverables. While the icons look the same as those in Figure 40, there are two differences. The first is that there is just one set for all three projects, not one set for each project as is shown in Figure 40.

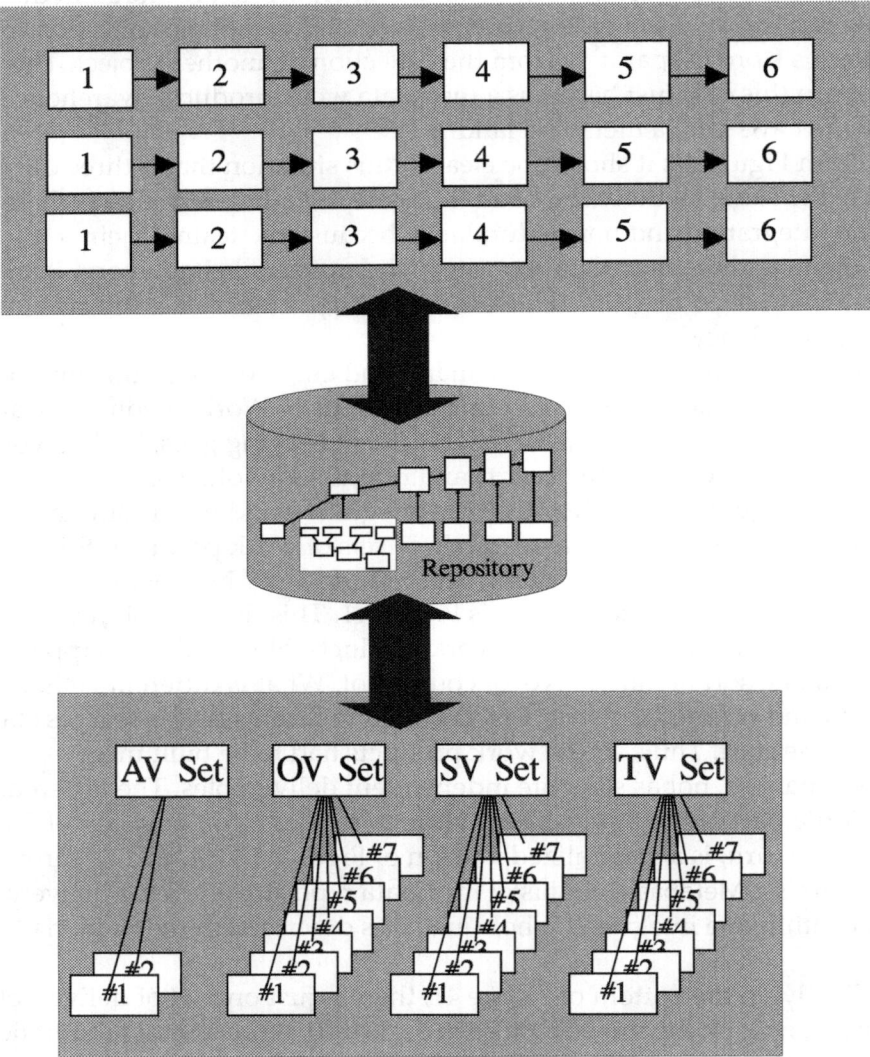

**Figure 41**. Three separate projects with one integrated set of metadata.

The second, and the more important difference is that because of the Metabase, these deliverables are "reports" from the Metabase. They are reports from the one integrated and non-redundant collection of metadata work products. If a data element is employed in a dozen entities that are, in turn, employed as semantics in 50 different database tables across the three different projects, then the data element is defined only once. Further, the dozen entities are defined only once. Each is used many times. In this case, the Data Element is reused from 150 to 1800 times. Now, that's integration and non-redundancy.

When this approach, that is, integration and non-redundancy is chosen, then Figure 26, Functional Distribution of Data Architecture Efforts, becomes dominant. Instead of having large multi-faceted teams that can and do everything, no matter how redundantly and how unintegrated, the enterprise can now make use of the Data Element engineering specialists, the functional data model specialists, the database designers, and the business information system builders. Teams are able to be crafted into a matrix-management fashion that employs just the right skills at just the right time. What truly makes this possible are three things: Metabase, methodology, and metrics. Collectively, these three things comprise a standardized, knowledge worker interoperable infrastructure.

Figure 42 shows the relative quantities of the metadata that is produced from a Figure 41 approach rather than from a Figure 40 approach. If the approach were Figure 40, the quantity of data elements would continue to grow as would the Specified, Implemented, Operational, and View Data Models. But under the Figure 41 approach, it is the very process of integration and non-redundancy that ultimately stops the growth of data elements.

Specified Data Model growth also slows and might even stop growing as well. The quantity of databases whether for implemented or operational will continue to grow, but they will only contain the already-known semantics from the specified and Data Element Models. So, while they are new in form, they will all have the same "semantic look and feel."

There are additional benefits from a Figure 41 approach. Phase 1 (Preliminary analysis) and Phase 2 (Conceptual Specification) can be accomplished with a larger scope than just one database or business information system project. Whole collections of projects can be accomplished because there is integrated and non-redundant metadata that supports all the projects. Similarly, the three Phase 6s (Production and Administration) can also be brought together and accomplished across a collection of installed and

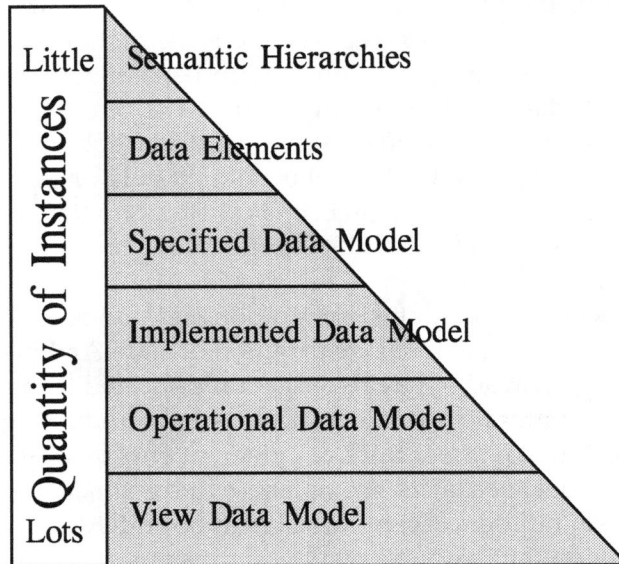

**Figure 42**. Relative quantities of metadata
across data model generalization levels.

operating databases and business information systems. If this strategy is set
into motion, Figure 41 is then transformed into Figure 43. The key difference
is to the tope part of Figure 43.

If this transformation occurs, the entire strategy for accomplishing
business information systems can change from a water fall approach that is
manifest in the six phases from Figures 40, 41, and 42 to one that looks like
Figure 33, Continuous Flow. This is especially true after a large collection of
projects have been implemented and the enterprise has transformed from one
of original development to continuous and incremental maintenance.

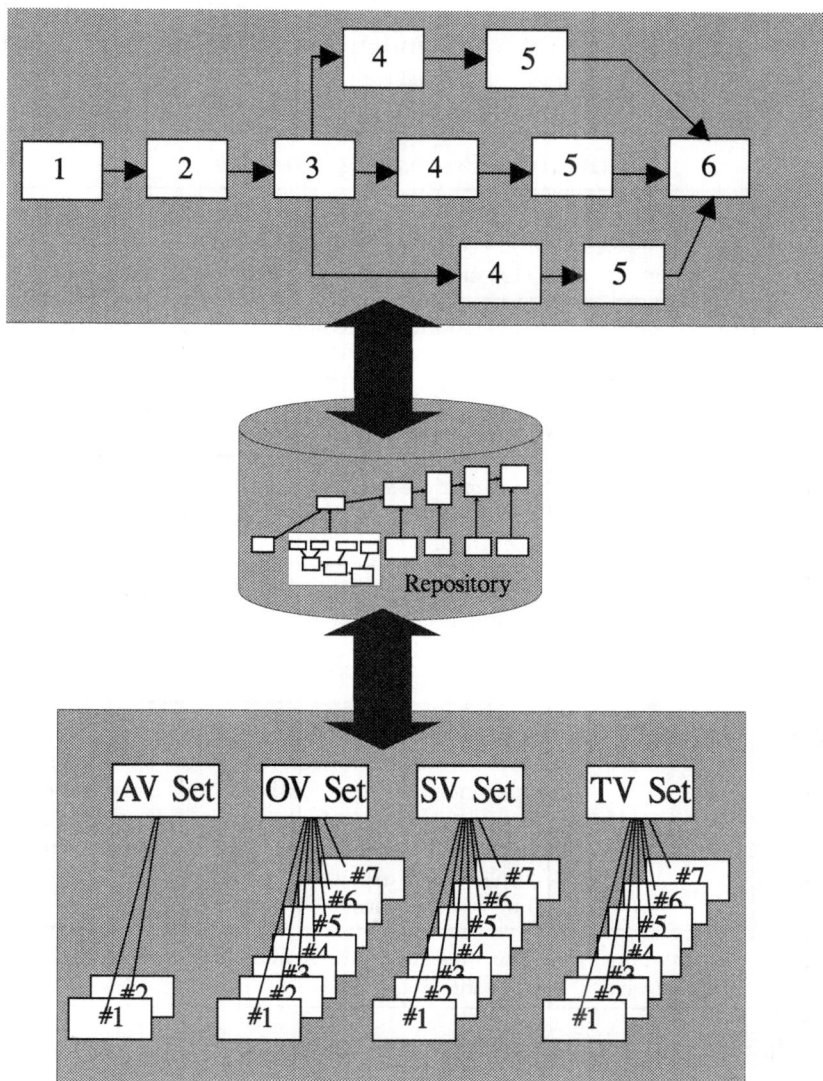

**Figure 43**. Integrated methodology phases because of a metabase.

## 9.4 Metabase Component Modules

The Metabase concept, implemented as a database application, naturally includes the architecture-based major and minor processing modules similar to those presented in Table 19.

| Metabase Processing Modules | | |
|---|---|---|
| **Major** | **Minor** | **Description** |
| Enterprise Architecture | Missions | This module stores and interrelates missions. |
| | Organizations | This module stores and interrelates organizations and relates them to various missions. |
| | Functions | This module stores and interrelates all functions and relates them to the various mission-organization pairs. |
| | Database Domains | This module stores and interrelates the database domains that are discovered with respect to the leaves of mission hierarchies. |
| | Position | This module defines and describes all positions, and if available stores persons and assigns them to positions. This module also assigns positions to mission-organization-function triples. |
| Information Needs Analysis | Information Needs | This module stores the descriptions of all the information needs determined necessary by the enterprise to support the functional needs of the various organizations that accomplish enterprise missions. This module also assigns information needs to the mission-organization-function triple. It also assigns information needs to the Resource Life Cycle Nodes. |
| | Information Characteristics | This module captures all the key characteristics about each information need. |

| Metabase Processing Modules | | |
|---|---|---|
| **Major** | **Minor** | **Description** |
| Database Objects Class | Database Object Class | This module identifies the Database Object Classes that result from the analysis of the database domains. If there are property classes as well, these typically become candidate database object tables. |
| | Database Object Table | This module associates Implemented Data Model tables as Database Object Tables. Most commonly a table resides in only one database object unless it's a factored table for reference data, or is an inter-database-object association table. |
| | Database Object Table Process | This module creates and associates the set of processes for each Database Object Table that governs quality inserts, modifies, and deletes ultimately executed by all business information systems. This guarantees uniform add, update, and delete behavior across an entire database regardless of the business information system or language agent. |
| | Database Object State | This module creates the names and specifications of the states that a database object proceeds through from the first valuation to deletion. This module also identifies the database object information systems that perform the database object transformation. Finally this module enumerates the conditions under which rows of database object tables participate in a certain state of the database object. |
| | Database Object Information System | This module creates and associates the set of processes for transforming a database object's collection of table rows from one state to another so as to achieve the required state. |

| Metabase Processing Modules | | |
|---|---|---|
| **Major** | **Minor** | **Description** |
| Data Models | Data Elements | This module creates the required metadata for an ISO 11179 data element. This includes concepts, conceptual value domains, value domains, value domain values, and mapping among the values. It includes creating data element concepts and finally data elements. It contains associated value domains and the semantic and data use modifiers for both data element concepts and data elements. Finally, this module supports the creation of compound and derived data elements and associates them with their atomic data element sources. |
| | Specified Data Model | This module creates the data models of the concepts necessary for the various databases that exist across the enterprise. Each Specified Data Model consists of subjects, entities, entity subtypes, attributes, primary, candidate, and foreign keys. It contains associated value domains and the semantic and data use modifiers. This module supports re-engineering of all its contained components, including the creation of data elements from attributes. Finally this module supports the importing and exporting of SQL DDL to create a Specified Data Model. |
| | Implemented Data Model | This module creates the data models of databases that are independent of any particular DBMS. Included in each Implemented Data Model is a schema, tables and subtypes, columns and nested column structures, primary, candidate, and foreign keys, It contains associated value domains and the semantic and data use modifiers. This module supports re-engineering of all its contained components, including the creation of data elements from columns, the importing of Specified Data Models to create Implemented Data Models, and the promotion of Implemented Data Models to create Specified Data Models. |

| Metabase Processing Modules | | |
|---|---|---|
| **Major** | **Minor** | **Description** |
| | Operational Data Model | This module creates the data models of operational databases. Included in each Implemented Data Model is a DBMS schema, DBMS tables and subtypes, DBMS columns and nested column structures, primary, candidate, and foreign keys, It contains associated value domains. This module supports re-engineering of all its contained components, including the importing of Implemented Data Models to create Operational Data Models, and the promotion of Operational Data Models to create Implemented Data Models. |
| | View Data Model | This module creates a View Data Model including its view columns, and the relationship between view columns from different views including transformation processes. This module supports mapping view columns to derived and compound data elements. Finally, the module supports the building of views from selections of DBMS tables. |
| Resource Life Cycle Analysis | Resources | This module creates and describes the resources that are essential for the enterprise. This module associates the resources with various missions. |
| | Resource Life Cycles | This module creates the resource life cycles for the resources. This module associates resource life cycle nodes with Database Object Classes and business information systems. |
| | Resource Life Cycle Structures | This module creates the interrelationships between resource life cycle nodes from different resource life cycles. |
| Business information systems | Business Information Systems | This module creates business information systems and their nested business information systems as appropriate. |
| | Business Events | This module creates business events, that is, the triggering event between a business function and a business information system. This module sets business events within business cycles and business events. |

| Metabase Processing Modules | | |
|---|---|---|
| **Major** | **Minor** | **Description** |
| | Business Cycles | This module defines the various business cycles and sets the business events within those cycles. An example is monthly closing, or quarterly reporting. There can be seasonal cycles such as Spring, Summer, Easter, Halloween, and the like. |
| | Calendar Cycles | This module defines the various calendar cycles and sets the business events within those cycles. |

**Table 19.** Metabase processing modules.


## 9.5 Functional Requirements for a Metabase System

The Metabase system is a database centered software system. Given the nature of this system, the following are the key functional requirements that must be satisfied at the very minimum:

- The Metabase system must support minimum redundancy and maximum reuse of all the components that comprise the managed interoperable data environment infrastructures.

- The Metabase system must be engineered to support the identification of common business facts, concepts, processes, business rules, value domains, and data structures across the providing or consuming business information systems.

- The Metabase system must support the identification, management and integration of common business facts including their meanings, value domains, and other supporting semantics across all uses of these facts.

- The Metabase system must be engineered to manage value domains employed exclusively within single business facts or across multiple business facts, and must manage the evolution value domains including value domain transformation mappings.

- The Metabase system must be engineered to identify, manage, and deploy standard data structures of standard business facts.

- The Metabase system must be engineered to support the discovery of redundant and/or conflicting business information systems that generate or process interoperable data.

- The Metabase system must be engineered to support the identification, exposition, and interrelationship of data generation and/or use within the operational schedules of business information systems included within the interoperable data environment infrastructures.

- The Metabase system must be engineered to identify, manage, and integrate authoritative sources of data for standard data structures.

- The Metabase system must be engineered to map standard data structures, business facts, and value domains across variant definitions and deployments of those data structures, business facts and value domains.

- The Metabase system must be engineered to support the importing and exporting of SQL schemas for databases.

- The Metabase system must be employable by database and business information system developers within the existing work efforts of quality-engineered database projects.

- The Metabase system must be employable as an integrating mechanism within communities of interest, and by the enterprise to identify conflicts across communities of interest, and by the enterprise as appropriate.

- The Metabase system must support the identification and management of projects that are creating and/or evolving aspects of the data environment infrastructure.

- The metadata must be contained within an SQL database of explicit tables that map directly to the tables so that the metadata can be accessed, explored, and reported through data mining, report writers, and Internet publishing tools.

- The metadata must support access through a variety programming languages which, in turn, can be employed to create embedded metadata processing rules that control and/or govern the fundamental processes of the Metabase System.

- The metadata environment must not result in proprietary data formats, and when the metadata is exported, it must be in a SQL "values" format on a table by table basis such that the content and meaning of the exported tables and values are clear, obvious, and unambiguous.

Beyond these core functions, the following additional functionality is also required:

- **Administrative Information.** Enables the association of organization, necessary creation and modification dates, and if appropriate, authorized person with Metabase work product trees.

- **Authoritative Data Sources.** Enables the identification of the source for a particular class of information such as reference tables.

- **Automatic Definition Creator.** These are for data elements, attributes, columns, DBMS columns and view columns so that no intellectual effort need be expended beyond the definitions associated with the constituent parts of these Metabase work products.

- **Automatic Name Abbreviator.** This is necessary for DBMS columns and view columns based on a name length parameter for those DBMSs that have a restricted name length.

- **Business Rules** (a.k.a. data integrity rules). Enables the central definition and allocation of data integrity rules to each other and to appropriate Metabase work products.

- **Business Terms**. Enables the definition and allocation of business terms to each other and to appropriate Metabase work products.

- **Configuration Management**. Enables the isolation of development from test, and test from production. There will be multiple production model instances and one development and test instance.

- **Metadata Management System Project Management**. Complete integration of project management and project deliverables, tasks, and earned value reporting.

- **Internet Presentation Layer.** Provides access to the Metabase system database through the Internet for reporting purposes.

- **Reference Data.** Forms the basis for establishing, tracking changes to, and cross referencing all restricted value domains including the organizations that establish and maintain them.

- **Transactions.** Enables the formalization of standard transactions that are to form the basis of data interoperability.

Broadly, the functions of the Metabase system enable its users to accomplish the processes set out in Table 19.


## 9.6 Metabase, The Architecture Integrator

Table 20 lists the work products by Enterprise Architecture. The objective of this table is to show that work products created in one architecture are employed in another. The cross reference cells contain letter codes. C is for create, E for employ, and R for refine.

From this table, many of the work product components (first column) are used within multiple architectures. The table shows that the components are created in only one architecture but may be refined, employed, and in the case of the Data Architectures, which includes five distinct types of data models, the components may both be employed and refined.

This type of cross reference shows that the five architectures are interlinked across the work product components. Thus, if these components are build in isolation then there would be metadata stove-pipes, which, of course is a condition to be avoided.

## Methodology Phases and Work Products vs Enterprise Architectures

1. Enterprise's Architecture
2. Database Objects Architecture
3. Data Architecture
4. Resource Life Cycle Analysis Architecture
5. Business Information Systems Plan Architecture

The cross reference cells contain letter codes. C is for create, E for employ, and R for refine.

| Component | Description | Enterprise Architectures | | | | |
|---|---|---|---|---|---|---|
| | | 1 | 2 | 3 | 4 | 5 |
| Attribute | An attribute is intended to be a data-value based partial descriptor of an entity. There are three classes of attributes. Those that represent the entity's content, for example, if the entity is address then the content attributes would be Street-1, Street-2, City, State, and Zip. There are attributes related to the instance of the entity. For example, the set of attributes which have a combined value such that only one row from the entity is found. This is commonly called the entity's primary key. The third set of attributes represent infrastructure needs such as who created or updated an entity's instance; what project caused the entity's instance to be added or changed; and finally, what was the date of the creation or change of the entity's instance.<br><br>Note: Specified Data Models are never database models and thus, there can never be "instances" of data. This third set of attributes is therefore just for completeness of the entity's definition. | C | | E R | | |
| Attribute Assigned Value Domain | An assigned value domain is a value-based constraint on the attribute. The assigned value domain cannot be the same as that assigned the data element. Nor can a value domain be more expansive than that assigned the data element. | | | C E | | |
| Attribute Assigned Meta Category Values | An assigned meta category value, whether a semantic or data use modifier is a "meaning" constraint on the attribute. The assigned meta category value cannot be the same as that assigned the data element. Nor can a meta category value be more expansive than that assigned the data element. | | | C E | | |
| Business Calendar | A Business Calendar Cycle is a set of recurring calendar-based dates that are of interest to the enterprise. For example, quarterly, bi-weekly, monthly, daily, and the like. Business Calender cycles are linked to Business Events so that the timing of business event triggering can be known. | C | | | | E R |

# Methodology Phases and Work Products vs Enterprise Architectures

1. Enterprise's Architecture
2. Database Objects Architecture
3. Data Architecture
4. Resource Life Cycle Analysis Architecture
5. Business Information Systems Plan Architecture

The cross reference cells contain letter codes. C is for create, E for employ, and R for refine.

| Component | Description | Enterprise Architectures | | | | |
|---|---|---|---|---|---|---|
| | | 1 | 2 | 3 | 4 | 5 |
| Business Cycle | A Business Cycle is a cycle during which business events occur such as financial reports, holidays, business planning and the like. A business cycle may be simple or complex. If complex, the business cycle actually consists of other business cycles as represented in the business cycle structure. | C | | | | E R |
| Business Events | A business event is an intersection between a business information system and a business function. A business event is a triggering event. It is invoked by the business function, and the business information systems execute in response. Business events may be set within business event cycles and calendar cycles, or both. | C | | | | E R |
| Business Functions | A business function is a set of hierarchically organization text that describes the activities performed by a position within an organization. Business functions are entirely human-based and if support is needed from a business information system then a business event is triggered. Business functions are independent of organizations and may be allocated to more than one business organization. | C | | | | E R |
| Business information system Assignment | The Business information system Assignment is an association between the business information system with one or more Resource Life Cycle nodes. | | | | C | E |
| Business Information Systems | A Business information system is a computer-based business information system that is being managed through the Metabase. It is known by its characteristics, its operation cycles (business and calendar), subordinate business information systems, employed databases, views, and associated Resource Life Cycle nodes. | C | | | E | E R |

## Methodology Phases and Work Products vs Enterprise Architectures

1. Enterprise's Architecture
2. Database Objects Architecture
3. Data Architecture
4. Resource Life Cycle Analysis Architecture
5. Business Information Systems Plan Architecture

The cross reference cells contain letter codes. C is for create, E for employ, and R for refine.

| Component | Description | Enterprise Architectures | | | | |
|-----------|-------------|:-:|:-:|:-:|:-:|:-:|
| | | 1 | 2 | 3 | 4 | 5 |
| Business Organizations | An Organization is a unit within an enterprise. It is hierarchical so any quantity of organizational levels can be represented. | C | | | | C |
| Column | A column, like an attribute of an entity, is intended to be a data-value based partial descriptor of a table. Columns can be complex, and thus represent arrays, groups, repeating groups, and nested repeating groups. Like attributes there are also three classes of columns. Those that represent the table's content. For example, if the table is CustomerAddress then the content attributes would be CustomerStreet-1, CustomerStreet-2, CustomerCity, CustomerState, and CustomerZip.<br><br>There are columns also related to the instance of the table. For example the set of columns which have a combined value such that only one row from the table is found. This is commonly called the table's primary key. The third set of columns represent infrastructure needs such as who did the table's creation or update; what project caused the table to be added or changed; and finally, what was the date of the add or change.<br><br>Note: Implemented Data Models are never database models and thus, there can never be "instances" of data. This third set of columns is therefore just for completeness of the table's definition. | | E | C | | |
| Column Assigned Meta Category Values | An assigned meta category value, whether a semantic or data use modifier is a "meaning" constraint on the column. The assigned meta category value cannot be the same as that assigned the data element or an attribute. Nor can a meta category value be more expansive than that assigned the data element or the column. | | | C | | |

# Methodology Phases and Work Products vs Enterprise Architectures

1. Enterprise's Architecture
2. Database Objects Architecture
3. Data Architecture
4. Resource Life Cycle Analysis Architecture
5. Business Information Systems Plan Architecture

The cross reference cells contain letter codes. C is for create, E for employ, and R for refine.

| Component | Description | Enterprise Architectures | | | | |
|---|---|---|---|---|---|---|
| | | 1 | 2 | 3 | 4 | 5 |
| Column Assigned Value Domain | An assigned value domain is a value-based constraint on the column. The assigned value domain cannot be the same as that assigned the data element or the attribute. Nor can a value domain be more expansive than that assigned the data element or column. | | | C | | |
| Concepts | Concepts are identified, described, and interrelated. Concepts are the root-semantic source for all data elements. These concepts may be similar to the concepts named in the subjects of the Specified Data Models, but that is merely a coincidence. Concepts may be complex in their relationships with other concepts forming either, hierarchies, networks, or both. An example might be resources, of which an example might be a materiel resource such as equipment, or supplies. There also then might be a non-material resource such as intellectual property or intelligence. | | | C E | | |
| Conceptual Value Domains | Conceptual value domains are identified, described, and interrelated. Conceptual value domains are the concepts behind value domains from which both data element concepts and value domains are derived. An example of a concept behind a value domain might be numbers, and within that, integers, floating point. Another might be descriptions, text and codes. Conceptual value domains can be either simple, or complex. If complex, they can be networks or hierarchies. | | | C E | | |
| Data Element Classifications | Data element classifications (not shown on Figure 16) are a way to assign data elements to certain classification schemes. A data element may be assigned to more than one classification scheme. | | | C E | | |

## Methodology Phases and Work Products vs Enterprise Architectures

**1. Enterprise's Architecture**
**2. Database Objects Architecture**
**3. Data Architecture**
**4. Resource Life Cycle Analysis Architecture**
**5. Business Information Systems Plan Architecture**

The cross reference cells contain letter codes. C is for create, E for employ, and R for refine.

| Component | Description | Enterprise Architectures | | | | |
|---|---|---|---|---|---|---|
| | | **1** | **2** | **3** | **4** | **5** |
| Data Element Concepts | Data element concepts are identified, described, and interrelated. Data element concepts are the conceptual forms of data elements. A data element concept is the association of a concept with a conceptual value domain.<br><br>A Data Element Concept is the joining of a Concept and a Conceptual Value Domain that, in turn, is a generalized representation of a collection of data elements. An example of a Data Element Concepts is real property characteristics. The Data Element Concept contained Data Elements that would result would be a real property name, description, dimensions, valuations, and the like. Data Element Concepts can be either simple, or complex. If complex, they can be networks or hierarchies.<br><br>Data element concepts are able to be assigned semantic and data use modifiers to specialize their general nature. Together, these enable automatic data naming, definitions, and abbreviations. | | | C E | | |
| Data Elements | Data elements are defined within the context of their data element concepts and their assigned value domain. Data elements are the semantic-laden business facts that are used to create either attributes of entities from subjects within Specified Data Models or columns of tables from schemas within Implemented Data Models.<br><br>Data elements are able to be assigned semantic and data use modifiers to specialize their general nature. Together, these enable automatic data naming, definitions, and abbreviations. All semantic, data use, and value domains that are assigned to a data element must be a subset of any previously assigned to a data element concept. | C | | E R | | |

## Methodology Phases and Work Products vs Enterprise Architectures

1. **Enterprise's Architecture**
2. **Database Objects Architecture**
3. **Data Architecture**
4. **Resource Life Cycle Analysis Architecture**
5. **Business Information Systems Plan Architecture**

The cross reference cells contain letter codes. C is for create, E for employ, and R for refine.

| Component | Description | Enterprise Architectures | | | | |
|---|---|---|---|---|---|---|
| | | 1 | 2 | 3 | 4 | 5 |
| Database Domains | A database domain is a hierarchically organized set of noun-intensive descriptions associated with a mission leaf. Analyzed database domains lead to the identification of Database Object Classes, enterprise data elements, and property classes. Property classes, in turn, often become tables in databases. | C | E | E R | | |
| Database Object Classes | A Database Object Class is a large collection of data and processes that are tied together for business-based reasons, and when instantiated, proceeds through well defined states. A database object can exist in two forms: a collection of interrelated database tables, or the set of a column-based nested structures within a table. The rows that comprise an object are transformed from one valid state to another via database object table processes and database object information systems. Database objects are related to one or more database domains. | C | R | E | E | |
| Database Object Information Systems | A Database Object Information System is a collection of processes defined within the domain of the DBMS usually as a stored procedure that transforms one or more rows of a database object from one valid state to another. A database object information system accomplishes one or more database object table processes. | | C | | E | |
| Database Object Information System | A Database Object Information System is a collection of processes defined within the domain of the DBMS usually as a stored procedure that transforms one or more rows of a database object from one valid state to another. A database object information system accomplishes one or more database object table processes. | | C | | E | |
| Database Object Assignment | A Database Object Assignment is an association between a Resource Life Cycle node and a database object. A database object may be assigned to one or more Resource Life Cycle nodes and a Resource Life Cycle node may be related to one or more database objects. | | | | C | E |

## Methodology Phases and Work Products vs Enterprise Architectures

1. Enterprise's Architecture
2. Database Objects Architecture
3. Data Architecture
4. Resource Life Cycle Analysis Architecture
5. Business Information Systems Plan Architecture

The cross reference cells contain letter codes. C is for create, E for employ, and R for refine.

| Component | Description | Enterprise Architectures | | | | |
|---|---|---|---|---|---|---|
| | | 1 | 2 | 3 | 4 | 5 |
| Database Object Class | A Database Object Class is a large collection of data and processes that are tied together for business-based reasons, and when instantiated, proceeds through well defined states. A database object can exist in two forms: a collection of interrelated database tables, or the set of a column-based nested structures within a table. The rows that comprise an object are transformed from one valid state to another via database object table processes and database object information systems. Database objects are related to one or more database domains. | C | R | E | E | |
| Database Object Class State | A Database Object State is a well-defined value state of a database object. States occur in a particular sequence, typically from the null state through a set of value states and returning to a null state. A database object state is accomplished through one or more database object information systems. | | C | | | |
| Database Object Class table process | A Database Object Table Process is a process such as insert, change, or delete that executes against one row of a single table within a database object. A table owns (and is thus acted upon by) one or more database object table processes. A database object table process may be invoked by one or more database object information systems. | | C | | | |
| DBMS Column Assigned Meta Category Values | There are no assigned meta category values because at this data model generalization level there should be no additional modification of semantic and data use modifiers. | | | C | | E |
| DBMS Column Assigned Value Domain | An assigned value domain is a value-based constraint on the DBMS column. The assigned value domain cannot be the same as that assigned the data element, attribute, or column. Nor can a value domain be more expansive than that assigned the data element attribute, or column. | | | C | | E |

# Methodology Phases and Work Products vs Enterprise Architectures

1. Enterprise's Architecture
2. Database Objects Architecture
3. Data Architecture
4. Resource Life Cycle Analysis Architecture
5. Business Information Systems Plan Architecture

The cross reference cells contain letter codes. C is for create, E for employ, and R for refine.

| Component | Description | Enterprise Architectures | | | | |
|---|---|---|---|---|---|---|
| | | 1 | 2 | 3 | 4 | 5 |
| DBMS Column | A DBMS column, like an attribute of an entity is intended to be a data-value based partial descriptor of a DBMS table. DBMS Columns can be complex, and thus represent arrays, groups, repeating groups, and nested repeating groups. Like columns, there are also three classes of DBMS columns, and those definitions are not be repeated again. | | | C | | E |
| DBMS Schema | A DBMS schema is a DBMS structure that encapsulates all its contained DBMS tables as well as containing other classes of DBMS schema objects such as data types, procedures, constraints, including the interrelationships of the various DBMS schema objects. The string, "DBMS" is attached to these components because at this data architecture level, these components are directly representative of the real and operating databases under the control of a specific DBMS. | | | C | | E |
| DBMS Table | A DBMS table is a database construct that exists within a DBMS schema to represent a collection of DBMS columns that are bound to a particular DBMS and represent a set of rows of data across those DBMS columns. DBMS Tables have precise specifications including constraints, primary and foreign keys, and other table centered features. Within the scope of the Operational Data Model generalization level for data architectures, these DBMS table specifications represent actual rows of data because this level is bound to a particular DBMS and is related to any specific business information systems.<br><br>Every DBMS table should relate back to a specific policy within the domain of the DBMS table's schema. DBMS Tables can be subtyped to represent collections of DBMS columns that have a common set and then several non-intersecting sets. | | | C | | E |

## Methodology Phases and Work Products vs Enterprise Architectures

1. Enterprise's Architecture
2. Database Objects Architecture
3. Data Architecture
4. Resource Life Cycle Analysis Architecture
5. Business Information Systems Plan Architecture

The cross reference cells contain letter codes. C is for create, E for employ, and R for refine.

| Component | Description | Enterprise Architectures | | | | |
|---|---|---|---|---|---|---|
| | | 1 | 2 | 3 | 4 | 5 |
| Entity | An entity is a collection of business facts that are commonly called attributes. Every entity should relate back to a specific policy within the domain of the entity's subject. Entities can be subtyped to represent collections of attributes that have a common set and then several non-intersecting sets. | C | | R | | |
| Implemented Data Model Column | Columns are the manifestation of the semantics of a data element within a table of a schema. Additionally, a column is a deployment of the semantics of an attribute. Columns may have additional semantics that further refine the column within the context of either the attribute or the data element. The order of processing these additional semantics is that the column must first be a subset of the attribute, which in turn must be a subset of the data element. Not all the columns of a table must map to attributes from a single entity. | | | C | | |
| Implemented Data Model Relationship | A relationship is a defined mechanism to relate one instance of on table to another. As with the Specified Data Model, the most common are the one-to-many, and one-to-one. The keys are almost always primary and foreign keys. Relationships cannot exist between tables in different schemas. | | | C | | |
| Management Level | Management level is a named and defined level of bureaucratic management within an organizational setting. Examples could be executive, senior, mid-level, and first-level. | C | | | | |

## Methodology Phases and Work Products vs Enterprise Architectures

1. Enterprise's Architecture
2. Database Objects Architecture
3. Data Architecture
4. Resource Life Cycle Analysis Architecture
5. Business Information Systems Plan Architecture

The cross reference cells contain letter codes. C is for create, E for employ, and R for refine.

| Component | Description | Enterprise Architectures | | | | |
|---|---|---|---|---|---|---|
| | | 1 | 2 | 3 | 4 | 5 |
| Meta category values | Meta category values are words or phrases that have a specific and controlled meaning in the enterprise. These words/phrases are either prefixed to the common business name of a data element concept, data element, attribute, or column, or are suffixed to the common business name. In the case of the former, these are semantic modifiers, and in the case of the later they are data use modifiers. An example of semantic modifiers is geography such as United States, New England, Rhode Island, and Providence. There can be other classes of semantic modifiers including for example, temporal, or precision. Only one semantic modifier of each class can be assigned. Data use modifiers are for example, data type or role. Only one data use modifiers of each class can be assigned. Assignments are always checked to ensure that proper semantic nesting is enforced. | | | C | | |
| Missions | Missions are hierarchically organized textual descriptions that define the very existence of the enterprise, and that are the ultimate goals and objectives that measure enterprise accomplishment from within different business functions and organizations. An enterprise is incomplete if one of its missions is not defined. Not all enterprises accomplish their missions simultaneously or in an ideal state. Missions are accomplished over time and are subject to revisions. | C | E | E | E | E |
| Operational Data Model Relationship | A relationship is a defined mechanism to relate one instance of one DBMS table to another. As with the Implemented Data Model, the most common are the one-to-many, and one-to-one. The keys are almost always primary and foreign keys. Because the Operational Data Model supports the SQL DDL for an actually operating database, a fourth key type, Secondary, is supported. This key type consists of one or more DBMSs columns such that when the values are supplied, a subset of rows is materialized from the table. | | | C | | |

## Methodology Phases and Work Products vs Enterprise Architectures

1. Enterprise's Architecture
2. Database Objects Architecture
3. Data Architecture
4. Resource Life Cycle Analysis Architecture
5. Business Information Systems Plan Architecture

The cross reference cells contain letter codes. C is for create, E for employ, and R for refine.

| Component | Description | Enterprise Architectures | | | | |
|---|---|---|---|---|---|---|
| | | 1 | 2 | 3 | 4 | 5 |
| Organizations Performing Missions | An organization performing missions, that is, a Mission-Organization is the association of an organization with a mission. There can be multiple organizations associated with a mission and an organization can be associated with multiple missions. The description contained within the Mission-Organization may be more refined than the description contained in either the mission or the organization. | C | | | | |
| Organizations Accomplishing Functions ... | An organization accomplishing a function in support of a mission, that is, a Mission-Organization-Function is the association of a mission-organization with a function. A mission-organization can be associated with multiple functions and a function can be associated with multiple mission-organizations. One or more mission-organization-functions may be associated with a business information system. When they are, business events are created. | C | | E | E | E |
| Positions | A named and defined collection of work tasks that can be performed by or more persons. Positions are often assigned to one or more organizations. | C | | | | |
| Positions performing missions ... | A Mission Organization Function Position Role is the assignment of a position to a particular function within an organization as it accomplishes a mission. Once a position is assigned, its role can be described. | C | | | | |
| Resource | A Resource is an enduring asset of value to the enterprise. Included for example are facilities, assets, staffs, money, even abstract concepts like reputation. If a resource is missing then the enterprise is incomplete. | | | | C | |
| Resource Life Cycle Analysis Node | A Resource Life Cycle Node is a life cycle state within the resource. If the resource is employee, the life cycle node may be employee requisition, employee candidate, employee new hire, assigned employee, reviewed employee, and separated employee. | | E | | C | E |

## Methodology Phases and Work Products vs Enterprise Architectures

1. Enterprise's Architecture
2. Database Objects Architecture
3. Data Architecture
4. Resource Life Cycle Analysis Architecture
5. Business Information Systems Plan Architecture

The cross reference cells contain letter codes. C is for create, E for employ, and R for refine.

| Component | Description | Enterprise Architectures | | | | |
|---|---|---|---|---|---|---|
| | | 1 | 2 | 3 | 4 | 5 |
| Resource Life Cycle Node Structure | The Resource Life Cycle Node Structure is the association of one Resource Life Cycle Node and another. The association represents a relationship between the two resources for some purpose. | | | E | C | E |
| Resource Life Cycle Node | A Resource Life Cycle Node is a life cycle state within the Resource. If the resource is employee, the life cycle node may be employee requisition, employee candidate, employee new hire, assigned employee, reviewed employee, and separated employee. | | | E | C | E |
| Resources | A Resource is an enduring asset of value to the enterprise. Included for example are facilities, assets, staffs, money, even abstract concepts like reputation. If a resource is missing then the enterprise is incomplete. | | | E | C | E |
| Schema | A schema is a database structure that encapsulates all its contained tables as well as containing other classes of schema objects such as data types, procedures, constraints, including the interrelationships of the various schema objects.<br><br>Implemented Data Models are cast within the domain of a schema. The set of all tables within a schema is not required to be taken from a single set of entities within a subject area. | | | C | E | E |
| Specified Data Model Relationship | A relationship is a defined mechanism to relate one instance of one entity to a set of instances of another entity. While there are eight classes of relationships, the most common are the one-to-many, and one-to-one. In the case of one-to-many, the relationship mechanism is the primary key attributes of one entity related to the foreign key attributes of the related-to entity. The term, foreign key, comes from the fact that it's really a "transplant" of the "related-from" entity's primary key. Relationships should always be named and defined to the extent that the real purpose of the relationship is clear. | C | | R | | |

| Methodology Phases and Work Products vs Enterprise Architectures | | | | | | |
|---|---|---|---|---|---|---|

1. Enterprise's Architecture
2. Database Objects Architecture
3. Data Architecture
4. Resource Life Cycle Analysis Architecture
5. Business Information Systems Plan Architecture

The cross reference cells contain letter codes. C is for create, E for employ, and R for refine.

| | | Enterprise Architectures | | | | |
|---|---|---|---|---|---|---|
| Component | Description | 1 | 2 | 3 | 4 | 5 |
| Subject | A subject is a area of interest from within the enterprise that is to be represented through structures of data values. Examples can include address structures, person name structures, contracts, purchase orders, and the like. Subjects can be hierarchical. Commonly, the subjects are related to policies accomplished by knowledge workers that require "proof of execution." Subjects are not databases, however. Nor are subjects the concepts from within the Data Element Model. | C | | R | | |
| Table | A Table is intended to be a well-defined expression of one policy within a schema. Ideally, the collection of all the tables within a schema area should define a coherent collection policy. Although unlikely, some tables and even some schemas may never be represented within Operational Data Models. Additionally, some columns within a table may never be employed. A table may contain columns that map to attributes from multiple entities. Tables can be sub-typed.<br><br>A table represents a collection of columns, which when bound to a particular DBMS and valued, represents a set of rows of data for those columns. Tables have precise specifications including constraints, primary and foreign keys, and other table centered features. Within the scope of the Implemented Data Model generalization level for data architectures, these table specifications do not represent actual rows of data because this level is not bound to a particular DBMS and is not related to any specific business information systems. These tables, and the entire Implemented Data Model is intended to be a data architecture design layer.<br><br>Tables can be subtyped to represent collections of columns that have a common set and then several non-intersecting sets. | | E | C | | E |

## Methodology Phases and Work Products vs Enterprise Architectures

1. Enterprise's Architecture
2. Database Objects Architecture
3. Data Architecture
4. Resource Life Cycle Analysis Architecture
5. Business Information Systems Plan Architecture

The cross reference cells contain letter codes. C is for create, E for employ, and R for refine.

| Component | Description | Enterprise Architectures | | | | |
|---|---|---|---|---|---|---|
| | | 1 | 2 | 3 | 4 | 5 |
| Value Domains | Value domains, along with their value domain values and relationships among value domain values, are identified, defined, described, and if appropriate, enumerated. Value domains are also associated with their parent conceptual value domains. Value domains are able to be assigned to data elements, attributes of entities of Specified Data Model subjects, columns of tables of Implemented Data Models schemas, and DBMS columns of DBMS tables of Operational Data Model schemas. | | | C E R | | R |
| View | A view is the interface between the Operational Data Model and the Business Information System. Views are defined within the scope of the Operational Data Model for a specific database within a specific DBMS. A key component of a retrieval view is that it can contain complex selection logic and also multi-table normalization logic that enable application programs to not have to know about the database's structure or to navigate the database. An update view can also contain constraint clauses that check the quality of the data prior to it being sent to the DBMS that in turn updated the database. | | | C | | E R |
| View Column | A view column is a "data" component of a view. Some view columns are the result of a computation that "goes on" inside the view involving multiple DBMS columns. | | | C | | E R |
| View Column and DBMS Column | A View Column and DBMS Column is relationship between a view column and the Operational Data Model. This enables a given view to be specified in the Metabase such that it is applicable to multiple DBMSs and multiple databases. An executing view, of course, is applicable to only one DBMS and one database. | | | C | | E R |

| Methodology Phases and Work Products vs Enterprise Architectures | | | | | | |
|---|---|---|---|---|---|---|

1. Enterprise's Architecture
2. Database Objects Architecture
3. Data Architecture
4. Resource Life Cycle Analysis Architecture
5. Business Information Systems Plan Architecture

The cross reference cells contain letter codes. C is for create, E for employ, and R for refine.

| Component | Description | Enterprise Architectures | | | | |
|---|---|---|---|---|---|---|
| | | 1 | 2 | 3 | 4 | 5 |
| View Column Process mapping | A view column mapping process is a mechanism to map between view columns of different views. This enables the specification of an input view from one database to an output view to another database, or even to several databases. | | | C | | E R |

**Table 20.** Metabase component reuse across Enterprise Architectures.

## 9.7    Metabase Benefits

The following is a partial list of benefits attained through the use of a Metabase. A Metabase will:

- Assist top management in identifying the resources required to build a business information system.

- Provide discipline and control for the database and business information system design process.

- Provide a structured approach to enterprise architecture engineering.

- Enhance the business information system development process through the utilization of prior work.

- Provide a management facility for engineering and monitoring database projects.

- Allow for the non-redundant storage of data definitions and business policies that produce greater consistency throughout the enterprise.

## 9.8    Role of Metabase Summary

This chapter stated that a Metabase is just a database encapsulated in a Metabase oriented business information system that has as its sole purpose the capture, manipulation, and reporting of metadata. The objectives of such a Metabase system are these:

- Capture requirements and design work products.

- Support the extraction of design work products to then feed business information system generators and schemas for database management systems.

- Capture of enterprise operational metadata

This chapter focused on the first objective because there are business information system generators to accomplish the second objective that, as a byproduct, automatically creates throw-away metadata.

The chapter did not focus on the third objective because there are a number of operational/technical metadata repositories that are more than adequate.

What remains are the metadata that if unaddressed represents 95% of all database and business information systems reasons for failures. Hence, the emphasis on that objective.

This chapter then stated the obvious, that is, that the metadata model of the Metabase has to map onto the metadata requirements of Chapters 3 through 8, as these metadata are critical for the enterprise architectures.

Thereafter this chapter provided the business rational for a Metabase by indicating that the data contained in the Metabase is parallel to the financial data contained in a company's finance databases. In short, if well ordered financial data is essential to a business then well ordered metadata is essential at the very minimum to information technology, and at the maximum, the entire enterprise.

This chapter enumerated all the different types of relationships that had to exist among all the different metadata products. It was clear from the descriptions that having adjacency-only relationships is far from sufficient. The Knowledge Worker Framework, seen top-down and left-right, while certainly valuable as a way to perceive the work products, is more a "reading" and "understanding" organization for these products than a "doing" order.

This chapter also pointed out that just having a methodology, a metadata repository, and well-defined product work products does not mean that "automagically" there is integrated and non-redundant metadata. It is delusional to believe otherwise. That step requires dedication and hard work. The payoff however can be a doubling of business information system creation and complete integration across all data and metadata. Finally, this will bring about integrated metadata which is the necessary first step in eliminated stove-pipe databases and business information systems.

In support of providing more the specifications for a quality Metabase system, this chapter briefly described the key functional modules that must exist and then an overall list of functional requirements that the Metabase system must satisfy.

This chapter presented a cross reference table between the work products and the five architectures as a way to show that these work products conform to the database core principle: Define once, use many times.

This chapter concluded with a short list of benefits that ultimately result in increased productivity, increased quality, lowered costs and lowered risks. While not explicitly addressed in this chapter, Metabase systems satisfying the requirements of this chapter, coupled with business information system generators have an overall negative cost to the enterprise. That, is, it always costs more to be without these systems than to have them.

The next chapter, Chapter 10, Summary and Conclusions, brings together the goals and summary of every chapter and sets out the way ahead: a work plan for success.

## 9.9 Questions and Exercises

1.  What is Computer Aided Systems Engineering (CASE) mean to you? What is its history? Did it succeed or fail, and why?

2.  What is a metadata repository and what does that term mean to you? What is its history? Did it succeed or fail and why?

3.  Is there a real difference between UpperCASE and LowerCASE? Is this difference important and valuable to the enterprise? If yes, what is the difference and why? If no, what's not different and why?

4.  Can a diagram-based tool be as comprehensive as a metadata repository based tool? If yes, then what must its characteristics be? If no, then what does the metadata repository typically have that makes it more valuable?

5.  Is there value in having all five architectures represented as integrated and non-redundant metadata in an enterprise-wide metadata environment? What is the value in terms of resources and business opportunities?

6.  Can and/or should there metadata development efforts be divided along the lines of the five architectures, and within the data architecture along the lines of the five data model generalization levels that are set out in Figure 26? If yes, why, and what are the benefits? If no then why not and what are the drawbacks?

7.  How would you engineer a federated metadata development environment? What are the likely problems? How could you use Enterprise Identifiers to engineer integratable metadata across the federation?

8.  Should the database of metadata be "open?" That is, accessible through ordinary ODBC-based report writers and 3GL programming languages? If yes, why? If not, why not?

9.      Are all the necessary metabase modules and requirements set out in Section 9.4 and 9.5? What is missing? How would you resolve what is missing?

10.     Compare and contrast the features, benefits, and drawbacks from having metadata stove-pipes versus an overall integrated non-redundant metadata repository?

11.     Compare and contrast an active versus passive Metabase?

# 10

# Summary and Conclusion

This chapter provides a summary of the book and also sets out a section on a way-ahead.

## 10.1   Enterprise Architectures

The objective of this book was to present an approach to the creation of the architectures that affect the knowledge worker and that should exist across the enterprise to ensure integration of data, semantics, and policy. To that end, this book presented the following architectures essential to the success of the knowledge worker:

- The Enterprise's architecture.
- Database Object Class architecture.
- Data architectures.
- Resource Life Cycle Analysis architecture.
- Business Information Systems Plans architecture.

Presented as well were the components of any well engineered architecture, a highly engineered framework within which the knowledge workers operate, and the characteristics, requirements, and processes that are necessary for a Metabase system.

This book showed that these five architectures are important to comprehensively accomplish the knowledge workers products and activities. This book further showed that the architectures are all interrelated, and that there are common products across them, and that these architectures and products reinforce each other, are integrated, and enable enterprises to understand their past, operate the present, and plan for the future.

## 10.2    Components of an Architecture

There's real engineering required for quality architectures. All the architecture work products must be thoroughly identified, engineered, and integrated. Because the knowledge worker environment is so complex, there's no practical way to have just one architecture. All five of the architectures must be such that their work products are able to be stored and integrated within one Metabase. Otherwise there will be more stove-pipes. The on-hand supply is more than sufficient. If the Metabase exists, is on the critical path of all knowledge worker efforts, and is of high quality, then overlapped work will not be done multiple times. That will also prevent the need for re-casting existing work because of work product conflicts.

Without quality engineering, bad architectures will result and be counterproductive. That will require significant rework because their underlying methodologies that have not been detailed, integrated across the architectures, or proven end-to-end.

In the end, the shortest route to success in terms of both times and money will be through good architectures that are fully detailed, have had their work products expertly engineered, are supported by high-quality methodologies, and are integrated with all the other work products within a Metabase.

Remember always that good architectures are just highly proceduralized common sense; else it is just very expensive non-sense.

## 10.3    Knowledge Worker Framework

Knowledge workers need a framework within which all their work products are created, stored, and interrelated. All the architectures are thus set within the Knowledge Worker Framework.

The Knowledge Worker Framework was fully described, row by row, and column by column. Every cell was detailed including a high level description of every work product that results for the cell contained work processes. All cells are, of course, completely integrated. Described also was a high level view of the processes necessary to create each work product.

The Knowledge Worker Framework is just that: a framework for the knowledge worker. The percent of reasons for information technology system failure from Table 4 clearly indicate the framework's real value. If all the cells' work products are accomplished appropriately, there's an almost certainty of success. But if collections of cells are not done or done inappropriately, there is a moderate to severe probability of failure. Table 21 again provides the key reasons for failure percents and summary descriptions of the reasons.

| U.S. General Accountability Office Reasons for Information Technology System Failure | |
| --- | --- |
| **Percent** | **Reasons for Information Technology Failures Description** |
| 41% | A lack of proper identification, analysis and configuration of enterprise architecture Scope and Business Rows across all six of the columns. That is, Missions, Database Object Classes, Business Information Systems, Business Events, Business Functions and Business Organizations. |
| 29% | A lack of proper identification, analysis and configuration of enterprise architecture Scope and Business Rows of just the Missions, Business Functions and Business Organizations columns. |
| 50% | A lack of proper re-engineering of the business functions and organizations as a consequence of re-engineered databases and business information systems. |
| 5% | A lack of proper engineering and development of databases and business information systems. |

**Table 21.** Summary of U.S. General Accountability Office Reasons for Information Technology System Failure

Table 4 shows that even if the "system" being contemplated is not an information technology system, there is still a very good reason to use this framework's cells as 66% of all the cells are outside the domain of IT. A close reading of the text from the non-IT cells describe non-IT activities. 91% of the GAO reasons for failure are still in effect even if the "system" being implemented has no information technology component at all.

All the columns and rows of Table 3 are integrated in some form as illustrated in Figure 9. In general the columns are all related in a many-to-many fashion. Additionally, there are relationships among products in adjacent cells and even between non-adjacent cells.

## 10.4 Enterprise's Architecture

The objective of an enterprise's architecture is to describe the entire enterprise. The key parts of the enterprise's architecture are its missions, organizations, functions, and database domains. The subsequent architectures that follow, for example, data architecture and resource life cycle architecture are dependent on the enterprise's architectures for context. They are dependent because their scope's depend on the content of the enterprise's architecture. All the data specifications, resource specifications, and resource life cycles are all bound by the scope of the enterprise's mission.

It is therefore appropriate that the enterprise's architecture is accomplished first, as it is from within this architecture that all other architectures should be derived.

However, if other architectures are being done in parallel, then that's acceptable just so long as the work products that exist across the architectures are reconciled. While there may be overlapping work products there must be only one definitive set. For example, if there's a resource and one or more of its life cycle nodes cannot be discovered from within the enterprise's missions, then an analysis error has been made. Such errors must be resolved.

The architecture class, Database Object Classes, sets out the major categories of enterprise data and identifies the most significant processes and states for these Database Object Classes.

## 10.5 Database Object Class Architecture

Database Object Classes were defined and contrasted with other types of object classes. The unique role Database Object Classes play in a database environment is that this object class is completely encapsulated within the DBMS schema definition layer and therefore cannot be avoided by any business information system regardless of its source language form.

There is a real business case for database objects as was shown by several examples. Presented also was how Database Object Classes can be implemented in SQL DBMSs that are not object-oriented, and how these classes can be implemented in SQL:1999 or more DBMSs that are object-oriented.

All the different Database Object Class work products were described and were interrelated. Shown also was how these work products fit with the work products of the other architectures.

## 10.6   Data Architecture

There are two dimensions to data architecture: Database Architecture Classes, and Data Model Generalization levels. The database architecture classes are:

- Original data capture.
- Transaction data staging area.
- Subject area databases.
- Data warehouses (wholesale and retail).
- Reference data.

The original data capture database architecture class represents the actual databases that reside within organizations within an enterprise and may provide data to other database classes. These database types are often called OLTP databases because they support on-line transaction processing.

The transaction data staging area database architecture class represents the data extracts from the original data capture databases that are recast, as necessary to meet the required precision, granularity, and other semantics for the other database architecture classes. Any interface between any database architecture class may proceed through a transaction data staging area.

The subject area database architecture class represents the subject-based integrated databases of data that, in turn, support some measure of analyses and reports, analysis results retention, and supports the generation of other classes of databases, that is, data warehouses.

The data warehouse (wholesale and retail) database architecture represents the transformed and likely redundant sets of data that serve special reports and analyses. The key set of differences between wholesale data warehouses and retail data warehouses are one of volume, duration and specialization. Data mart data warehouse designs are commonly created along the lines of "star schemas" or "snow-flake schemas," and when compared to wholesale a data warehouse have smaller volumes, shorter durations, and are more specialized.

The reference data database architecture class represents data that form the critical characterization and discrimination characteristics of data from within the entire set of business facts. Included, for example are genders, city names, state names, all codes, and like. Ideally, all reference data would be exactly the same across all the other four data architecture classes.

Realistically, different agencies and providers have different reference data value versions for the same reference data and different data value versions across time. All reference data must be managed centrally and then distributed in so far as it is possible to all databases of the other data architecture classes.

Every one of these databases employs and/or proceeds through the following data model generalization levels:

- [11179] Data elements.
- Specified Data Models.
- Implemented Data Models.
- Operational Data Models.
- View data models.

Database Object Classes are defined within the Implemented Data Model and made operational during the Operational Data Model.

The Data Element level provides the ability to have enterprise-wide business facts combined with semantic, data use modifiers, and language independent data types.

Specified Data Models are value-based representations of the various concepts included in databases throughout the enterprise. These Specified Data Models can be employed in the development of databases that are used throughout the enterprise such that these databases are integrated and non-redundant.

Implemented Data Models are models of specific databases of one or more classes such as original data capture, transaction data staging area, subject area databases, warehouses, and reference data. Some of the subject area databases, also called Operational Data Stores (ODS) may contain data that is classified as master data, which is also known as strategic data, golden source data, and authoritative data sources.

Operational Data Models are the database models of the databases that are actually govern the structures and data value domains of enterprise data.

In general, an enterprise-wide effort can be made to discover data elements through an analysis of any number of enterprise documents including database schemas, manual and computer generated reports, policy and procedure manuals, and forms. This type of effort can largely proceed independently of any functional data modeling effort, or any database and/or business information system effort. A more comprehensive treatment of the contents of data elements is treated below.

Similarly, functional data administrators can begin efforts to create subject-based data models of common seen data structures within their functional area.

The various data model generalization layers are interrelated within the Database Object Classes column, and for the Operational Data Model level, there are relationships with other Knowledge Worker Framework columns such as the Business information systems.

The data model generalization layers are interrelated with the enterprise's architecture as the data architectures are derived from database domains that are created from missions. The Implemented Data Model layer contains all the database tables defined within Database Object Classes. These database objects are directly related to the Resource Life Cycle Analysis (Chapter 7), and Business Information Systems Plan (Chapter 8).

Finally, the chapter set out the work products that must be created for each data model generalization layer, and then how all these work products are thoroughly integrated one with the other.

## 10.7   Resource Life Cycle Analysis

Resource Life Cycle Analysis enables business mangers to participate in the identification of the resources, their life cycles, and then enablement vectors among the life cycles.

The information technology staff has a business management defined network against which it can allocate the existing business information systems and databases. Once allocated, information technology can root out the conflicting and redundant systems and databases. Information technology projects, representing advances in the sophistication of its support to the business, can be identified and resource-estimated through standardized methodologies and metrics.

Once a set of information technology projects are estimated, the entire enterprise-network of information technology projects can be scheduled through project management software. At that point, management re-enters the picture and makes the hard choices, what, when, and why. Information technology is left with the How. That's how it should be.

It is again important to note that while valuable in their own right, Resource Life Cycles also serve as a key linking mechanism between the Enterprise's Architecture, Database Object Classes, and Data Architectures on the one hand and Business Information Systems Plans on the other hand.


## 10.8   Business Information Systems Plans

Business Information System Plan architectures are both blueprints of all information technology database and business information system projects and also the battle plan for their accomplishment. Given that Knowledge Worker Framework based enterprises spend about 5% of its budget on Information Technology, 3% of that, or 0.15% to develop the enterprise's Business Information Systems Plan is not out of line.

A quality Business Information Systems Plan must, of course, be timely, useable, maintainable, able to be iterated into a quality product, and reproducible.

The book's 10 step Business Information Systems Planning strategy was described. For this strategy to be successful, it must be supported by a database project methodology, and an already existing set of architectures for the Enterprise, Data Architecture, Database Object Classes, and Resource Life Cycles. The reason these architectures should already exist by the time the business information system planning effort begins is because if done, the plan will be seen as a capstone and integrator of the other architectures, and the plan will be much more readily accepted because the other architectures, accomplished by collaborative enterprise organizations will represent a consensus-based foundation.

In contrast, if the Business Information Systems Plan is accomplished in isolation and within its scope is the creation of the Enterprise's Architecture, Database Object Classes, and Data Architectures, and Resource Life Cycles architectures then there will be two unrecoverable problems. The first is that the plan's development time will greatly exceed the 3% of the information technology budget, and second, these encapsulated architectures will have a much lower probability of being of value to the enterprise as a whole. There will have been no enterprise-wide sweat-equity and ownership in the architecture products. In short, Business Information Systems Plans done this way take longer, cost more, and most often become "shelf-ware." This is not good.

The necessary characteristics for Business Information Systems Plans to be successful, efficient and effective were set out in Chapter 8. Unfortunately, these characteristics have been glaringly unfilled by other Business Information Systems Plan development methodologies. Notwithstanding the bad reputation of Business Information Systems Plan efforts, they need to be done. This book outlines a better way that in the end will make Business Information Systems Plan part of the standard planning steps of a well run information technology organization.

Information Technology organizations, once they have completed their initial set of databases and business information systems will find themselves transformed from a project to a release environment. That necessitates a transformation from either of two standard development life cycles, waterfall and/or spiral to one of continuous flow.

The continuous flow environment becomes the only viable alternative for moving the enterprise forward. It is precisely because of the release environment that enterprise-wide Business Information Systems Plans that can be created, evolved, and maintained are essential.

Finally, the very process of configuring a final Business Information Systems Plan involves intense database and business information system project planning. This process too can be largely automated through the use of sophisticated project planning software where the PERT chart is the Resource Life Cycle Node network, and the individual projects associated with the nodes are easily estimated because of a large quantity of project plan and metric templates.

If project plan and metric templates are subsequently refined over time, the ability to automatically generate new Business Information Systems Plans will become quite easy. Further, these generated plans will be reliable, repeatable, and are malleable as new technologies unfold.

## 10.9    Role of the Metabase

The Metabase is just a database encapsulated in a Metabase oriented business information system that has as its sole purpose the capture, manipulation, and reporting of metadata. The objectives of such a Metabase system are these:

- Capture requirements and design work products.

- Support the extraction of design work products to then feed business information system generators and schemas for database management systems.

- Capture of enterprise operational metadata.

The first objective is the most important because it addresses the highest percent of GAO reasons for failure. It is important to note, one more time, that most of the GAO reasons were outside the proper boundaries of information technology.

The second objective is largely accomplished by business information system generators, which, as a byproduct, automatically create throw-away metadata.

Not emphasized as well was the third objective because there are a number of operational/technical metadata repositories that are more than adequate. What remains is the first objective, that is, metadata that, if unaddressed, represent 95% of all database and business information systems reasons for failure. Hence, focus on that objective.

Metadata repositories that store just operational or technical metadata miss almost all the true value of metadata to the enterprise. Clearly, if the focus is solely on the optimization of the past, enterprises will never be able to plan, see, and accomplish the future. It is through the exposition, optimization, and recasting of our missions, organizations, functions, database objects, databases and business information systems that the future will be unfolding in ever better forms. Consequently, the database design of a metadata repository should closely match the metadata requirements of Chapters 4 through 8.

There is also a very compelling business rational for the Metabase. The data contained in the Metabase is parallel to the financial data in a company's finance databases. In short, because well ordered financial data is essential to a well-ordered business, well-ordered metadata is essential at the very minimum to information technology, and at the very maximum, the entire enterprise.

Just having a methodology, a metadata repository, and well-defined product work do not mean that there is integrated and non-redundant metadata. It is delusional to believe otherwise. If multiple databases and business information system projects develop their own metadata in isolation without achieving integration and non-redundancy, there will just be an increase of stove-pipes, but this time, the stove-pipes will be of metadata.

The overall requirements, functions, and processes of any Metabase system closely follow the sequence and content of the architectures that are constructed. Any quality Metabase must be able to build these architectures independently, and then have facilities to integrate and reconcile the inevitable disconnects.

In support of providing more specificity to a quality Metabase system, the key functional Metabase modules and the list of functional requirements were set out.

Over the past 20+ years, quality Metabase systems have always increased productivity, increased quality, lowered costs and lowered risks. Additionally, when Metabase systems, which fulfill the requirements set out in Sections 9.4 and 9.5, and are built through business information system generators, they have an overall negative cost to the enterprise. That, is, it always costs more to be without Metabase systems than to have them.

## 10.10  Enterprise Architecture Way Ahead

The way ahead involves answering the following questions:

- Do you want to increase productivity?
- Do you want to increase quality?
- Do you want to decrease cost?
- Do you want to decrease risk?

If the answers are yes, and certainly they are, time and effort must be invested in establishing a knowledge worker environment. Is the Knowledge Worker Framework set out in this book perfect? Certainly not. Is the set of architectures identified in this book the definitive and complete list? Certainly not. The Knowledge Worker Framework and the architectures represent a good starting place that while not perfect is based on 30 years of experience-fired evolution. Waiting for perfection means never starting.

Key to the way ahead is to embrace the "meta-world." That is, get comfortable in designing and building tools that make knowledge work easier, cost effective, repeatable, reliable, integrated, and non-redundant.

In the 1960s, computers (32K words and 12 tape drives with no disks) cost $650 an hour to operate. Monthly staff costs were $650. Clearly staff was the most common and the least expensive resource. Large quantities of staff were the solution to the overall computer hardware costs. Days or weeks between program compiles were common. No more. Today, very sophisticated and profoundly powerful computers (2 gig memory, 210 Gig of 15K RPM SCSI disk drives, and two dual-core 2.5 megahertz processors) can cost just $5,500 dollars to purchase. Over a 4 year period, that's $0.53 per hour to use. Staff costs are $125 per hour for the "journeyman."

It should be abundantly clear that it's the knowledge worker that needs to be optimized and made more productive. That is where the biggest payoff is. This book addresses the architectures that directly affect the quantity and quality of the work of the knowledge worker.

The bottom line to this book, and certainly the recommended way-ahead is to maximize the productivity of the knowledge worker. That is where the payoff is. Such a working environment is illustrated in Figure 44. In this environment, as the "happy" knowledge worker does his job via some methodology set within one or more frameworks, he is able to access one or more Metabases to create, employ, or evolve work products that are of value on the project, or that will be of value for other projects. The Knowledge Worker Framework, the architectures, and the Metabase, all described in this book are a great place to start.

What are you to specifically do? Simple. Now that you have read the book, take it and put it onto your manger's desk. Ask that it be read and acted upon. Your enterprise's very existence may depend on it.

Finally, it needs to be said, and remembered that this book is not a theory book. If it had been, it would have been written 25 or more years ago when all this was untested and unrefined by many industry and government organizations through many information technology projects. Rather, this book is the consequence of the evolution and development of enterprise architecture and data management practices that have been conducted in industry and government since the early 1970s.

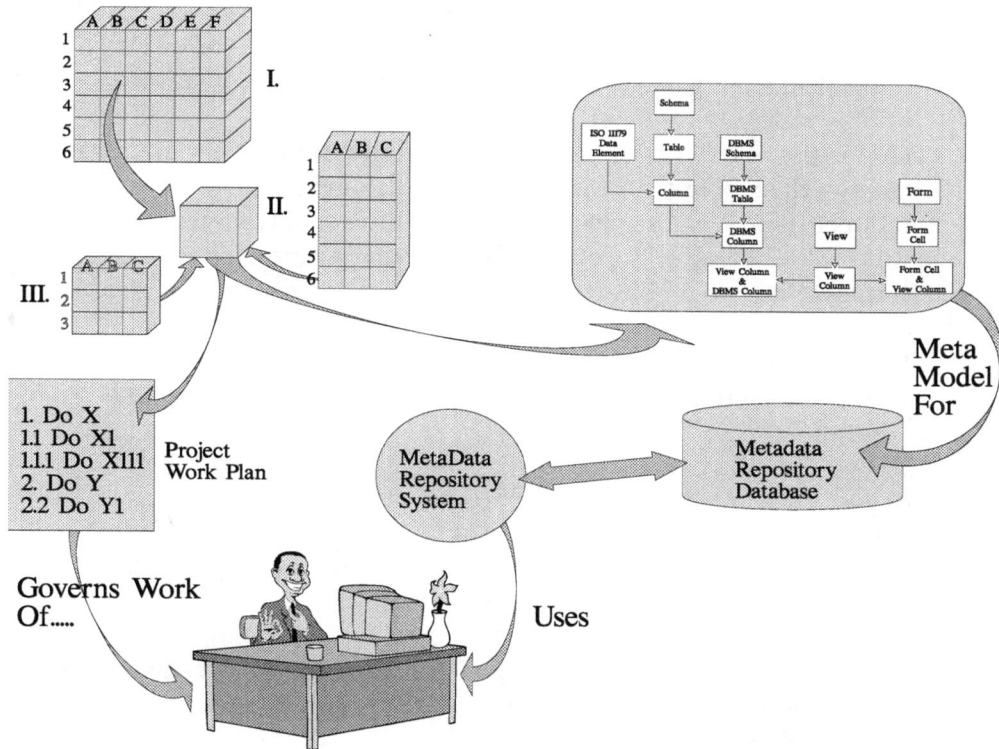

**Figure 44**. Unified operating knowledge worker environment with frameworks, metabase (metadata repository), and methodology.

Every product in every chapter of this book is fully detailed in other Whitemarsh books, and is fully supported by detailed methodology, courses, workshops, and of course, the Metabase, Metabase. In short, this book is another integral component in the Whitemarsh Data Management Series.

## 10.11 Questions and Exercises

1       Why are the five architectures important in your enterprise? Do you have all five? Which are missing and what's the effect from their absence?

2    Are the architectures that exist integrated with one another? If yes, how and what are the benefits? If no, how do you keep the architectures integrated? What is the effect of non-integration?

3    What is the role of the Knowledge Worker Framework? Does such a framework exist in your enterprise? Does it encompass all your architectures? What are the key features of such a Knowledge Worker Framework? What is the effect of not having a Knowledge Worker Framework as an architecture integrator?

4    Do you have formal change management? Is it part of every project? What have been your experiences when change management is forgotten?

5    Do you have an enterprise's architecture? Has it been helpful? Are all your projects set within its context? How often is it updated? If you don't have a enterprise's architecture, how do you keep projects organized, integrated, and non-conflicting?

6    Have you been implicitly accomplishing database object classes? Will this book's recognition and definition help? Will you undertake database object class formalization? If yes, why? If no, why not?

7    Do you see and recognize the need for different database architecture classes? Is there value in classifying databases? If yes, what is the value? If no, when why not?

8    Do you have a TDSA environment for regularizing precision, granularity, temporal characteristics, and value domains? If yes, what's the benefits? If not, what's the cost of not having a TDSA environment?

9    Do you have something akin to the five levels of data model generalization? How do you create and maintain enterprise-wide data elements and functional data models? Are your databases guided by these models? If yes, what is the benefit? If not, what's the cost?

10   Do you do top-down or bottom-up data modeling? Why one versus the other? Compare and contrast the benefits and costs.

11      How do you integrate ERP data models with the overall collection of enterprise data models? Do you use a TDSA approach whereby the ERP system puts and gets standardized data from a database that's "bolted onto" the ERP system?

12      Do you have something like Resource Life Cycle Analysis network that acts as a lattice-work for inventorying and organizing databases and business information systems in a business-rationale based order? If yes, how has it helped? If no, then how do you account for all your databases and business information systems?

13      Do you regularly develop and maintain a Business Information Systems Plan? If so, compare and contrast the process and work products contained in this book with the products you develop. Do you develop the Business Information Systems Plan from a basis of already existing work products or from a blank slate? Which is quicker? Which is more accurate?

14      What is your approach to a Metabase? A stand-alone metadata repository? A series stand-alone entity-relationship and process modeling tools? Compare and contrast either of these two approaches with an integrated and non-redundant CASE/Repository environment that's on the critical path of database and business information system development and maintenance.

15      How have you benefitted from a Metabase? Does it save time and resources? Which kind and how?

16      Overall, are the five architectures set out in this book necessary and of value so you can better understand, manage, develop, and maintain your enterprise and its databases and business information systems?

17      If this book has been of value, what is your next step? How about putting it onto your manager's desk and ask that the book be turned into an action plan.

# Attachment 1
# Application for Employment

## Sample Employment Application Form

| PLEASE PRINT ALL<br>INFORMATION REQUESTED<br>EXCEPT SIGNATURE | |
|---|---|

**APPLICATION FOR EMPLOYMENT**

**APPLICANTS MAY BE TESTED FOR ILLEGAL DRUGS**

PLEASE COMPLETE PAGES 1-4.                             DATE _____

Name _____
        Last                    First                    Middle                    Maiden

Present address _____
              Number          Street          City      State      Zip

How long _____          Social Security No. _____ – _____ – _____

Telephone ( )_____

If under 18, please list age _____

                                                Days/hours available to work
Position applied for  (1) _____    No Pref _____    Thur _____
and salary desired   (2) _____    Mon _____    Fri _____
(Be specific)                                    Tue _____    Sat _____
                                                 Wed _____    Sun _____

How many hours can you work weekly? _____    Can you work nights? _____

Employment desired    __ FULL-TIME ONLY    __ PART-TIME ONLY    __ FULL- OR PART-TIME

When available for work?_____

| TYPE OF SCHOOL | NAME OF SCHOOL | LOCATION<br>(Complete mailing<br>address) | NUMBER OF YEARS<br>COMPLETED | MAJOR &<br>DEGREE |
|---|---|---|---|---|
| High School | | | | |
| College | | | | |
| Bus. or Trade School | | | | |
| Professional School | | | | |

HAVE YOU EVER BEEN CONVICTED OF A CRIME?          __ No          __ Yes

If yes, explain number of conviction(s), nature of offense(s) leading to conviction(s), how recently such offense(s) was/were committed, sentence(s) imposed, and type(s) of rehabilitation. _____

| PLEASE PRINT ALL INFORMATION REQUESTED EXCEPT SIGNATURE | |
|---|---|

**APPLICATION FOR EMPLOYMENT**

DO YOU HAVE A DRIVER'S LICENSE?  __ Yes __ No

What is your means of transportation to work? _____

Driver's license
number _____  State of issue _____  __ Operator __ Commercial (CDL) __ Chauffeur
Expiration date _____

Have you had any accidents during the past three years?        How many? _____
Have you had any moving violations during the past three years?   How Many? _____

| OFFICE ONLY |
|---|

|  | __ Yes |  |  |  | __ Yes | Word |  | __ Yes |  |  |
|---|---|---|---|---|---|---|---|---|---|---|
| Typing | __ No | _____ WPM | 10-key | __ No | Processing | | __ No | _____ WPM | | |
| Personal | __ Yes | __ PC |  | Other _____ | | | | | | |
| Computer | __ No | __ Mac |  | Skills _____ | | | | | | |

Please list two references other than relatives or previous employers.

Name _____        Name _____

Position _____      Position _____

Company _____      Company _____

Address _____      Address _____

_____              _____

Telephone ( ___ ) _____    Telephone ( ___ ) _____

An application form sometimes makes it difficult for an individual to adequately summarize a complete background.  Use the space below to summarize any additional information necessary to describe your full qualifications for the specific position for which you are applying.

| PLEASE PRINT ALL INFORMATION REQUESTED EXCEPT SIGNATURE | | |
|---|---|---|

**APPLICATION FOR EMPLOYMENT**

| MILITARY |
|---|

HAVE YOU EVER BEEN IN THE ARMED FORCES? ___ Yes ___ No

ARE YOU NOW A MEMBER OF THE NATIONAL GUARD? ___ Yes ___ No

Specialty _____ Date Entered _____ Discharge Date _____

| **Work Experience** | Please list your work experience for the **past five years** beginning with your most recent job held. If you were self-employed, give firm name. **Attach additional sheets if necessary.** |
|---|---|

| Name of employer<br>Address<br>City, State, Zip Code<br>Phone number | Name of last supervisor | Employment dates | Pay or salary |
|---|---|---|---|
| | | From | Start |
| | | To | Final |
| | Your last job title | | |

Reason for leaving (be specific)

List the jobs you held, duties performed, skills used or learned, advancements or promotions while you worked at this company.

| Name of employer<br>Address<br>City, State, Zip Code<br>Phone number | Name of last supervisor | Employment dates | Pay or salary |
|---|---|---|---|
| | | From | Start |
| | | To | Final |
| | Your Last Job Title | | |

Reason for leaving (be specific)

List the jobs you held, duties performed, skills used or learned, advancements or promotions while you worked at this company.

<table>
<tr><td>PLEASE PRINT ALL<br>INFORMATION REQUESTED<br>EXCEPT SIGNATURE</td><td></td></tr>
</table>

**APPLICATION FOR EMPLOYMENT**

| Work experience | Please list your work experience for the **past five years** beginning with your most recent job held. If you were self-employed, give firm name. **Attach additional sheets if necessary.** |
|---|---|

| Name of employer<br>Address<br>City, State, Zip Code<br>Phone number | Name of last supervisor | Employment dates | Pay or salary |
|---|---|---|---|
| | | From | Start |
| | | To | Final |
| | Your last job title | | |

Reason for leaving (be specific)

List the jobs you held, duties performed, skills used or learned, advancements or promotions while you worked at this company.

| Name of employer<br>Address<br>City, State, Zip Code<br>Phone number | Name of last supervisor | Employment dates | Pay or salary |
|---|---|---|---|
| | | From | Start |
| | | To | Final |
| | Your last job title | | |

Reason for leaving (be specific)

List the jobs you held, duties performed, skills used or learned, advancements or promotions while you worked at this company.

May we contact your present employer?     __ Yes  __ No

Did you complete this application yourself     __ Yes  __ No

If not, who did? _____

# Attachment 2
## Database Architecture Class Descriptions

| Database Architecture Persistent Data Classifications and Characteristics | | | | |
|---|---|---|---|---|
| **Persistent Data Classification** | **Persistent Data Characteristics** | **Process Characteristics** | **User Considerations** | **Technical Considerations** |
| Original Data Capture | Detailed atomic data<br><br>Accurate as of the last update<br><br>Well defined, long lasting database designs<br><br>Normalized database designs<br><br>Uses reference data<br><br>No invalid data updates allowed | Tuned for transaction capture, storage and update<br><br>Application oriented<br><br>Transaction driven<br><br>Processing supported by well known data integrity and business processing rules<br><br>Understands, creates, and maintains TDSA databases through Original Data Capture system extract and TDSA loading software.<br><br>Source data for TDSA | Original data source entry personnel<br><br>High availability<br><br>Supports day-to-day operations | Amount of data for processing is small<br><br>Multiple vendor packages<br><br>Package specific<br><br>May or may not be controlled by SQL DBMS |

| Database Architecture — Persistent Data Classifications and Characteristics | | | | |
|---|---|---|---|---|
| **Persistent Data Classification** | **Persistent Data Characteristics** | **Process Characteristics** | **User Considerations** | **Technical Considerations** |
| TDSA: Transaction Data Staging Area | Transient data/short lived<br><br>Foundation data source for all operational data systems<br><br>Enterprise-wide standard semantics<br><br>Package independent database designs<br><br>Denormalized Full business transaction<br><br>Does not use reference data | Accepts, stores, and then pushes forward function<br><br>Only refreshed with changes from previous version<br><br>Operations application data system daily update event driven<br><br>Translation and transformation | Users cannot access | Multiple platforms<br><br>Interface monitoring<br><br>Applications insulation<br><br>SQL DBMS controlled |

| Database Architecture | | | | |
|---|---|---|---|---|
| Persistent Data Classifications and Characteristics | | | | |
| **Persistent Data Classification** | **Persistent Data Characteristics** | **Process Characteristics** | **User Considerations** | **Technical Considerations** |
| ODS: Operational Data Store<br><br>"Subject Area Data Store" | Detail level data<br><br>May be lightly summarized<br><br>Current or nearly current<br><br>Rolling histories<br><br>Broad subject area database scope<br><br>Normalized database designs<br><br>Redundant data from across enterprise<br><br>May contain derived data from "outside"<br><br>Uses reference data<br><br>May receive and/or send data to databases within class<br><br>Data source for all warehouse databases | Updated daily via TDSA data transaction files<br><br>Accepts and stores data from TDSA<br><br>Supports comprehensive reporting and generalized ad hoc query | End-user detailed level analysis<br><br>Used for up to the minute decisions<br><br>Used for detailed decision making | Requires fast response time<br><br>Large volume<br><br>SQL DBMS controlled |

| Database Architecture<br>Persistent Data Classifications and Characteristics | | | | |
|---|---|---|---|---|
| **Persistent Data Classification** | **Persistent Data Characteristics** | **Process Characteristics** | **User Considerations** | **Technical Considerations** |
| Warehouse: Wholesale | Summarized and some detail<br><br>Rolling Histories<br><br>Load/replace, no end-user update<br><br>Enterprise-wide standard semantics<br><br>Narrow/subset of one or more subject areas<br><br>Redundant data from across enterprise<br><br>May contain internal derived data<br><br>Reference data fully embedded<br><br>May receive and/or send data to databases within class<br><br>Data source for all retail data warehouses | No end-user updating<br><br>Regular, periodic updates<br><br>Supports standardized, on-demand reports<br><br>Supports general complex business data analyses such as trends and forecasting<br><br>Views data from multiple subject areas | Supports managerial community<br><br>Used for broad direction and positioning<br><br>Used to formulate and assess long term decisions | Availability not on business' critical path<br><br>User workstation access<br><br>Large data volumes per query<br><br>High processing power required<br><br>SQL DBMS controlled |

| Database Architecture Persistent Data Classifications and Characteristics | | | | |
|---|---|---|---|---|
| **Persistent Data Classification** | **Persistent Data Characteristics** | **Process Characteristics** | **User Considerations** | **Technical Considerations** |
| Warehouse: Retail | Light to highly summarized and some detail

Rolling histories

Load/replace, no end-user update

Enterprise-wide standard semantics

Denormalized and highly designed to specifically favor one or more reporting formats

Redundant data from across enterprise

May contain internal derived data

Reference data fully embedded

May receive and/or send data to databases within class | Availability not on business' critical path

Regular, periodic updates

Highly designed, end-user on-demand reports

Supports very specific simple to complex business data analyses

Views data from multiple subject areas | Supports managerial community

Cannot update

Used for direction and positioning

Used for long term decision making

Specific reporting need | Relaxed availability

User workstations

Large volume

High processing power

SQL DBMS controlled |

| Database Architecture<br>Persistent Data Classifications and Characteristics | | | | |
|---|---|---|---|---|
| **Persistent Data Classification** | **Persistent Data Characteristics** | **Process Characteristics** | **User Considerations** | **Technical Considerations** |
| Reference Data | Durable codes and long value alternatives with policy definitions and full descriptions<br><br>Enterprise-wide standard semantics<br><br>Source of all valid and invalid values including alternatives for different countries and languages<br><br>Multiple group data field constructors suitable for different countries and languages<br><br>Definitive source for multi-use data in all other databases<br><br>Changed data history supported by conversion mappings<br><br>Long lasting, seldom updated | Simple updates<br><br>Update mappings required for reference data value migration | Needed by all levels in the organization<br><br>Used by all systems<br><br>Enables understanding and conversion of historical data | Supports the concept of single source<br><br>Integration with all data store types |

# Attachment 3
## U.S. Department of Defense Architecture Framework

| | | | U.S. Department of Defense DoD Architecture Frame Framework | |
|---|---|---|---|---|
| **View** | **Frame work Product** | **Frame Product Name** | **General Description** | **IT Specialization and Database Sub-specialization** |
| All Views | AV-1 | Overview and Summary Information | Scope, purpose, intended users, environment depicted, analytical findings | Mission, Database Domains |
| | AV-2 | Integrated Dictionary | Architecture data repository with definitions of all terms used in all products | Business Terms, Data Element Model |
| Operational | OV-1 | High-Level Operational Concept Graphic | High-level graphical/textual description of operational concept | Mission, Database Domains, Functions, and Organizations |
| | OV-2 | Operational Node Connectivity Description | Operational nodes, connectivity, and information exchange need lines between nodes | Business Event, Business Calendar, Business Cycle, Business information systems, Organization, and Function |
| | OV-3 | Operational Information Exchange Matrix | Information exchanged between nodes and the relevant attributes of that exchange | TDSA via operational data model, with Business information systems, Business Event, Business Calendar, and Business Cycle |
| | OV-4 | Organization al Relationships Chart | Organizational, role, or other relationships among organizations | Organization, Function, and Business Event |
| | OV-5 | Operational Activity Model | Capabilities, operational activities, relationships among activities, inputs, and outputs; overlays can show cost, performing nodes, or other pertinent information | Business Function, Business Events, Operational ata Model, and View Data Model |

| | U.S. Department of Defense DoD Architecture Frame Framework | | | |
|---|---|---|---|---|
| View | Frame work Pro-duct | Frame Product Name | General Description | IT Specialization and Database Sub-specialization |
| | OV-6a | Operational Rules Model | One of three products used to describe operational activity—identifies business rules that constrain operation | Business Functions, Business Events, Operational Data Model, Views, Data Integrity Rules, Business information systems, and Database Objects. |
| | OV-6b | Operational State Transition Description | One of three products used to describe operational activity—identifies business process responses to events | Projects (To Be and As-is) That Identify Business Functions, Business Events, Operational Data Model, Views, Data Integrity Rules, Business information systems, and Database Objects. |
| | OV-6c | Operational Event-Trace Description | One of three products used to describe operational activity—traces actions in a scenario or sequence of events | Mappings Regarding Business Functions, Business Events, Operational Data Model, View Data Model, Data Integrity Rules, Business information systems, and Database Objects. |
| | OV-7 | Logical Data Model | Documentation of the system data requirements and structural business process rules of the Operational View | Data Element Model, Specified Data Model, and Implemented Data Model. |
| Sys-tems | SV-1 | Systems Interface Description | Identification of systems nodes, systems, and system items and their interconnections, within and between nodes | Business information systems, View Data Model, and Inter-view Mappings |
| | SV-2 | Systems Communications Description | Systems nodes, systems, and system items, and their related communications lay-downs | Not in the Current Domain of Data Asset Products. |

| View | Frame work Product | Frame Product Name | General Description | IT Specialization and Database Sub-specialization |
|---|---|---|---|---|
| | | | U.S. Department of Defense DoD Architecture Frame Framework | |
| | SV-3 | Systems-Systems Matrix | Relationships among systems in a given architecture; can be designed to show relationships of interest, e.g., system-type interfaces, planned vs. existing interfaces, etc. | Business Information Systems, View Data Models, and Operational Data Models |
| | SV-4 | Systems Functionality Description | Functions performed by systems and the system data flows among system functions | Business information systems, Database Objects Model, and Implemented Data Model |
| | SV-5 | Operational Activity to Systems Function Traceability Matrix | Mapping of systems back to capabilities or of system functions back to operational activities | Business Information Systems, Business Events, Business Functions, and Optionally to Organizations and Missions |
| | SV-6 | Systems Data Exchange Matrix | Provides details of system data elements being exchanged between systems and the attributes of that exchange | Business information systems, View Data Model;, and Inter-view Mappings |
| | SV-7 | Systems Performance Parameters Matrix | Performance characteristics of Systems View elements for the appropriate time frame(s) | Not in the Current Domain of Data Asset Products. |
| | SV-8 | Systems Evolution Description | Planned incremental steps toward migrating a suite of systems to a more efficient suite, or toward evolving a current system to a future implementation | Projects Relative to the "To Be" and "As-is" That Identify Business Functions, Business Events, Operational Data Model, View Data Model, Data Integrity Rules, Business information systems, and Database Objects. |

| U.S. Department of Defense DoD Architecture Frame Framework | | | | |
|---|---|---|---|---|
| View | Frame work Pro- duct | Frame Product Name | General Description | IT Specialization and Database Sub-specialization |
| | SV-9 | Systems Technology Forecast | Emerging technologies and software/hardware products that are expected to be available in a given set of time frames and that will affect future development of the architecture | Not in the Current Domain of Data Asset Products. |
| | SV-10a | Systems Rules Model | One of three products used to describe system functionality—identifies constraints that are imposed on systems functionality due to some aspect of systems design or implementation | Business Information System, Database Objects, Data Integrity Rules and Implemented Data Model. |
| | SV-10b | Systems State Transition Description | One of three products used to describe system functionality—identifies responses of a system to events | Business Events and Database Objects |
| | SV-10c | Systems Event-Trace Description | One of three products used to describe system functionality—identifies system-specific refinements of critical sequences of events described in the Operational View | Mappings among Business Events and Database Objects |
| | SV-11 | Physical Schema | Physical implementation of the Logical Data Model entities, e.g., message formats, file structures, physical schema | Operational Data Model and View Data Model |
| Tech- nical | TV-1 | Technical Standards Profile | Listing of standards that apply to Systems View elements in a given architecture | Not in the Current Domain of Data Asset Products. |

| U.S. Department of Defense DoD Architecture Frame Framework | | | | |
|---|---|---|---|---|
| View | Frame work Pro- duct | Frame Product Name | General Description | IT Specialization and Database Sub-specialization |
| | TV-2 | Technical Standards Forecast | Description of emerging standards and potential impact on current Systems View elements, within a set of time frames | Not in the Current Domain of Data Asset Products. |

# Attachment 4
# Cross Reference Between Methodology, Architectures, and the Knowledge Worker Framework

This attachment contains two tables. The first table represents a general cross reference between the work products of the phases and the enterprise architectures. The second tables contains a general cross reference between these work products and the columns of the Knowledge Worker Framework.

**Note**: Not every product is allocated because Architectures are not really methodologies. This suggests that architectures, while valuable, do not replace a full methodology.

The cross reference cells contain letter codes. C is for create, E for employ, and R for refine.

| Methodology Phases and Work Products vs Enterprise Architectures | | | | | | |
|---|---|---|---|---|---|---|
| 1. Enterprise's Architecture<br>2. Database Objects Architecture<br>3. Data Architecture<br>4. Resource Life Cycle Analysis Architecture<br>5. Business Information Systems Plan Architecture | | | | | | |
| | | Enterprise Architecture | | | | |
| **Phase** | **Major Product** | 1 | 2 | 3 | 4 | 5 |
| Preliminary Analysis | Mission | C | E | E | E | E |
| | Organization | C | | | | E |
| | Function | C | | | | E |
| | Database Domain | C | R | E | | |
| | Specified Data Model | C | | E | | |
| | Data Elements | C | E | | | |
| | Database Objects | C | R | | E | E |
| | Business Information Systems Plan | C | E | | | E |

234

## Methodology Phases and Work Products vs Enterprise Architectures

1. Enterprise's Architecture
2. Database Objects Architecture
3. Data Architecture
4. Resource Life Cycle Analysis Architecture
5. Business Information Systems Plan Architecture

| Phase | Major Product | Enterprise Architecture | | | | |
|---|---|---|---|---|---|---|
| | | 1 | 2 | 3 | 4 | 5 |
| Conceptual Specification | Refined mission, organization, database domain, and Specified Data Model | R | | | | |
| | Refined Specified Data Model | R | | | | |
| | Refined Data Elements | R | R | R | | |
| | Detailed Database Objects | | C | | | |
| | Implemented Data Model | C | | C | E | C |
| | Specified Business information systems | | E | | | |
| | Specified Business Events | | | | | |
| | Iterated Business information system Prototype | R | R | R | E | E |
| | Identified human support systems | | | | | |
| Binding | Select database management system | | | | | |
| | Determined Implementation Strategy | | | | | |
| Implementation | Operational Data Model | | | C | | |
| | Designed Business Information Systems | | R | | R | R |
| | Engineered training and hotline, and test data | | | | | |

| Methodology Phases and Work Products vs Enterprise Architectures | | | | | | |
|---|---|---|---|---|---|---|
| 1. Enterprise's Architecture<br>2. Database Objects Architecture<br>3. Data Architecture<br>4. Resource Life Cycle Analysis Architecture<br>5. Business Information Systems Plan Architecture | | | | | | |

| Phase | Major Product | Enterprise Architecture | | | | |
|---|---|---|---|---|---|---|
| | | 1 | 2 | 3 | 4 | 5 |
| | Unit and System tests | | | | | |
| | Acceptance Testing | | | | | |
| | Revised Human Supports | | | | | |
| Conversion and Deployment | Procured and installed hardware | | | | | |
| | Converted data | | | | | |
| | Conducted training | | | | | |
| | Installed hotline and maintenance organizations | | | | | |
| Production and Administration | Commencement of business information systems operations | E | E | E | E | E |
| | Emergency maintenance | R | R | R | R | R |
| | Standard maintenance | R | R | R | R | R |
| | Standard Revision | R | R | R | R | R |
| | System optimization | R | R | R | R | R |
| | System auditing | E | E | E | E | E |

Table 22. Methodology Phases with Work Products versus Enterprise Architectures.

This table contains a general cross reference between these work products and the columns of the Knowledge Worker Framework.

**Note**: Again, not every product is allocated because Architectures are not really methodologies. This suggests that the Knowledge Worker Framework, while comprehensive, does not replace a full methodology.

The cross reference cells contain letter codes. C is for create, E for employ, and R for refine.

| Methodology Phases and Work Products vs Knowledge Worker Framework | | | | | | | |
|---|---|---|---|---|---|---|---|
| 1. Mission<br>2. Database Object Classes<br>3. Business information systems<br>4. Business Events<br>5. Business Functions<br>6. Business Organizations | | | | | | | |
| | | Knowledge Worker Framework Column | | | | | |
| Phase | Major Product | 1 | 2 | 3 | 4 | 5 | 6 |
| Preliminary Analysis | Mission | C | | | | | |
| | Organization | | | | | | C |
| | Function | | | | | C | |
| | Database Domain | | C | | | | |
| | Specified Data Model | | C | | | | |
| | Data Elements | | C | | | | |
| | Database Objects | | C | | | | |
| | Business Information Systems Plan | | | | | | |
| Conceptual Specification | Refined Specified Data Model | | R | | | | |
| | Refined Data Elements | | R | | | | |
| | Detailed Database Objects | | R | | | | |
| | Implemented Data Model | | R | | | | |

| Methodology Phases and Work Products vs Knowledge Worker Framework | | | | | | | |
|---|---|---|---|---|---|---|---|
| 1. Mission<br>2. Database Object Classes<br>3. Business information systems<br>4. Business Events<br>5. Business Functions<br>6. Business Organizations | | | | | | | |
| | | Knowledge Worker Framework Column | | | | | |
| Phase | Major Product | 1 | 2 | 3 | 4 | 5 | 6 |
| | Specified Business information systems | | | C | | | |
| | Specified Business Events | | | | | | |
| | Iterated Business information system Prototype | | | | C | | |
| | Identified human support systems | | | R | | | |
| Binding | Select database management system | | | | | C | |
| | Determined Implementation Strategy | | | | | | |
| Implementation | Operational Data Model | | C | | | | |
| | Designed Business Information Systems | | | C | | | |
| | Engineered training and hotline, and test data | | | C | | | |
| | Unit and System tests | | | C | | | |
| | Acceptance Testing | | | C | | | |
| | Revised Human Supports | | | | | R | |
| Conversion and Deployment | Procured and installed hardware | | | R | | R | R |
| | Converted data | | C | | | | |
| | Conducted training | | | | | C | |

238

| Methodology Phases and Work Products vs Knowledge Worker Framework | | | | | | | |
|---|---|---|---|---|---|---|---|
| 1. Mission<br>2. Database Object Classes<br>3. Business information systems<br>4. Business Events<br>5. Business Functions<br>6. Business Organizations | | | | | | | |
| **Phase** | **Major Product** | Knowledge Worker Framework Column | | | | | |
| | | 1 | 2 | 3 | 4 | 5 | 6 |
| | Installed hotline and maintenance organizations | | | | | C | |
| Production and Administration | Commencement of business information systems operations | | | | | | |
| | Emergency maintenance | R | R | R | R | R | R |
| | Standard maintenance | R | R | R | R | R | R |
| | Standard Revision | R | R | R | R | R | R |
| | System optimization | R | R | R | R | R | R |
| | System auditing | E | E | E | E | E | E |

**Table 23.** Methodology Phases with Work Products versus Knowledge Worker Framework..

# Index

www.ingramcontent.com/pod-product-compliance
Lightning Source LLC
Chambersburg PA
CBHW061400210326
41598CB00035B/6048